KIMJONGILIA

A TRUE STORY

I0446155

VICTOR FOX

KIMJONGILIA

A TRUE STORY

VICTOR FOX

For man in the park.

AUTHOR NOTE

After North Korea allegedly hacked Sony pictures, many publishers were afraid to publish this explosive book. To them, it was just too risky. Regardless of the warnings and threats, I have decided to go ahead and make this book available to you without censoring any information.

ACKNOWLEDGMENTS

Heidi Nisar
Karen Davis
Laya Salar Behzadi
Jen Tran
Carlos Kim
Andrew Hong
Betty Domingo

PROLOGUE

I smiled when I saw him. He sat in his usual spot, a wooden bench next to the playground. I didn't know anything about him, but I felt as if I'd known him all my life. Every time I went to Glen Park, there he was, tall and wrinkled, smiling at the kids or talking to other park-goers. We'd never spoken, until one morning when I jogged by.

"You don't come to the park every day."

I stopped. *So he does notice me.* "You're right. I've been busy." It was an excuse. The truth was I wasn't motivated to get out of the house that early, and if it weren't for my expanding circumference, I would never have exercised. I hated it. "By the way, I'm Vic." I held out my hand.

"I'm Ron," he said, "You look heavy."

No need to be too honest. I faked a smile. Lately I'd been eating junk food from sheer necessity. I was having a so-called writer's block and in no mood to monitor what went down my throat. "*You* look good." I was being honest. He looked the same as when I'd first noticed him a few years before.

He smiled and looked around furtively, "Guess how old I am." He sounded proud.

I sat down beside him. It was a good excuse to stop running. I wasn't enjoying it anyway. Summer was weeks away, but it felt like July. At seven, the sun already shone brightly and had dispelled the morning fog. Even in my knee-length black shorts and white tee shirt, I swore it felt closer to eighty-five degrees. I was sweating as if I'd run miles. "Seventy?"

"More than ninety," he whispered.

I was taken aback. I'd seen sixty-year-old men who looked older than he did. "Did you say more than ninety?"

He beamed, a twinkle of joy in the small brown eyes behind his thick glasses. "I'm getting close to a century."

"Wow!" I didn't know of anybody in my family who'd lived to be a hundred. The only one who had passed the eighty-year mark was my Greek grandma. She died ten years after my grandfather at the age of eighty-seven. "Maybe you can teach me how to live as long as you."

~

As the days passed I exercised less and spent more time talking to Ron, who told me he was from Korea and lived a block from the park. One thing I found particularly fascinating about him was that he never asked me personal questions.

"Would you be offended if I asked what you do for a living?" he finally ventured, a little nervous.

"I'm a writer."

"Oh. I'd never have guessed it. You look like a businessman." Ron smiled, missing a few teeth.

I laughed. I didn't have a business bone in my body. Even my childhood lemonade stand, which I ran out of my parents' garage, didn't go anywhere. My only customers were my seven-year-old friends who promised to pay but never did.

After two days my dad—who'd worked as an accountant for Arthur Andersen & Co. until it was dismantled by the Enron scandal and then started his own small accounting firm—seized my operation and reassigned me to mowing the lawn and doing other small chores around the house that summer.

"I love books. I wrote one, too."

"You did?" I loved meeting fellow authors. "Tell me about it. I'll read it."

"I've never shown it to it anyone." His eyes darted around stealthly.

"Why not?"

"Don't know. Maybe one day I'll let you read it," he said, rising slowly. It took him a while to fully stand. I offered him a hand but he refused it.

~

The following Sunday morning I saw him again, dressed in a full-sleeve white shirt, loose khakis, and old white sneakers, a brown briefcase on his lap. He looked anxious.

"How are you, Ron?" I studied his face. His squared jaw line looked firmer than usual and his thin gray hair was neatly combed sideways.

"Good, good. Sit down, please. I want to show you something," he said, looking around. The park wasn't too busy, but I knew that would change once the children arrived to play. "I brought you my book." He smiled, tapping his briefcase.

"That's great," I said politely. I'd stopped writing on Sundays when my late mother (a devout Orthodox Christian) chastised me for working on a holy day. I wasn't religious but I took her advice to heart and spent weekends reading and cleaning my cluttered apartment.

"You sure you want to read it?" He scrutinized my face. "I'm not a good writer."

"I'd be delighted." I was sincere. Before coming to the park, I was actually thinking about hitting the bookstore to get something new to read. The old man offering me a free book to read was nothing short of a delight.

"Here." He opened his briefcase and handed me a stack of loose papers.

I noticed the odd fonts. He had used a typewriter. My father had had one on his desk at home. "Thanks," I said, studying the title page. "What's Kimjongilia?"

"It's a flower named after Kim Jong. Do you know him?"

"Not really." I knew he was a North Korean dictator but nothing more. "When do you want this back?"

Ron hesitated. "Go ahead. I'll wait."

I smiled. "Now? If you don't mind I'll read it today and bring it back tomorrow."

Ron stared, debating whether to trust me. As a writer, I understood his dilemma clearly. I wouldn't want to surrender my unpublished writings to another author either.

"You keep it," he said after a brief silence. His face was a lot calmer.

"Thanks. Your book is safe with me."

"I know." He looked up at the sky. "I want you to keep this book with you, and if one day I die... you publish it."

"You're very generous!" I smiled. I glanced at only a few pages before I decided it wasn't for me. I had no real interest in Asian culture. But I would read it anyway. It wouldn't be the first time I read something I didn't like.

Later that afternoon I put aside everything I'd planned to do and began reading *Kimjongilia*.

CHAPTER ONE

"I can't believe your parents want you to work. What are they going to do with all that money?" eighteen-year-old Fen Fang said, rolling her eyes.

"Who told you that?" Peter Chang snapped, breathing hard. He hated to be interrupted during his exercise routine, especially when he was practicing *Qigong*, but he was willing to make an exception for this new girlfriend.

"It's true, I can tell by your face." Fen Fang sat on a Li Park bench, looking piqued that he wasn't paying attention to her.

"I'm not worried. I know how to make money." Peter removed his damp shirt. His chiseled body, all muscle and no fat, glistened with sweat. His dark, short hair was wet at the temples, back, and front. The sun was hot and he'd been in the park over an hour.

"Really?" She raised her eyebrows in a sizzling taunt. Disbelief was written all over her face. And he recognized it.

"What the hell is that supposed to mean?" he frowned, walking up to her. His five-foot-eight frame, which looked taller, loomed over her.

"You don't have the education or skills to earn money." She stood, firmly planted next to him. Her gaze was unflinching. This wasn't the first time she'd come across someone gauche. She had six brothers. She knew how to talk them down.

"If I don't have anything to offer then why do you follow me around like a puppy?" He laughed, looking over her shoulders. The Yangtze River was only a few yards away. He could hear the muted voices of fishermen, returning from a night-long fishing trip.

His parents owned a small textile company and hadn't been concerned with his schooling. All they cared about was his happiness. But too much freedom and an unchecked allowance had brought out the worst in him and he started asking for more money. Tired of his unreasonable demands and growing expenses, his struggling parents thought he should start working. The factory wasn't doing well because of climbing labor costs and sprawling new competition.

"Are you calling me a bitch?" She stepped back. Her round, dimpled face was red hot. No one had ever been disrespectful to her outside the family. She was the youngest child. Her brothers called her spoiled and demanding but no worse.

"Don't be so stupid," he grunted. There wasn't any shortage of potential girlfriends in a neighborhood with a conspicuous female majority. A long face, wide forehead, and broad shoulders made him one of the more handsome boys.

"Hey! Don't bark at me. Go home and show your anger to your parents," Fen Fang shot back, her light brown eyes filled with hate.

"Watch your ugly mouth!" He leaped forward, fists clenched.

"You want to hit a girl, coward? Go ahead! My brothers

will feed you to the pigs," she said, jutting out her chest boldly. Her pink cheongsam looked too tight around the tiny waist and bosom.

"Fuck your brothers!" He growled.

"Bastard! Your mother—"

"Get lost before I ruin your fat face." He reached out his hand but then dropped it to his side, remembering the promise he'd made his mother about not hitting a woman again. She had forced him to take such a pledge after an ex-girlfriend's mother had come to her, crying. The girl had lost a tooth after he'd slapped her hard. He'd caught her in bed with his friend.

"You swine! My brothers will teach you a lesson for insulting me." She stomped her feet hard, her fists clenched tightly, and left.

"I'll be waiting right here!" He kicked at the overgrown patch of grass in her direction. He wasn't afraid of anybody. He sat down on the bench. Two old men gave him an angry look and shook their heads as they walked by him. He thought about telling them it wasn't his fault. She had provoked him. But he found it unnecessary. Nobody would side with him. People often sympathized with the weaker person in a fight, regardless of the issue.

Peter stayed a little longer, hoping to demonstrate his bravery. The park in Nanjing wasn't big like most of the others close to his home, but it was one of cleanest, maybe because not too many people came. It had only five benches and no trees or flowerbeds. But the grass was thick and green and that's all he cared about.

He arrived home late and was surprised to see his neighbors gathered outside his house. He lived on one of the busiest streets in Nanjing, filled during the day with vendors and pedestrians on their way to the nearby train station.

"What are you people doing here?" he asked a bystander, who responded by yelling, "Look! Peter Chang is here."

"Where were you? Some thugs beat your parents and burned down their factory."

"Move!" He knocked down a few elderly, fragile people while making his way to his father, who sat on a wooden bench, his head wrapped in white cotton bandages.

"Who did this to you?! Where is Mother?!" Peter jolted his father's shoulder, his mouth foaming with rage.

"Calm down, Peter! Your mother is in the other room," one of his father's friends said, gently lifting his hand off the old man's shoulder. His father never looked up.

"Do you know who did this?" Peter asked the man who still held his hand, but loud wailing and crying suddenly distracted him, which grew louder as he ran.

"Mother! Mother! Who hurt you?" Peter cried, wading through a crowd of women. But he was too late. She could no longer prolong her life, waiting for her only son. He dropped to his knees and kissed her lifeless grey cheeks. Her silver hair was matted with dried blood. Someone tried to pull him away. He pushed the hand from him and placed his head on his mother's chest, as if she might awaken any second to wipe his tears. No one had ever seen Peter Chang cry before, at least not since they'd moved to Nanjing.

His mother's death had a deep impact on Peter. The loud-mouthed and insolent boy became a quiet and subdued young man who spent most of his time at home waiting for his tight-lipped father to reveal who'd killed her.

One morning Peter was filling a small garment bag with dirty laundry to give to his neighbor, who'd offered to wash his clothes if he'd teach her five-year-old son karate, he confronted his father.

"Tell me who is responsible or I'll never come back in this house again," he threatened, the garment bag slung over his left shoulder.

The old man, who'd been avoiding eye contact with him since his wife's passing, looked straight into his eyes and opened the front door.

Peter was stunned.

"You want me to leave?" he asked, seesawing his gaze between the door and his catatonic father. He felt his heart plunge into his stomach. The man who had loved him and carried him around on his shoulders to see the city as a young child now wanted him to leave. *My mother would never do this,* he thought sorrowfully. He missed her.

His father looked the other way. He'd never done that before. He was always there when he needed him. Every time Peter's mother wanted to discipline him for his roguish behavior, it was his father who would rescue him and tell her not to be so hard on the boy. His mother always listened to his father. She loved her husband and never said a word against him. Unlike other married men in the neighborhood, his father never raised his voice to his wife or hit her. He always spoke to her with respect. "You have learned nothing from your father. Can't you be like him? You see how he talks so politely," his mother would remind him persistently. Deep inside, Peter admired his father's serene manners and some days wished he were more like him. But he convinced himself that there were so many stupid people around he was bound to lose his temper.

"I respect your decision," Peter sighed, slouching. They'd lived in this house since coming from Shanghai, where so many new textile factories had popped up that his parents could no longer afford to compete with skyrocketing wages. "I am leaving."

Peter shuffled along the floor and left his home. *Maybe he's testing me, like I was testing him.* A ray of hope shone in his eyes as he turned back, but his father had already shut the door.

~

Fen Fang was right. I don't have any skills, he said to himself when a distant relative refused to hire him in his restaurant. "You cannot be a good waiter. You have too much anger," he'd told Peter after escorting him out and handing him a small money offering.

"Thank you," he said with great effort. It was the fourth time in a week that someone he knew well had refused to hire him. *I have an anger issue? At least I am not thick-skinned like you, who doesn't care if your relative sleeps in the park.*

By late afternoon, after another unsuccessful day, he was back in the park on the same bench. He'd left the house three days before, and even though one of his neighbors had offered him a place to stay, he'd refused. He didn't want his father to think he was weak and helpless.

Maybe someone will tell my father and he'll come to get me. He was still hopeful that his ordeal was temporary. *Why do some people think I'm an angry man? Is it wrong to always be right and to let people know it?*

He remembered his relative's remarks and grew angrier. *You can all go to hell! I am who I am. You don't want me? So be it! I don't want you either!* He clenched his fists and kicked the grass. "I'll move to a bigger city where people aren't as stupid and narrow-minded as in this dump!" He looked around self-consciously to see if anyone had heard his outburst. He had hated this neighborhood since they'd moved here. People were much nicer back home, he'd told his mother over and over again. Back in Shanghai, he had a lot more friends to play with and the neighbors loved him. He wondered if his life would have been better had they not moved to this city. Everything was so different here: the dialect, food, streets, parks, and bazaars. Even the girls were prettier back home, he often bragged, thinking it would somehow impress neighborhood girls.

"I must disagree with your description of the town," said a male voice, laughing.

Startled, Peter jumped up from his bench. He didn't see anybody. All the nearby benches were empty. "Who's there?"

"I'm sorry. I didn't mean to scare you."

Peter's eyes followed the sound. A man lay on the grass close to the hedges behind him. He walked around the bench. The man was in his fifties or sixties, the same height as him. His eyes were closed but he had a strange smile on his face, as if he knew Peter was standing over him with a set jaw and closed fists. "Nobody scares me. Who are you and why are you talking to me?"

"I apologize, young man." He opened his eyes. They were

brown, shiny, and penetrating. They caused Peter to take a step back.

Still smiling and lying flat on his back, his arms tucked behind his neck as if they were his pillows, the man lifted his head. "I didn't mean to interrupt your leisure."

"Too late for that." Something about the man's voice assuaged his anger. That had never happened before. "I want to be left alone." He went back to his bench. The man got to his feet and followed.

"I'm sorry to intrude on your privacy. My name is Shao Peng."

"Oh, I get it! My father sent you to talk some sense into my empty brain!" Peter stared. Shao Peng wasn't wearing a brightly colored *changshan* robe like his father and most of the other men in Nanjing. He was dressed in a gray *Zhonshan* suit. The jacket was cinched at the waist and had four front pockets, two on top and two on the bottom. Peter knew they didn't merely carry money and conveyance tickets but represented the four basic principles of Chinese philosophy: probity, hard work, equity, and penitence. The five centered front buttons symbolized the body of pure government: governance, guidance, inquisition, legal aid, and representation. The three buttons on the cuffs signified country pride, felicitousness, and liberation. The man was certainly a Communist and this was his uniform.

Peter recalled seeing people wear this type of clothing in Shanghai a few years before. His father had told him they were insecure Chinese people trying to give up their traditional clothes to the Western ideology so they could blend in with the rest of the world. Peter privately liked the clothes and hoped to wear them one day. *How did my dad become friends with him?*

"No, son. I'm afraid I don't know your father."

"I see." *I guess my father doesn't miss me,* he thought sadly. In Shanghai, when he was about ten, his father would come back from the factory and spend hours teaching him Kung Fu, or take him to the local park to teach him to ride a bicycle, or sometimes take him to the nearby river to give him a swimming lesson. His mother complained that he was spoiling him, but he laughed it off. "Don't worry about him. He is my only son." Peter noticed that every time his father used that phrase she wouldn't complain again for months.

"I really don't have much time. I need to go for a job interview."

"Are you unemployed?"

"Why? You hiring?"

Shao Peng gave him a curious look. His fingers were interlocked on his chest and his grey head was tilted over his right shoulder. "Matter of fact, I'm looking for strong and motivated men."

"To do what?"

"Mind if I sit down?"

Peter dropped his gaze and scooted aside. In his head he was planning what to do with his stipend. A room with a bed was first on his list.

The trace of a smile still lingering on his face, Shao Peng sat on the right end of the bench. "Have you heard of the Communist Party of China, or CPC?"

He nodded and crossed his arms. "I've heard about it." His parents talked politics all the time, even though they didn't belong to any party. They were afraid to pick sides.

The winners weren't always too gracious to handle the victory and the losers weren't too forgiving to eat the defeat, Peter's father told him once after watching two neighbors fight over some politician.

Shao Peng's face lit up with curiosity. "What have you heard?"

Peter's brain wandered back in time when he had heard his parents discuss communism. Neither of them had anything positive to say about it. After listening to his father's comments Peter had concluded it was a system that made people do evil things to others. But today things were different. He was facing the real world where he had to make his own choices without anybody's help and then live with them. He had to forego his parents' beliefs and opinions, and forge his own. Living by someone else' life lessons wasn't enough. "Not much. But I'm willing to learn more about it."

"Excellent!" Shao Peng cheered. "You're a wise young man. I'm glad I ran into you."

"What are you doing in the park?"

"Just resting before I go looking for some strong men to join us."

Peter observed the man's tranquil body language. His tall shoulders and forward face confirmed that he took great pride in his work and wasn't lying. It was an odd choice for an important man to lie on the grass. There were plenty of places in the city to relax and drink tea. Dandan served the best pork dumplings out of her street stall by the Quinhuai River. Locals and outsiders raved about her culinary skills. "What do you pay?"

He laughed. "We don't pay."

"What's so funny?" Peter frowned.

"Sorry, I didn't mean to insult you. We don't pay anything to our members, but we do compensate if we ask someone to do a particular job outside the realm of our party charter."

"I don't understand you."

"You will if you join us. By the way, what was your name again?"

"I never told you my name."

"You remind me of someone I knew a long time ago," Shao Peng said, looking up at the clear blue sky. "So what do you say? Would you be interested in working for us or do you prefer to live in this park?"

Peter looked down at his tired feet. He had walked miles in search of a job. Now he had to make a decision. After his father turned his back on him, there was nothing left in the city for him. His mother's death had broken the bond that kept his family together. And now his own father had become a stranger to him. *Perhaps joining the communists might force him to come after me. There is no way he would let his son become one of them.* "I don't have any education or skills. All I know is Kung Fu."

Shao Peng smiled, revealing a chipped front tooth. "Don't worry, we will teach you all the skills you need. But you have to move to Shanghai. Would that be a problem?"

"No," he shook his head. This place had offered him nothing but pain and suffering. He wished the Yangtze would change its course and wash the city away.

"Excellent! If you like, we can travel to Shanghai later this evening."

"I need to take care of some business first. Can I meet you tomorrow morning at the train station?"

"Of course, of course." Shao Peng moved his head like a

rooster pecking on a piece of bread. "I understand. You probably want to say good-bye to your family and friends. How about the ten o'clock train?"

"I'll be there," he said, walking away.

"I still don't know your name."

"Peter Chang!"

The distance from the park to his parents' burned-down textile factory was less than a mile. He stared at the rubble silently. The street was busy, full of shops and small factories, with lots of people walking, talking, and riding bicycles. He'd considered asking the factory employees who were responsible for the assault until he heard it happened after all the workers had gone home for the day.

"Hey, boy, why are you standing there?"

Peter lifted his head and noticed a shopkeeper, sitting behind open bags of spices, eyeing him suspiciously. He crossed the street. "This was my parents' factory."

"Oh, you must be Peter." His gaze softened.

"Yes." His father had asked him so many times to come to the factory and help him out, but he'd always had a good excuse not to come.

"Your mother was a good woman. She bought all of her spices from me and talked about you all the time."

Peter remembered his mother complaining about adulterated spices and cursing the shopkeeper. "I've heard about you, too."

"It's not fair that these rich people get away with things so easily. I heard…"

Peter's heart quickened. Something told him he was

getting close to finding out what his father had been hiding. He felt a warm sensation on the back of his neck.

"But don't worry—time will punish them. I'm just happy they didn't go after you." He fanned the flies off a sugar bag. The day was hot.

Peter was sweating, his anxiety overbearing. "My father didn't tell me much about that night. Could you tell me more?"

"Your father isn't much of a talker. But he's a good family man." The shopkeeper shook his pudgy face.

"Did you see what happened that night?" Peter swallowed hard. The spice seller was right about his father. He was a man of few words who went to work and then came right home to his family. Peter had seen his mother advising him to go out and hang out with his friends. However, his father would smile and say, "Who needs friends when I have a beautiful wife and handsome son at home?" Peter thought about his mother, a petite woman with long lashes, black hair, and an attractive almond-shaped face. Her big brown eyes reminded Peter of a deer, penetrating and gloomy. He never knew why there was so much sadness behind them. She had a husband who loved her and never looked at any other woman, and a son who cared about her.

"Of course." He looked out at the charred factory. "I always close my shop late. Your father was shutting the front door when Chow Fang's eldest son appeared with his friends and asked for you. Your father asked why they wanted you and one of them slapped him and said you had dishonored Fen Fang. The argument got heated. Before I realized it, both your parents were lying in blood and the factory was on fire. I took them home. You weren't— Are you okay?"

Peter was trembling with anger. "I didn't know it all happened because of me."

"I heard that your father agreed to forgive your mother's blood for your life. Otherwise, they would—" He paused to wipe his sweaty face. "Peter? Peter? Where did the boy go?"

⁓

Most wealthy families lived in the eastern part of the city near Zhong Avenue. Here the street was paved evenly with bricks and clay, and cypress trees on both sides shadowed it from the blazing heat in summer. In winter, when the weather turned extremely cold, people wished the trees didn't block the sun.

The sun had just set when a young man, walking as if the stray dogs were chasing him, bumped into an elderly Tao priest. The priest fell on the ground with a moan, but the young man didn't offer any help and continued his journey. It wasn't normal. Most Chinese revered Tao priests for their blessings and good luck. Ignoring them or hurting them was considered blasphemous. The young man, dressed in gray changshan and wooden slippers, realized his mistake and looked back. A street wonton seller was helping the priest. A sigh of relief escaped his thin lips as he turned into an unnamed side street and stopped. Before him was a grand house with a big wooden door. He took a deep breath and knocked at it as hard as he could, then stepped back. Although his heart was beating faster than ever before, he was doing a good job of not letting his carping anxiety show on his round face.

Soon a girl came to the door. Her pretty face twisted with anger, she examined the man head to toe. One hand was on her waist and the other was on her dark-colored chignon. "What do you want?"

"Is your older brother home?" he asked, narrowing his eyes. It wasn't the first time she, repulsed, had opened the door for him. He never understood why she was so mean to him. He'd never wronged her. Friends said that she was belligerent and discourteous.

"How many times have I told you to let the servant answer the door?" a crisp voice admonished. "Who is there?"

"Your stupid friend Dao." The girl moved away. A man in his early twenties appeared.

"What are you doing here?"

"I need to talk to you. Can you come?"

"I was about to sit for dinner…"

"It won't take long. I have to show you this girl. She got a big—"

"Shush! Wait here."

The man outside the house looked around nervously.

"Let's go. She better be good. I left my favorite meal on the table."

"She is."

After walking around the twisted brick streets a few minutes, the two men entered a dark alley. Their body language suggested it wasn't the first time they'd gone there, where one of the famous brothels in the city was housed. Unlike the brothels next to Xuanhu Lake, here the girls were younger and prettier, and went the extra mile to attend to their clients' needs.

"How big is she? You hardly find a Chinese girl with big breasts."

"I am so sorry."

"For what? Hey! Hey! Why are you running away? Dao!"

"He is running away from you." A shadow emerged from the wall. "I gave him two choices—his life or yours. He picked you."

"P-p-p-...." The man stuttered, staggering backward. The last thing he saw was a long knife plunging into his heart.

CHAPTER TWO

A few months after Peter Chang accompanied Shao Peng to Shanghai, Japanese soldiers pillaged his hometown of Nanjing, killing over three hundred thousand people, raping thousands of young girls, and looting whatever was available to loot. All that happened under the watchful eyes of the Japanese commanders, who made every effort to hide their atrocities by executing scores of news reporters and traveling church missionaries. Western and American nationals were strictly prohibited from entering the city without advance permission and an army escort.

Despite strict news blackouts and brutalities, stories of horror and pictures of dead men, women, and children found their way to newsrooms around the world. The Japanese government blamed the CPC for the leaks and assembled a death squad to hunt down underground Chinese organizations. It had little success stopping the flow of news.

Within months of joining the CPC in Shanghai, young Peter Chang became a fearsome guerrilla fighter. News of his heroism and adventures reached across borders. His superiors joked that he didn't need weapons to kill the Japanese—his hands were steel blades. Peter was unimpressed by such accolades. All he wanted was to rid China of Japanese invaders. He often fantasized about drowning them in the bottom of the Yangtze River and then setting it on fire. An impossible feat. It puzzled him why his mother thought the Japanese were civilized people. She often told him that when he was young. Good thing she wasn't around to see these bastards and their heinous acts, he thought regularly before bed. Japanese soldiers were nothing short of monsters.

After he heard about the Japanese atrocities in his hometown, the increased ferocity of his attacks scared even his comrades.

On several occasions Peter sent men to locate his father, but none came back with positive news. He had disappeared as if he didn't exist, presumed murdered by the Japanese, as were most of his other relatives. One of the men told Peter that a relative who owned a restaurant insulted a high-ranking Japanese officer and later that night a soldier went to his house, raped his wife and thirteen-year-old daughter, and then chopped him into pieces and threw his remains in a boiling pot.

By late 1939, although the Japanese had killed millions of innocent people in China and neighboring Korea, their tyrannical control was abating rapidly. The Chinese and Koreans joined the CPC under the leadership of Mao Zedong and developed into a significant guerrilla force, the primary cause of Japanese fatalities in the region.

After months of military humiliation, Japanese forces lost control of China. Shao Peng was delighted, picturing his future as CPC head council. At the same time, he was concerned about CPC's reluctance to acknowledge Peter Chang's heroic role.

"So I'm now a useless tool?" Peter complained. He and a few others were dining at the Shao home. Two months had passed since Li Kenong, his commander, asked him to stay idle and let the politicians deal with things. Peter wanted to scream and disobey his commander and remind him what took place in Nanjing, but then he knew he was nothing without CPC. They had plucked him out of depravity and despair. If it weren't for them, he would have been dead by now. Just like many people whom he had left behind. And now he was going to do what he was told. But it wasn't easy.

His parents had raised him without any strict discipline. His friends envied him, most Chinese parents saw corporal punishment as the only viable discipline of children. He had refused his parents' orders so many times but no one ever hit him. Of course, on occasion, his mother yelled and screamed, but that was the end of it. His father hardly ever raised his voice. There were times when Peter deliberately ignored his parents to test their forbearance. He wanted to be like other kids in the neighborhood, who bragged about their beatings, and showed off their red faces and raw backs with pride. A sign they were tough. "The reason you don't get beatings is because you are delicate like a girl. You follow whatever your parents tell you," a boy in the neighborhood teased him. Peter had to beat him to the ground to show him he was not a weakling.

"Why don't you hit me when I do wrong? All the other parents do," he asked one evening when his father returned from the factory. His question made them uncomfortable. He saw the deep lines appear on their faces and foreheads. They looked at each other briefly and then his father left to wash up without answering and his mother went to the kitchen. Surprised, Peter concluded that his parents didn't discipline him because he had no other siblings and they didn't want to hurt him. There was no other explanation.

Accustomed to such forbearance, it took Peter a while to get used to taking orders and then fulfilling them. He had seen comrades willfully disobey orders and disappear from the battlegrounds. Nobody said anything about it. But Peter knew the CPC equated a disobedient person to a quisling.

"This isn't the right place to address your concern," Li said. He blamed the scorching sun and stresses of war for excessive facial wrinkles that made him look ten years older than his real age——late thirties.

"I have to agree with Commander Li. The dinner table should be reserved for pleasure and happiness," said a chubby man sitting directly across from Peter.

"Your size tells me you're always happy at the dinner table." Peter laughed alone. Faces around him were as stern as biltong.

"You lack table manners," the man glared.

Peter opened his mouth to speak again when Shao looked at him askance and steered the conversation to his least favorite topic, politics. The table was suddenly charged and everyone began talking over each other. Peter sat across from Shao, silently drinking his tea and nodding if someone looked to him for support. A few hours later the noisy political dustups turned to whispers, grimaces, and the men with tired jaws began yawning.

"We should go home. It's getting late," Li said, lifting his arms in the air. Other men agreed and chairs rattled.

"Peter, could you stay? I need to talk to you," Shao said, noticing Li was studying him. His eyes were saying it was about time to discipline the brute. He had complained several times in the past to Shao that he was too lenient with him. The boy needed a good kick in the balls.

"Of course. I've no one waiting for me. You know, actually there is one girl who might come over tonight to get some of this…"

"Ah, the arrogance of youth," Li said wryly.

Peter smiled. "Whatever you say, grandpa."

Li spun around and glared with hostility.

"Don't mind him. He's fooling around." Shao reached for Li's elbow to escort him.

Peter was filing his teacup when Shao came back. "What do you want to talk about?"

Shao gave him a long, hard look. "I know you're a great warrior but, son, to move forward you have to learn how to communicate with other people. Your tongue is the most powerful weapon you have. Learn how to use it."

"If you're referring to kissing people's behinds, you're absolutely right," he snarled. "I sure lack those skills."

Shao sighed in despair. This wasn't the first time they'd had this conversation. "Peter, go home and think calmly about this. I've asked a most important person to help you find a new assignment. I know you are bored."

"You've been saying this for weeks." He pushed back his chair.

"I'm doing my best. But you need to improve your behavior. You scare people and that's not a good thing."

Peter left, mumbling under his breath.

~

A few weeks of persistence enabled Shao to convince his friend Kang Sheng to come to dinner. The third-highest ranking member of the CPC, he was very close to Mao Zedong. Shao never understood how Kang Sheng had moved up the ranks so fast. They had joined the CPC at about the same time and were almost the same age.

"I should recommend you for a medal for recruiting Peter," Kang praised while they sipped oolong before dinner. He was average height with small shoulders, and wore a thin mustache over a glabrous chin.

"Merely doing my duty. Peter is a great fighter." Shao set his *gaiwan* on the table.

"You should introduce him to me. How did you find him?"

"It's an interesting story. I was led to him." Shao smiled. "I received an anonymous letter saying I should hire Peter Chang and pointing me to him."

"Where did the letter come from?"

"Nanjing."

"Still, you are the one who molded him into a warrior. I would love to meet him."

"I'll arrange it as soon as possible," Shao said. His purpose was accomplished.

"No hurry. I hear the Japanese are looking for him."

"There's a huge reward for his arrest."

"I'm sure," Kang smiled.

"I wish we could acknowledge his affiliation with us

formally. He's concerned that we might abandon him after the war."

"Tell him he has Kang Sheng's word that we'll take care of his needs and status."

"I'll give him your message. I'm sure he'll be thrilled," Shao said exuberantly but then fell silent. There was something else on his mind.

"You look lost." Kang smiled, his unaligned teeth stained with tea. Shao had never seen someone drink this much tea. In just under an hour he had downed four *gaiwan*.

"I'm sorry, I was just thinking—"

"I know what you're thinking, Shao. Don't worry. Your name is already being mentioned in our head council meeting."

"I am honored," he bowed his head. His heart was racing with sudden excitement but it was better not to show to it. Eagerness was a sign of weakness. All these years he'd been waiting patiently to be part of the thirteen-member head council of the Communist Party of China. "Let me go and see if our dinner is ready."

The next day Kang Sheng met four top members of the CPC at one of their secret meeting places. All men wore traditional Chinese garb and talked in voices not to be heard outside the room. Secrecy was important and strictly practiced. Members were barred to share information outside the party circles. Violators were stripped of their status and lives.

"How was Shao?" the eldest asked.

"A bit concerned, but overall in good spirits."

"Concerned about what?"

"Peter Chang. His own future."

"What did you say?"

"I told him we'd do something about it. Peter Chang did a lot for this country."

"I wish you hadn't," another man sighed, dropping his shoulders. "We can't afford to bring these uncivilized men among us. They'll take over, and who knows where they will lead us?"

"How can you call them uncivilized?" Kang frowned. "They protected our lands, our families."

"You're right, but the decision has already been made," the eldest man said.

"What are you talking about?"

"You'll find out soon."

CHAPTER THREE

Weeks later Peter Chang received a dinner invitation from Shao Peng. He was thrilled and hopeful. Walking around the neighborhood idly and chasing girls was the way he used to spend his days in Nanjing, but now those days were behind him. He wanted to be useful and busy. His mother's death and Japanese incursion had transformed him forever.

"You don't listen to me now and waste your life. But you will regret all this when you grow old like me." His mother had warned him days before her death when he refused to go with her to the factory. His father was sick that day. Peter knew he couldn't go back in time to correct his past and now the only way to honor his mother was to live as she had wanted him to live. Existence with purpose and dignity. Fighting the Japanese had facilitated both.

"Am I the only guest?" Peter asked Shao, entering his big, orange courtyard. Unlike its neighboring single-story mud-brick homes, it was two stories and built of wood and stones.

"You are. I wanted to discuss something private and important."

"I see. Please go ahead." This was the first time Peter had been invited here alone.

"Not now. We'll talk after dinner."

Peter nodded and followed him into the dining room. He had been too excited to eat his lunch and was hungry.

The male servant had set the table and was leaving the room. Shao touched his shoulder. "Everything smells so good. What did you make?"

"*Saozi* noodles, *mapo* tofu, and *zong zi*. I hope your guest likes it. I'll prepare tea," the servant replied without lifting his head.

Shao watched him leave. "He's an excellent cook."

"I believe you." Peter smiled, noticing his host looked a little chunkier than the last time they'd met.

When they'd finished eating, Shao said to Peter, "I like your appetite. Now let's go to the sitting room."

"Can I ask you something?"

"Go ahead." Shao was only five feet five but walked with long strides.

They entered the sitting room. It was decorated with two large benches, six chairs, and one rectangular wooden table. The walls were bare and a wide cobweb hung a few feet above a fireplace. The blazing fire and two kerosene-oil lanterns hanging from the ceiling provided light. Japanese soldiers had cut down most of the power lines in the city.

"Why don't I ever see any of your family members?"

"Hu is my family," Shao replied, pointing to the servant busily shoving wood onto the fire. He was in his seventies and his face was crisscrossed with unruly wrinkles. His posture was crooked from the waist up like an old tree, tired of carrying the burden of its heavy branches.

"I'm sorry. I thought he was your help," Peter whispered in an apologetic tone. He was certain the old man had heard him.

"Master! You want me to bring you tea here?" Hu turned away from the glowing fireplace, trying to stand straight.

"That will be fine." Shao waited for the servant to leave the room. "Hu Yaobang is more than help."

Peter felt easy as Shao cleared the air. The man was just a servant. But it was nice of Shao to consider him family. There were people in the world who didn't care about their own blood let alone the help. He thought about his father. "It's good to have a loyal person around you."

"I agree. Now tell me what else is on your mind?" Shao ran his hand over his smooth face. At fifty, he stood like an arrow. His small eyes always seemed curious. He spoke slowly and often took breaks between sentences. His words seemed planned and well rehearsed. He appeared to be a man who spent hours thinking about the right words. Too few words showed disinterest and too many left the door open for mistakes and confusion. However, Shao had mastered balancing the two in perfect harmony.

Peter shot him a quick glance. He hadn't come to complain. "I feel like you guys didn't fulfill your side of the bargain and have abandoned me. I resent you think I'm not good enough to sit with you at the same table."

"It's not true. Didn't I invite you to my house?" Shao said, walking up to the fireplace and staring into it.

"You know what I mean. Don't tell me you didn't see the looks on your friends' faces the minute I walked into your house last time."

"I'm sorry you felt that way." Shao picked up a wooden stick and used it to gather the charcoal embers in a red pile inside the hearth. The fire got louder and brighter.

"Nobody can deny your great service to the people of China, Peter. It's only a matter of time before people recognize your greatness."

"I don't care about greatness. I just want to live a respectable life."

"I admire your choice. I'll make sure you get everything you desire, but…" Shao kept his eyes on the fire a few seconds and then turned back. "I have to ask you one last favor."

"Ask me anything. You're the only friend I have left." Peter was willing to do anything for him. He was the man responsible for saving him. He was the man who'd shown him the path of salvation. From the time they'd met in the park, he decided to trust him. Peter didn't know why he felt that way. He remembered his mother telling him, in tears, "Select your friends with utmost care and don't trust them blindly. They could betray you when you need them the most."

Peter had smiled and told her not to worry. He knew how to pick his friends and enemies. Sometimes he wondered why his mother spoke so much wisdom. He never saw her reading or having intellectual conversations. She didn't even socialize with neighborhood women. All she did was take care of her family and accompany her husband to the factory,

"Do you know Kim Il-Sung?"

Peter thought momentarily. "The Korean?"

Hands clasped behind his back, Shao nodded gravely, his jaws tense.

"I've heard about him, but never met him in person."

"How about Kim Jong Suk?"

"Yes, I know her," Peter said.

"How do you know her?"

"I've seen her at the headquarters once or twice." Several Koreans had fought the Japanese alongside the Chinese. "She is his wife, right?"

"True. You know more than I thought."

"I'm not a fool. Who doesn't know the Korean? People say he is full of shit and a coward. How can a man like him become important?"

"Don't pay attention to gossips. Nobody is perfect," Shao waved his finger. "Our job is to do what's good for China. And he is good enough."

"What if he is bad for his own people?"

"We can't carry the burden of others. Our concern is only for the CPC."

"I'm afraid I don't see things your way. How can you support someone like him to rule his people when you know he's no good?" Peter had heard reports that Kim Sung was asking Koreans to call him their leader. Still there was some resistance from elder Korean warriors to accept him. Kim Sung's war credits were as questionable as his morality. "I don't know what has got into you tonight, but you sound so different. Didn't you lecture me that a man should be recognized by his place in society and his virtues? Unfortunately, I have none of those. But at least you should stick to your own philosophy."

"Don't judge me. It's not in my power to make such decisions." Shao said, subdued. Suddenly, he looked older and feebler, and his pointy shoulders drooped. "The Soviets are determined to install him as the leader of Korea as soon as the Japanese leave. We have no choice but to support him. We don't want him to become a Soviet puppet."

"So you want him to become *our* puppet?" Peter laughed.

"It's in our best interest that he remains loyal to us, not them."

"If Soviets are going to make him the leader, why should he listen to us?" Peter said, studying Shao's face, "To be honest with you, I don't understand any of it."

"You will, after I give you this letter." He took a neatly folded paper from his front shirt pocket.

"What's this?" Peter hesitated to reach for it.

"Don't be afraid, son. This letter will change your life." Shao grabbed Peter's right hand, forcing him to take it, and whispered, "Read it! Then we'll burn it."

Peter gave Shao an incredulous stare and unfolded the letter. Suddenly he jumped up from his chair. His eyes widened and his face turned white, as if he'd encountered the ghost of someone he'd once killed. He swallowed, wiping his sweaty forehead, staring at the golden seal prominently affixed to the top right corner. "Is this real?"

"It is. Now read."

Peter finished and stood motionless for several minutes.

"I understand you're shocked, but we must talk about this quickly before we burn it."

"Why me? I can't do this!"

"The Party likes you! You've proven your loyalty beyond any doubt. Now the council has chosen you for something important. You must succeed, Peter, and earn the Party's respect."

"If I do as the letter says, the council will take care of me for the rest of my life?" Peter paced back and forth. The words had built a storm inside him. It was the first time CPC had addressed him in writing, but this was not what he had expected or hoped. He looked at his hands, then at Shao, who was composed, and then at the door. He could walk away from all this and no one could stop him. Shao couldn't force him to do anything. Peter had enough strength in is hands to snap his neck within seconds.

"If that is what they promised, then they'll take care of you and your future family... You're not planning to leave, are you?"

"No, I'm not leaving. It's hard to breathe without any windows and a closed door." Peter opened the top button on his white-collared shirt. He also wore gray slacks. Some of the locals, including a few members of the CPC, hated the way he dressed and often labeled him a Westerner. Shao never took issue with his choice of clothing.

"I'm sorry, but this is the safest place to have such a meeting. Let me have this letter."

Peter wiped his sweaty face against his upper arm and handed the letter back. Shao threw it in the fireplace.

"What are you doing?" Peter ran to the fire.

"Don't!" Shao ordered. "It has to be done."

Peter watched the letter turn to ashes, his heart beating out of rhythm. He wished Hu could come with a cold glass of water. His throat was so dry. It was the same feeling he had had when his father shut the door on him and estranged him. Why would a loving father do such a heartless thing to his only son? He struggled to find an answer, but there was none. The man who could supply the answer was gone, without a lead or clue. Was he the victim of Japanese savagery or something else?

"You should think everything over very carefully, because once you accept this offer there's no turning back," said Shao, standing behind him. "You can never leave this assignment, unless..."

"Unless what? I'm dead?" Peter was thinking he knew CPC better than they knew him. "I know how to take care of myself. I'll tell you my decision tomorrow. It's getting late. Tell Hu I'm sorry I couldn't stay longer to enjoy his tea."

Shao nodded silently and fell into his creaky chair, looking at the open door. *I wish it wouldn't end this way.* He thought about the events that had led up to this night.

One afternoon, exactly two weeks and two days before his meeting with Peter, a messenger knocked at his door, confirmed his identification, and handed him a sealed envelope. Shao observed that the envelope looked far more professional and formal than any other he had received from his friends and comrades. He tore it open and was shocked to see the invitation inside. It asked him to attend an emergency meeting of the head council of the Communist Party of China. Excited and happy, Shao Peng was first to arrive. The security guards allowed him to enter headquarters two hours earlier than the scheduled meeting. He was sitting on a bench by the entry door, engrossed in the Party newspaper, when someone called his name. He lifted his eyes in disbelief. Mao Zedong was directing him to follow him.

Hu's voice brought him back to present.

"Master, I brought tea. Sorry it took so long. I was having a problem with the stove." He looked around for Peter.

"He's gone. It was getting late. I'm going to bed. You may drink it if you want."

The next day Shao woke early, even though he'd tossed and

turned most of the night worrying about Peter Chang. He continued to worry while sipping his favorite morning tea. *What if he refuses? What'll happen to me if he doesn't follow the wishes of the council? I'm an evil man, but what can I do? I have no other choice.*

The day passed quickly. He spent most of it watching the door, hoping Peter would appear. *He's never refused an assignment before so why would he decline this?* Shao had been sitting in the courtyard since late afternoon, watching the door with dwindling hope. *Is he not coming?* His trembling hand reached for his forehead.

"Master, you haven't eaten all day. Shall I bring some soup or roasted sweet potatoes?" Hu asked, knowing Shao loved sweet potatoes, roasted on open fire or boiled in hot water.

"I'm not hungry," he said. It was the fifth time Hu had come out to ask him the same question. "You go to bed now. I'm going to sleep, too," he said, looking up at the stars. In a few days, it would be a full moon.

"You want me to bring a lantern? It's hard to see out here," Hu asked, squinting. Recently he'd complained about seeing dark circles out of his left eye.

"I like it better this way. The sky is so peaceful tonight." He kept his gaze turned upward where the moon kept playing hide and seek with clouds. "Go to sleep."

"Yes, master. Please call me if you are hungry."

Shao went to bed late and woke up early. Hu was arguing with someone at the door.

"Who knocks at someone's house so early? Master is sleeping. Come back in three hours."

What's going on this early in the morning? Shao rushed from his bed and ran to the door barefoot. "Peter! Please come in.

I've been waiting for you since yesterday," he said. Hu was still blocking the doorway and Peter looked more frustrated than angry.

"He wouldn't let me in," Peter said, pushing past.

"I'm sorry. It's my fault. I should have told him you might come." Shao led Peter into the room where they'd spoken before. Hu remained at the door.

"I was worried you might not come. Have a seat, please. I'll make us some nice hot tea—"

"I brought tea." Hu entered carrying a small tray with a big pot and two cups.

"Thank you, Hu. Could you close the door behind you? Never mind. It might get too dark. Leave it open."

Hu turned back with an uncertain look, then left. Hu never complained about any of the guests who came to the house, but Shao knew by his expression whom he liked or disliked. And Peter Chang sure brought more wrinkles to his forehead than any other visitor.

"Let me pour you some tea," Shao said, noticing Peter staring at the pile of cold ashes in the fireplace. "What are you thinking?"

"The letter," he replied, shifting his weary eyes to the rim of the steaming cup. His clothes were excessively wrinkled, as if he had slept in them.

"Your presence means you've decided to take up this cause." Shao curbed his enthusiasm but the glint in his eyes was revealing. "Am I right?"

Peter smiled as if his jaw were hurting. There was no passion or willingness behind it. He had spent his night tossing and turning, and thinking. The words in the letter were permanently etched on his brain. He had evaluated all the possibilities and outcomes his decision would render. "I will do it."

"I'm so proud of you, Peter." Shao patted him on the shoulder.

Peter nodded..

"You'll play a great role in the future of our country and the prosperity of Korea." He smiled, remembering Mao Zedong's words: "If you can do this job with great precision and secrecy, we will have no choice but to add another chair to our head council."

Peter noticed him drifting. "You look happy."

"Of course! Wait here! I have something for you. Let me bring it," he said sheepishly and left the room. Five minutes later, he returned carrying a small leather satchel. Peter was pacing the room, mumbling. "I can't hear what you're saying."

Peter shrugged. "Ah, nothing ... talking to myself."

"Don't do that! People will think you're crazy. Now sit close to me. This is very important."

He spent all day listening to Shao's directions and instructions. At the end of the meeting he said soberly, "I'm only doing this so I can live happily."

Shao tried to brighten his mood. "You're a good warrior. Don't forget that a huge reward awaits you in Chinese history."

"I don't care much about the future. I like to concentrate on the present."

"Don't worry. Take this satchel. It contains two detailed files on Kim Il-Sung and his wife, Kim Jong-Suk. Read them carefully while I arrange for your job at their house."

CHAPTER FOUR

Late in the evening Peter returned home, exhausted. He lived in a tiny house behind a costume-making factory. The Chinese owner said he could live there free if he protected his business from the thieves who often struck at night. After one month, Peter had successfully deterred all thieves. He was happy with his living arrangements, even though the place consisted of one small room and a cramped kitchen, and his bathroom was inside the factory.

Someone gently knocked on the door.

"Who is it?" Peter asked, hiding the satchel under his bed. *Who is knocking at this hour?* He opened the door.

"Hello, Peter." His landlord's nineteen-year-old daughter, Cui, smiled at him.

"What are you doing?" He grabbed her wrist and pulled her inside. "Your father will kill both of us if he finds you here." Her arrival was unexpected but at a time like this, he could use a female companion. She smelled like jasmine, ready to bloom.

"I thought you were strong. You killed many Japanese," she taunted. She was the youngest of nine girls and had no brother. "My father is out of town."

"So you want to know how strong I am?" He pinned her against the wall. He had only met her four months ago, when she came to his apartment to deliver a message from her father. The physical attraction was instant. Within minutes, she was riding him like an equestrienne.

"I am ready," the girl whispered through her full lips.

He lifted her into the air and threw her svelte body on the bed. She spread her legs open. Her thighs were slim and smooth. He took off his pants while she pulled down her top. Then he climbed on top of her. She moaned with pleasure as he circled his tongue around her neck.

"You're so hard!" she moaned, wrapping her arms around him. He put his tongue in her mouth to stop her making too much noise, and twenty minutes later rolled off her, panting. The girl gave him a satisfying kiss on his lips and after an hour of chat, which he hated, left.

Tired, Peter looked at the ceiling and then peeked under the bed at the satchel. It was open. He wondered if he'd forgotten to close it or if nosy Cui had looked inside when he went to use the latrine. He briefly considered asking her, but then decided to go to bed instead. He was too drained, just the way he liked it.

In the morning, he removed the satchel from under the bed and dug out two red-covered files. This first, the thicker of the two, belonged to Kim Il-Sung. He sat down on the wicker chair beside the bed to read.

Kim Song-ju was born in 1912, the oldest of three brothers. His father was a Presbyterian minister, kicked out of the church for stealing funds. Even though Kim never fought in a guerrilla war, many stories about him circulate on the Korean Peninsula. No one really knows how these stories came to light, but there is strong evidence that Soviet leaders, desperately looking for a Korean ally, might have been behind the tales. In reality, Kim Song is an insecure man who loves to spend his time with loose women rather than with men of respect and honor. He loves to tell family stories to impress people, and often misrepresents his real family background. Many people in Korea, China, and the Soviet Union believe that he is a God-loving Christian man, but in point of fact Kim Song is an atheist who believes in aliens. He loves astrology and often makes absurd claims, such as seeing aliens and meeting them in his home. He believes firmly that he was born an exceptional man who is destined to rule the world. The Soviet Union and China know about his weaknesses but support him because he is the most gullible Korean public figure available. Both countries believe that Kim Song-ju will be easily controlled, and they use his incapacities to their advantage. An unspoken war is in progress between the two countries to get full control of Kim Song-ju, and unfortunately, from the Chinese point of view, our position is weakening and deteriorating. Kim Song is getting closer to the Kremlin and has even adopted his new name, Kim Il-Sung. We don't know why the Soviet Union convinced him to change his name, but we think it was to hide his military records. Lately we have confirmed that he has become a big consumer of vodka and drinks heavily in the evenings. Our source also tells us that alcohol consumption is having a terrible effect on his health, and some Soviet doctors are trying to stop him from drinking too much. He also suffers from numerous sexual diseases. While the Soviets were busy throwing beautiful women at him, we arranged for him to marry one of our finest agents.

Peter sighed as he finished the last page. He was surprised that the CPC knew so much about Kim Sung. *I wonder how much they know about me?* He picked up the second file on Kim Jong-Suk.

Kim Jong-Suk has Korean blood in her veins, but her soul belongs to China. At an early age she moved to China, where she dedicated her youth to the Chinese cause. She is a true communist and believes in the leadership of Mao Zedong. Kim Jong has sacrificed her youth to marry a scoundrel. She is a great asset to our country. Recent news from Korea suggests that Kim Sung is physically abusing her by constantly hitting her. Our party is sad knowing that, although Kim Jong is capable of defending herself, but because of the sensitive nature of the political arrangements, she is unable to defend her honor. The CPC and the leaders of its head council cannot sit idly by and let their finest agent suffer. Kim Jong-Suk's primary assignment has been to keep Kim Sung away from Soviet influence, but unfortunately, her mission has been compromised because of her husband's infidelities and volatile temper. The Party once thought Kim Jong would be able to influence Kim Sung, but now feels she needs help protecting herself.

"So I'm being sent to protect Kim Jong-Suk," Peter said aloud, remembering the letter Shao gave him.

He heard a noise outside his door and threw everything under the bed. When he opened it, no one was there. "Who—?" He looked around, and then felt something soft under his bare foot. He picked up the freshly cut jasmine. *Must be from Cui.* He smiled broadly, returned to his room, and began searching for a box of matches to burn those files.

CHAPTER FIVE

"**M**y time is coming. Soon I will be the supreme leader of Korea," Kim Sung said, thrusting out his chest. He was in his late twenties.

He'd invited his closest confidants to his house in *Vyatskoye*, a small fishing village in *Kharbarovsk*, Soviet Union. He'd been living with a few close Korean friends to avoid being caught by Japanese forces, who ruled most of the Korean peninsula. The CPC had offered him a place to live in China but he'd decided to stay in the Soviet Union. The majority of exiled Koreans living in China didn't understand Kim Sung's logic, but there were rumors that Stalin had granted him special privileges and safety. Most of the news of his heroic encounters with the Japanese originated in the Soviet Union and were broadcast by the Soviet news media.

"You work so hard for your people. You deserve every honor," one of his friends said while filling his mouth with pork dumplings. Others at the table nodded in confirmation. None of his comrades dared challenge any of Kim's claims, regardless of their merits. They were afraid of his close connections with the Red Army and didn't want to be ostracized from the man who was being vetted by the Soviets and Chinese to be the next Korean leader.

"Let's not talk about politics over dinner anymore," Kim Suk said, looking at her husband. She was weary of his constant boasting and pipe dreams. Since no one at the table would stop him from gloating, she had decided to take matters into her own hands, mindful of the rancorous outcome.

The table went silent. The guests looked down at their plates as their hands froze and their jaws dropped. The last time anyone spoke against Kim Sung was two years ago, at a similar gathering, before he was married. Kim Sung was telling the story of how he'd rescued Korean farm workers about to be executed by Japanese soldiers. His friend had laughed and challenged his narrative, saying that someone from his battalion had seen him hiding behind the rocks during the fight. Before leaving, he pointed at his chest. "You're a great storyteller, but leave the fighting to the warriors." Hours later his decapitated body was found a few miles from his house. His head was a few feet away and one of his sawed-off hands was shoved in his mouth.

"This woman is so stupid! She even trivializes my politics." Kim Sung slammed his fork on the table. Unlike his other dinner guests, nine men and one woman, he was dressed in a Soviet uniform. The others wore traditional Korean *hanbok*.

"I'm sorry, Sung-Ju," his wife said. "I thought we should talk about something different. We hardly ever have such dinners." She stared at her plate, her cheeks flaming. Never before had he screamed at her in front of other people. Maybe the two empty *takju* bottles were to blame. She and her servant had spent hours preparing for the dinner and had made *samgyetang*, *bulgogi*, *dakgalbi*, and *kimchi jjigae*.

"You see! Look at the mouth on this woman. She calls me Sung-Ju! She thinks she owns me. Maybe later I'll teach her how to talk to me in front of my friends." He spit a few food particles out of his mouth. He'd warned her never to use his real name in public. He preferred his new adopted name, Il-Sung. He was part of the Soviet 88th Brigade, which mostly consisted of Chinese and Korean expatriates whose main job was spying on the occupying Japanese. They also functioned as rumormongers.

"Please don't be angry. We all know about your greatness," an older man said, giving Kim Suk a disdainful look that accused her of provoking her husband's tirade.

"I'm glad you all see the right way. I hope she also sees the true way before it's too late for her." His last words were so cold and menacing that even his staunchly supportive guests looked at each other in disbelief.

"Why don't you get us more fruit?" His aunt Ko Hee gave Kim Suk a way to leave the room.

Kim Suk thanked her with a quick look and went to the kitchen. She instructed the servant to take the fruit bowl to the dining table, and went to her room. She didn't think any of the guests would miss her, not after her husband's meltdown. *I can't blame anyone. I dug my own grave,* she thought, collapsing on her bed. Why had she married a man she disliked so much?

She had been at home when she received the message to come to the CPC's central office in Shanghai. She was excited and intimidated at the same time. Why was an ordinary girl who cooked meals for Chinese guerrilla fighters invited to such an important place?

She confided in one of her Chinese friends who worked in the same kitchen. "What do you think? I'm not even Chinese." Born in Japanese Korea, she was only ten when her mother took her to China in search of her missing husband. Her poor mother never told her, but Kim Suk knew her drunkard father had sold their only source of income, the chicken farm, to his younger brother and had eloped with a younger girl. Kim Suk was much happier in China. Her mother worked all day at the local fish market and earned enough money to give them a comfortable life. A few years later, the Japanese invasion of China forced her mother out of work permanently and pushed Kim Suk to join the CPC. Her mother died a few months later of tuberculosis.

"Maybe they want to give you an award for your excellent work." The entire kitchen workers from dishwasher to head cook admired her industriousness. Even though her job was cutting vegetables and preparing soup, she came to work an hour early and left after everybody else, helping the dishwasher clean and stack his dishes and the cleaning girl mop and sweep.

"Awards and honors are for fighters, not kitchen helpers." She smiled at her friend's naivety.

When she arrived at the CPC's office, five men awaited her, seated around a table in a small room. She didn't recognize any of them.

"We have heard good things about you," one said.

"Thank you. I do my duty."

"What do think about China?" he asked. The other four sat silently.

"I love this country. This is my home."

"And what about social justice and equality?"

"I don't understand your question."

"Let me rephrase," another man said. "Commander Kang Sheng is asking your views about communism."

"I think capitalism is the root of all evil and communism is the right medicine to get rid of the evil."

All the men looked at each other and smiled. Kang Sheng leaned forward. "If I asked you to pick between China and communism, which would you pick?"

"You're asking me to separate fish from the ocean," she said. "They need each other."

Kang Sheng sat up straight, a gleam of praise and admiration in his eyes. "We would like you to work in our northern office."

"How many people do they feed there?" she asked half-heartedly. She liked her current place of work, not to mention coworkers. Among them she felt as if she were no longer an orphan.

The men smiled.

"It's not a kitchen. You'll be in charge of our women's committee."

"What would I do there?" Her heart was racing. Her first promotion!

"You would teach our political doctrine to young girls and their mothers. Can you handle this responsibility if we train you?"

"I am honored."

For the next two months, she went through grueling training, learning everything about communism. The first week was focused on the harmful effects of the capitalist and free markets. The second explained the differences between Marx and Lenin's versions of communism. The third described Maoism. The CPC leader Mao Zedong had redesigned the communist ideology to meet the need for an agricultural China. He had invoked Russian dictator Lenin's theory of imperialism. Finally, Kim Suk learned how to reach out to others to spread Mao's ideology.

Six months passed in the blink of an eye. While preparing for a local conference, Kim Suk was called back to CPC headquarters. She thought it was for another promotion. This time she was a lot calmer, confidence having taken over anxiety.

Kang Sheng was alone in the meeting room.

"Do you know Kim Sung?" he asked.

"Yes." She'd talked to him briefly at a political gathering he attended to show his support for Korean women, but she caught him making eyes at them. She disliked him thoroughly.

"What do you think about him?" Kang Sheng looked down into her brown eyes. This medium-height girl spoke softly, with manners.

"He is a Korean leader." She dropped her gaze and began to feel nervous—the feeling she thought she had put behind.

"True. Do you know he is getting closer to the Soviets?"

"No. I didn't know that," she said quietly. Preaching communism to women had kept her so busy, she hardly got around to reading the newspapers. It overwhelmed her to see how much communist literature she had to read. At first she thought it was impossible to absorb such voluminous information in just a few months and then go out and teach, but then hard work and determination paid off, and she was ready weeks before the end of her training.

"Mao Zedong has convinced him to get married so people will take him more seriously. Married politicians are considered more stable and trustworthy."

She stayed silent. Her father was married, but he wasn't stable or trustworthy. Perhaps politicians were cut from a different cloth. While working in the kitchen, she'd heard stories about respectable married men taking advantage of kitchen girls, but there was no evidence of it. Her mother had told her every day she was pretty, but no one ever courted her. She was still pure.

"Now that he is looking for a suitable wife, our leader believes…"

He paused deliberately, causing her to look up.

She turned crimson. She hadn't thought about marriage. She considered herself unworthy to be married to a man of wealth and power. She had come from a broken home where food was scarce and misfortunes abundant. When girls of her age dreamed of princes and riches, as her few kitchen girlfriends had told her, she had dreamt of struggle, poverty, and a hard life.

"Me?" Her voice sounded as if someone were plucking a broken pipa, vibrating without a proper tune.

"Yes. This country needs your help to strengthen her power and spread her ideology across the borders."

Her jaw tightened. She could feel perspiration on the soles of her feet, on her palms, and on the back her neck. The man she admired the most had chosen her destiny. And she wouldn't let him down. Not today, or ever. A man of such high moral doctrine could never be wrong. He was the totem of an ideology she subscribed to passionately. "I'll do what China wants me to do."

"You are an honorable woman. China will never turn her back on you."

When Kim Suk revealed her intentions to one of her close friends, the girl panicked.

"Don't marry Kim Sung! His reputation... he fools around a lot." The girl beat her chest as if mourning the death of her beloved.

"Most men do before marriage."

"He has a bad temper. And he is so ugly."

"He isn't ugly." Kim Suk recalled her last encounter with him. They were attending a gathering at Shanghai's CPC office. Her first impression of him wasn't flattering. She thought he was trying too hard to look important. He kept talking over people and interrupting them rudely. She remembered feeling sorry for the woman who lived with him, but later when an attendee told her he was still single, she sighed so comically that a few people standing near her grimaced.

A few weeks later, she married him in front of a small gathering and moved to Vyatskoye. None of her friends came to her wedding. She felt so lonely, and her wedding night wasn't any different. She stayed up all night waiting and later crying, because he never came to the room. A few days later she learned that he had spent their wedding night with another girl not too far from her room, decorated with fresh lilies, orchids, lotus, and chinoiserie. But who was to blame? She saw the writing on the wall.

She had heard losing virginity was painful but rewarding

afterward. Four or five days passed before she saw him again. She was in a deep sleep when he woke her up with a grunt. Her heart almost jumped out of her mouth. He stared at her with glassy eyes and then put his hand inside her sleeping gown and ripped it off. Frightened, she began to cry. He didn't care. He was too drunk. When he was done, she didn't know if sex was supposed to feel this awful the first time. "Sex between husband and wife is sacred," an old woman had told her when she was getting into her wedding dress. She spent the next hour vomiting and trying to understand the sacred aspect of consummation.

"Kim Suk."

She shook off her memories and opened the door, where Ko Hee stood smiling.

"Sorry. I had a headache. I was coming back." Kim Suk faked a smile. It wasn't easy at first, but over time she had mastered the skill. Living with Kim Sung was harder than forgiving her reprobate father, whom she blamed for her misfortune. Had he not abandoned his family and eloped, she might have led a very different life. Possibly her mother would still be alive. It wasn't the tuberculosis that killed her, it was the lack of medicine and hospital care brought about by an unjust society, she often thought.

Ko Hee entered the room, her narrow eyes wandering around as if looking for something. They stopped on Kim Suk's face. "I know my nephew has a temper. But his heart is like a child's. Don't let him upset you. Warm him well tonight and he will forget his anger by morning."

Warm him? He hadn't touched her in months. It was

obvious to her that he was getting warmed elsewhere. "I'm not upset. Let me come with you to the table."

"I'm leaving, but listen to me before I go." She squeezed her hand and looked in her eyes. They were the same height and body frame. The only things that set them apart were age, Ko Hee was in her late fifties, and makeup. Kim Suk hardly wore cosmetics. She didn't have any reason to——her husband didn't even look at her. The old woman's face was always coated with thick layers of maquillage. "Be a good wife. You are married to a very important man."

Why don't you tell your nephew to be a good husband? Kim Suk thought about telling her but decided not to. Unlike her soulless husband, who never spoke kind words to his aunt, Kim Suk was at least polite to her face. She saw her out and went to the dining room. The guests were gone. The table was cleared except for half a bottle of Vodka and a tipped-over empty glass. Kim Sung was slumped over the table, snoring. She decided to leave him there, knowing he would only be enraged if she woke him. It had happened a few times before when he'd fallen asleep on the couch. He had slapped her across the face.

How can you influence a man who is already under the influence? She gave her husband a look of hatred and returned to her room, wondering how her marriage would be if he wasn't a womanizer. From the beginning, Kim Sung had treated her like a subhuman. Her marriage was like being tied to a tree while rats tore her flesh, slowly and painfully, and death was imminent. Some days she wondered if her mother had felt the same way and if her father was just like Kim Sung. Her father never brought other women home, at least she'd never seen or heard it, and her mother never kept secrets. Kim Suk deplored the night Kim Sung had shown up with a couple of street girls wrapped in his arms. She could not control her temper at such humiliation and chased the women with a broomstick. Her husband was too intoxicated to defend his courtesans, so he went straight to his bedroom shouting profanities.

Kim Suk had received all kinds of warnings and advice regarding her husband's sexual escapades, but she'd never thought he'd bring those affairs into her bedroom. She changed into her nightgown in front of the mirror and noticed that the large, dark bruise above her chest was fading. He had punched her when she asked him, after he'd been gone two days, his whereabouts. She had gone to bed sobbing.

One morning she went to the basement to get a new set of meat-cutting knives. The night before the servant had had a hard time cutting the meat and she had promised to get him a sharper knife. She looked around the poorly lit room.

"Where is that knife?" she mumbled, accidentally tipping over a giant *kimchi* jar and losing her balance. She grabbed for a termite-infested bookcase to break her fall, but it came tumbling down on her head, knocking her unconscious.

"Are you okay?" a male voice asked.

She opened her eyes slowly, and for the first time looked at her servant carefully. He was in his early twenties, a few inches taller than her husband, with a strong jaw and broad shoulders. Her husband had hired him a few days before to help around the house. "I'm fine. My head hurts. You brought me to my room?"

"Yes, ma'am. Should I call the doctor?"

She waved her hand dismissively and then touched a bump on her forehead, the size of a walnut. "My clothes smell like fish."

The servant turned red. "I'm sorry. I had just returned from the fish market when I found you in the basement."

She remembered that she was the one who had told him to buy fish before he came to work. "There isn't enough light in the basement. Could you do something about it? I almost broke my neck."

"Yes, ma'am, I'll take care of it."

"How did you find me?"

"I came home and saw the basement door open. I went to close it and saw you passed out on the floor. I picked you up and carried you to your room."

"Don't tell Kim Sung."

"You have a big red bump—" he said, pointing at his forehead.

"Don't worry. Go now. I want to rest before he comes home." She knew her husband never came home before midnight.

Kim Suk closed her eyes. For the first time she did not dislike a servant. Her husband had hired several nosy ones. She always found an excuse to fire them after about a month, and did so, one by one, as if waiting for someone perfect—like this new Chinese servant, Peter Chang.

~

"Do you think it was wise to send him under his own name?" The man asked the other two men at the table.

"Don't worry. Hundreds of young men have the same name."

"Did he ask you anything?"

"No. He thanked me for getting him a good servant."

"We should thank you."

"Thank my wife. She's the one who trained him."

They laughed.

CHAPTER SIX

"You clean house better than you cook," Kim Suk said, sampling a rainbow trout. "Have you ever cooked a fish before?"

Flustered, Peter Chang nodded without conviction. He'd spent more than two hours cleaning and frying it, although he'd also done a fair bit of daydreaming about his future. Now he wished he had tasted the fish before serving it. To him, the trout looked crispy and appetizing.

"Huh!" She walked around the kitchen, hands clasped at her waist, her black hair coiled on top of her head with *dwikkoji*. "I guess it's edible. Never use so many fennel seeds again."

"Yes, ma'am," he replied, avoiding eye contact. "Should I make something else?" He stared at the platter filled with a flour-coated, ready-to-fry fish.

"No, it's okay." She smiled, facing him. "I'll see you later. I need to do some work."

"I'll be more careful. Should I set your lunch on the table?" He stole a glance at her perfectly round buttocks. This was the first time she'd come down to the kitchen wearing her nightgown and the second time he was able to see her curves properly. He had first noticed her body when he carried her out of the basement a few days ago. He'd been embarrassed by his erection when he placed her on the bed.

"I'm not hungry." She caught him adjusting his crotch.

"Umm, yes, ma'am," he stuttered.

"Keep it up," she smiled, turning back to the door. "Good work."

"Shit! I wish I could just cut you off," he said, looking down at his tented pants. Not having any female companionship was taking its toll. With pounding heart and red face, he wondered if she had noticed his arousal and would fire him for it. He promised himself to constrain his thoughts, especially the sexual ones. It had been a lot of trouble to learn this household stuff.

He'd been working at the Kim house in *Kharbarovsk* over a month. His commander, Li Kenong, had brought him here.

"Why can't I be a gardener or chauffeur instead of a house servant? I don't know anything about cleaning or cooking," Peter complained. He hardly ever cleaned his own place, nor cleared his dishes after a meal when his mother was alive. His father was the same. Men worked outside the house and women took care of the inside. To Peter it seemed fair and balanced.

"It wasn't my decision. I'm following orders, and I would highly suggest you do the same."

"But I don't know how to cook."

"Take this file," Li said, handing him a thick stack of papers.

"What's this?"

"Korean food recipes. Follow the directions and you'll soon cook like my wife." Li suppressed a smile. His wife was a terrible cook.

"I guess I can try." Peter flipped through the pages. "How about that cleaning?"

"My wife will teach you, but make sure you don't tell her anything about yourself."

"Won't she ask me why a man wants to learn what women are supposed to do?"

"Don't say such a thing in front my wife or she'll hit you on the head with a broom. She's a quiet person. She won't ask you much."

Two days later Peter went to Li Kenong's house. He hated Li's wife the minute she invited him inside her living room. In anticipation of teaching him house cleaning, she hadn't done any and the house looked as bad as Peter's own apartment.

What a damn liar! He cursed Li Kenong for misleading him about the chubby woman. True, she rarely spoke, but her hands were never quiet. She constantly pointed her finger, and during those two days, he never saw it at rest for more than a minute. *I wish I could break her damn finger!*

He never worked so hard in his entire life. When Li asked about his wife's training, Peter almost said, *your stupid wife is impossible to please!*

Kim Sung interviewed Peter without asking too many questions and hired him the same day. "My friend told me you are a reliable and loyal person. Come to work tomorrow." He didn't introduce him to his wife or anybody else in the house.

When he arrived the next morning, he was pleasantly surprised to see Kim Jong-Suk at the door.

"You must be Peter Chang," she said, as if she'd known him for ages. "Come in. I am Kim Suk. My husband told me that you come with good references."

"Thank you for your kind words." He took off his coolie hat.

"Your face looks familiar. Have I met you somewhere before?" she asked, leading him into a big kitchen.

"No, ma'am," he replied, hoping she'd change the subject.

"Let me show you the rest of the house. It won't be an easy job." She turned to see his reaction. None of the previous servants had cleaned the four-bedroom house well. Two of the rooms had cobwebs hanging from the ceiling. She could have removed them herself but she was afraid of spiders. Sometimes she laughed at the notion that death didn't frighten her but a small eight-legged creature did.

"I've cleaned bigger houses. You will be very happy with my work," Peter boasted, but the immensity of the house worried him. It would take him at least two hours to clean the courtyard alone.

She laughed and turned the other way. "We'll see."

Kim Suk's voice interrupted his thoughts. "Peter, come outside. I need something from the basement." He put the fish platter on the kitchen counter and ran to the door.

During the next two months, Peter hardly saw Kim Sung and spent most of his days cleaning and cooking. He was getting bored with his monotonous life until one day Kim Suk approached him after he'd arrived late for work.

"Why don't you move in with us? We have an extra room available. It will save you rent and traveling time," she said.

Peter liked the idea but said nothing.

"I'll talk to my Kim Sung tonight. I'm sure he'll be happy. He always complains you come late to make his breakfast. He hates my cooking."

"I'm sorry. I have to ride my bike for an hour to get here," Peter explained. His rented apartment was in the cheaper part of the village. "I could leave earlier."

"That won't be necessary. Finish these dishes. I'll see what I can do."

Several days passed and Peter grew nervous. *Maybe he doesn't trust me. Why would he let a young stranger live in his house with his pretty wife?* He thought, rearranging the spice cabinet in the kitchen.

"Could I talk to you, Peter?" A heavy male voice called out.

A jar of cinnamon sticks almost slipped out of his hands. Kim Sung had never come home this early in the evening. Dinner was still a few hours away. He wiped his hands with the towel and hurried out of the kitchen.

Dressed in a white shirt and black pants, Kim Sung was in the middle of courtyard talking to Kim Suk. Something about their body language told him they weren't too happy standing close to each other. When his parents talked, they had stood inches apart and looked affectionate.

"Yes, master?" Peter asked, looking down and crossing his hands over his crotch.

"My wife tells me it takes you more than an hour to ride your bicycle here. Is that true?"

"Yes, master. I have no problems riding my bike. If you want I can leave my home earlier."

"I want you to move in here. It'll save you time and will be good to have a man in the house."

"You are very kind, master."

"I like your manners. Don't disappoint me. I must go now. People are waiting for me."

Peter bowed deeply. Kim Suk looked pleased.

After his first week living at the house, Peter wondered if Shao Peng was wrong about the Korean couple. So far, he'd seen no sign that Kim Sung abused his wife. His room was close enough to theirs to hear anything that might be amiss.

Late one night, as Peter lay in bed wondering whether he should try to contact Shao Peng and get out of this degrading assignment, he heard angry voices. He jumped out of bed and moved closer to the door, his heart beating faster.

"Shame on you! Bringing all these whores to my house," Kim Suk's furious voice echoed in the courtyard.

"*Your* house? You see the way she talks to her husband." Kim Sung's voice sounded as if he had been drinking all night.

"Hey, bitches! Get out of my house! Don't you know he is married?"

"You don't know how to take care of him," a female voice mocked.

"You should be thanking us for helping you. Why don't

you join us in making him happy?" Another female voice said, laughing, but the sound of a slap quieted her.

"Get out of my house!" Kim Suk yelled.

Peter crouched and peeked through the small crack in the door. His mouth dropped open. Kim Suk was dragging two heavily made-up women by the hair to the front door. Kim Sung was intoxicated and sitting on the floor. *Wow! She's strong! How could someone abuse her?* Kim Suk picked up a wooden broom he'd forgotten to put away and headed toward Kim Sung, who was smiling. *There's no way she'll hit him!* He was wrong. She pounded him relentlessly until he curled up in a fetal position, begging for mercy. After the beating, she left him groaning and went to her room. *I thought I was supposed to protect* her *from* him*, but it seems the other way around. How could Shao and the Party be so wrong?*

He scratched his head and moved away from the door. It was too risky to help Kim Sung. "This is crazy," he mumbled, slowly climbing back into bed.

˘

The next morning Peter woke up feeling guilty he wasn't able to help Kim Sung. *I should make him white rice for breakfast. He loves rice,* he thought, walking to the kitchen. "So what if he brought a couple of girls home? You can't beat the crap out of a man who is going to be the leader of a country."

"Who are you talking to, Peter?" Kim Sung asked, entering the kitchen.

Peter gave him a quick, furtive glance and then lowered his chin. "Nobody, master. I was just remembering something I read in the Bible."

"Are you a Christian?" He asked.

Troubled by his smarmy politeness, he looked up. Smartly dressed and shaved, Kim Sung looked like an entirely different person from the night before.

"What's wrong? You look confused." Kim Sung stepped closer.

"I'm Presbyterian," Peter lied, knowing Kim Sung's childhood background. In reality, he flip-flopped between Buddhism and Confucianism.

"Very good! My parents were also Presbyterian." Kim Sung smiled. "I'm a little hungry. What're you making for breakfast?"

"White rice." Peter couldn't believe that a man beaten by his wife could wake up this cheery. How could he not be embarrassed knowing his servant witnessed him on his knees, crying? Perhaps alcohol had made him forget.

"You are the best. I think I underestimated your talent. One of these days, I will sit here and talk about your past. For a Chinese man, you speak Korean very well. Where did you learn it?"

"From neighborhood boys, master." Shao Peng had also been surprised when he first heard Peter talking to a Korean guerrilla fighter. Peter didn't even remember picking up the language. He only remembered playing with the Korean kids in Shanghai when he was little. There were plenty of them in his neighborhood.

After Kim Sung hurriedly ate his breakfast and left the house happy, Peter turned his attention to Kim Suk. Her bedroom door was still closed. If he told anybody about last night, they would call him a liar. Even those who knew him well. He shrugged and cleaned the kitchen.

Four hours later, with most of his cleaning done, he

wondered about her again. Usually she was awake before her husband and told Peter what to make for breakfast.

"I should wake her. It's almost noon," he mumbled, standing outside her door and then knocking. "Ma'am! Are you okay? It's late. I was wondering if you're going to have breakfast or I should make you some lunch."

She didn't answer. He waited a few seconds and then repeated himself, this time louder.

"Don't shout, Peter! I heard you the first time. Go to the kitchen. I'll be there in a few minutes," she said groggily.

"Ye-ye-yes, ma'am," he babbled, stepping away from the door. *What is her problem? Wants to broom my ass, too? Maybe she saw me peeking through the door last night. Who cares!* He shuffled angrily all the way to the kitchen and began peeling onions.

"I'm sorry if I raised my voice at you." Kim Suk's soft voice caught him by surprise. He fumbled the onion back into the sack and gave her a smile.

"Why are you putting the peeled onion back in the bag?" she asked, scooting toward him. She was dressed in her revealing pink nightgown.

"Oh, sorry." He pulled the onion out and turned his eyes to the floor.

"What's wrong, Peter? Why don't you look at me?" she chuckled.

"I am, ma'am," he said, looking up. He was able see her naked body in the bright sunlight. She wasn't wearing a bra or underwear. Her breasts were small but perky, her waist was small, and her hips were wide.

"Why are you so nervous?"

"What should I cook?" He moved behind a chair to hide his full-blown erection.

She moved the chair and sat on it, facing him. "I'm so hungry, I could eat anything."

"I'll make you something good." Peter swallowed. She was inches from his crotch. He had pleasured himself numerous times, fantasizing an event like this one, but now he was sweaty and embarrassed. Her pouty red lips were so close.

"What are you hiding in there?" she laughed, pointing at his tented pants.

"I'm so sorry!" His face was on fire.

"Don't be," she said flirtatiously, and started rubbing her fingers against his pants. "I know you've been watching me," she whispered, biting her lower lip.

"Ma'am, you shouldn't," Peter moaned, without resisting or moving away. His body needed this. A moment like this hadn't happened since he left China. "What if someone…?"

She looked up beaming, as if she didn't care who saw them, and pulled him forward by his hips. She took out his cock and began licking the sticky tip. She then slowly put his long shaft in her mouth and began rolling her tongue around it.

"I'm coming!" He squeezed his butt forward and grabbed her head. The sensation was too strong, but she didn't let him escape until he'd filled her mouth.

"Where did you learn this?" he said, breathing loudly. The intense orgasm had left him trembling. Of all the women he had been with, she was the second who had pleasured him this way. The first woman was a whore. He had begged Cui to do it but she had told him it was disgusting and unhealthy.

She gave him a pressed-lip smile and swallowed. That had never happened before.

He pulled up his pants and stared between her legs, but she gently shook her head and walked away smiling. He had forgotten last night's commotion. If clobbering her husband had made her this wild, he wanted to see Kim Sung's buttocks at the end of that broom every night. He was getting hard again.

A week passed uneventfully. Peter Chang was chagrined Kim Suk had been ignoring him since the last encounter and didn't come to the kitchen to see him or tell him what to cook. He was on his own. Because Kim Sung was hardly ever home to eat and Kim Suk was barely eating, his workload was cut in half.

During his free time, which was ample because nobody interrupted him, he stared at her closed door intermittently and tried to come up with a plausible explanation for her peculiar behavior. Had he done something wrong? He hadn't forced her into anything. She even smiled afterward. Maybe she was feeling guilty and was ashamed of herself. Whatever the reason, he was getting tired of thinking about it. He wasn't remorseful. He would do it again if she offered. She deserved to have fun, too.

He was resting when she burst into his room.

"I already finished my chores," he said, jumping off his bed. He had never seen her hair spread all over her shoulders before. She was wearing red lipstick and smelled like a rose.

"Don't panic. We have unfinished business," she said, pulling off her fetching pink gown.

Shocked, Peter ogled her gorgeous five-foot-three nude body … her tapered legs and her pointy breasts with enlarged areolae.

"You like it?" she teased. Her small brown eyes glittered lustfully.

"You are so beautiful." He gulped down his hesitation and swept her off her feet. "You're going to remember this," he said, dropping her on his bed and quickly undressing.

Licking her lips seductively, she spread her legs wider.

He grabbed her ankles and pulled her body forward, then put her legs on his shoulders. He was too horny for foreplay.

When they were done exploring each other's bodies, she wrapped her wiry arms around him and confessed shyly, "I never had an orgasm before."

He raised his head and smiled, "It doesn't look that way. You seem pretty skilled."

She pinched his nipple.

"Ouch!" he cried, "What's that for?"

"Not believing me," she frowned. "When you are married to a man who wants to court every woman he lays eyes on, you try to learn the skills of professional women so you can provide him the same service at home. But sadly, no matter what you do, nothing is enough."

Peter pitied her sad mien. "I didn't mean to upset you."

"Forget about it," she said, combing his hair with her fingers. "I'm so glad you are here. What did they say about me?"

"Who?" He asked.

"You know. Don't pretend. I know who sent you here."

"What are you talking about?" His eyes flew open as if she'd hit him on the head with a sledgehammer. She wasn't supposed to know him. Had he revealed something during the moment of weakness?

"I know who you are and…"

"And what? And what?" He asked frantically, glancing over her naked, coiled body. He stood a few feet away, his penis wilted.

"I personally chose you," she smiled slyly.

"You are mistaken about me."

"Stop pretending! No need to hide anything from me. We're on the same side," she said, stretching her body. Her hard nipples had also collapsed.

Unsure of the consequences of a confession, he asked, "You really asked for me to be your servant?"

She nodded. "I did."

"But why? I hardly knew you. I saw you once at Party headquarters."

"I know. You were so cold. Every time I looked over, you looked in the opposite direction."

"So you liked me?" He asked, but then realized his question was stupid. "What I mean is, why didn't you try to meet me? I thought you were a snob who kept giving me dirty looks."

"*Snob?*" She furrowed her brow. "To answer your first question, yes, I liked you. But…" She turned her eyes away.

"Go on." He sat beside her. How could a woman this important want him?

"My fate had already been sealed before I saw you." She exhaled deeply. "When CPC leaders asked me to marry Kim Sung for the good of China and Korea, I didn't resist the idea."

"Did you know what kind of man you were marrying?"

"I knew. Sometimes we have to make a decision regardless of the consequences." She put her hand on his bare back. "You're a man, much stronger than I am, yet you took this assignment knowing it might kill you."

"My circumstances are different. What gives you the idea that I'm here to get killed?"

"You are naive! You took this assignment to protect me, right?"

He looked at her face carefully and nodded.

"How could you possibly stop a man, who is backed by a heavily armed Soviet army and Korean guerrillas, from hurting me?"

"I thought, if he tried to hurt you, I'd stop him and take you back to China."

"We can never leave this place alive without his permission. Soon he'll be the leader of Korea and everything will be under his control."

"If you knew this place was unsafe, why would you get me into this mess?"

"I did you a favor," she replied, her eyes teary.

"What favor? I'm stuck here with you in some Soviet town I can't even pronounce. I had a bright future in China."

"Who told you that?" She looked puzzled.

"Shao Peng!"

"Oh, Peter!" she gasped. "You had no future in the CPC. The minute the Japanese threat weakened, you and other tough men like you became the Party's liability. The same people who hired you to kill Japanese are scared of you now, and they got rid of you one by one."

"Scared of us?"

"Yes! They thought men like you could cause

serious trouble in the Party, so they shipped you off on different missions."

"Missions to get killed?"

She nodded.

"You'd better not be lying to me."

"I will never lie to you, Peter Chang." She looked at him sadly. "They gave me few choices for a servant. I picked you because I liked you and didn't want you to die. You have a much better chance of surviving here with me than on another mission."

"I guess I should thank you for saving me," he mumbled, disgusted.

"You should trust me. I'm the only friend you have."

"Trust you? You lied that Kim Sung beats you. I saw you with my own eyes beating the shit out of him."

"Oh, you saw that?" she sighed.

"What do you think? I live five feet from your door."

"I'm sorry you had to see," she said, closing her eyes. "I have to do what he likes."

"What's that supposed to mean? He likes a broom up his ass?"

"Kim Sung is an algolagniac."

"Good! He'll be dead in a few months."

"No, you fool. He's not dying." She laughed. "He likes to be beaten up to get his sexual satisfaction, and sometimes the other way around."

"Are you pulling my leg? I'm not stupid!"

"I know it sounds strange but it's true. He's a sick bastard. I didn't know this until a few months ago."

Peter studied her face. She was telling the truth. Now it was clear why he had been so uncharacteristically congenial and pleasant in the following morning. "But why was he crying for mercy?"

"Oh, that's his signal to hit him harder. It stimulates him."

He shook his head.

"I should go back to my room now," she said, staring at her gown on the floor.

Peter said nothing and watched her dress and leave silently. He knew it wasn't the last time he would make love to her. She would come back for more. In the war fields, his peers called him a relentless warrior because he fought fearlessly, and in bed, he performed with the same passion and zeal. He knew his weaponry well.

Two hours later he stood calmly in front of the kitchen stove and wondered how he could get his hands on Shao Peng's neck. An old Chinese folk song played in his head. *The man who betrays his friends deserves dadao in the heart.*

CHAPTER SEVEN

A few months had passed since Shao Peng sent Peter Chang to Vyatskoye. Though his odds of getting appointed to the CPC head council had improved significantly, he didn't feel any joy knowing he might never see Peter again. After all, he was his best find, a rough diamond.

He had liked Peter from the first day he laid eyes on him in that park. Few people outside the CPC knew that he was in charge of recruiting members for the Party, and unlike other party members he was allowed to travel at will. Over the course of his member-hunting years, he'd discovered that the parks, bus stations, and train stations were the best places to find new blood. Most hopeless and vulnerable young men loitered around those places to escape their despair. To them, Shao's words were a beacon of hope and a new future. He often preached to young men, destitute of wealth and education, that their impecunious lives were the direct result of the evils of capitalism, and that communism was the only light at the end of the tunnel. Men who had nothing left to lose came in droves.

Late one afternoon he was taking his routine nap when

he heard Hu's apologetic voice. "Master, a man wants to see you. I tried my best to make him leave but he insists."

He opened one eye. "Go ask his name."

"His name is Bo Wang."

"*What?*" He asked, remembering his past.

Shao Peng had been born into a family of hardworking farmers. His father and mother worked side by side in the cornfields and barely made enough money to feed their thirteen children. They all lived in a small, two-bedroom house on the outskirts of Shanghai. His mother spent most of her youth pregnant and never showed any signs of slowing when working in the fields under the scorching sun.

Shao escaped his three brothers and nine sisters by becoming a loner. He spent most of his time walking through the fields, wondering why his parents had to work so hard for so little. *Why do some people have so much money, and others have none?* He often thought, watching his parents and others work from dawn to dusk.

He frequently asked his exhausted mother before bed, "Why can't rich people just share their money with us?"

"Come here, big thinker. I will ask you the same question when you become rich," she responded playfully, rubbing his head. "Why can't you be like your brothers and sisters? They never ask silly questions."

Afterward he thought about it, looking at his twelve siblings sleeping peacefully. They were so different from him. They enjoyed life as it was offered to them and were happy. However, he never truly felt happy among them. There was more to life than vast cornfields, dilapidated houses, and charred skins. How could one change all this? Was it even possible to have such a dream? The seeds of utopian ideology were growing in him.

Shao Peng didn't like to waste time. He was more interested in reading and writing, even though his parents couldn't afford a school or books. He was eleven when his father introduced him to Chao Chang, a farmer who was a former schoolteacher. Chao was in his early thirties. He had had to quit teaching because of the lack of students. Most parents preferred their kids to work with them on farms and in factories. Learning a skill was more important than wasting time in school. Enlightened parents, who sought education for their kids, because they thought it would bring them prosperity, were considered dreamers.

Shao was elated when Chao agreed to teach him. A few days later, he was taken aback when he visited Chao. The house was filled with books. "You read all these books?" He asked, spinning in circles. It felt like a cornfield of books.

"Most of them," Chao smiled. "You can borrow them when you know how to read them."

Shao's face lit up. How long would it take to read all these books? He picked up a hardcover. "What does this word mean? It's written on so many books." He recognized the word from a pamphlet his father once brought home.

"Communism," Chao said, taking a seat on the wicker floor mat.

"What does it mean?"

"Equality and happiness. Don't worry… I'll teach you from all these books."

A month later two other neighborhood children, one boy and one girl—Bo Wang and Yuan Young—joined them. Chao was a dedicated teacher. Even though he labored hard during the day, he never showed any hint of tiredness during class. "I wish we could start a school here," he would often lament at the end of the sessions.

Almost a year passed. The children, who by now had become inseparable friends, began asking their parents to start a regular school in their neighborhood, like the one they had seen in central Shanghai when their parents took them to the New Year carnivals.

"Everybody listens to you. Why can't we have our own school? Can't we use Chao's house?" Shao asked his father late one night.

"I don't like the way he teaches you. I was thinking you should stop going there," he responded with anger.

"Why are you saying that? He is a great teacher." Shao was surprised. This was the first time his father had said anything negative about his teacher.

"He doesn't teach you anything. He is just brainwashing you and your friends with communism. Some folks are very unhappy with the way he talks."

"He is a good teacher. He says after we finish reading his books he will teach us other things, too."

Two days later Shao was preparing to go to Chao's when Bo Wang ran to tell him their teacher had left town for good. Shao felt betrayed that he had abandoned them without any explanation.

Shao's childhood friendship with Bo and Yuan changed when the puberty years arrived. He fell in love with Yuan and started spending more time with her. Bo wasn't happy about it. On Yuan's sixteenth birthday, Shao was planning to give her a perfect gift. After months of collecting small colorful stones around the neighborhood, he was finally able to make her a beautiful necklace and was now waiting impatiently to give it to her. Bo had asked him several times about the gift but he'd refused to tell him. He didn't want him to come up with a better gift. She was his girlfriend.

Yuan will love this, he thought, looking at his necklace one last time before carefully placing it in his pocket. He had asked her to meet him at their favorite park so he could surprise her. He hadn't told Bo about it.

"What are you going to give her?" He heard Bo's voice.

Shao wasn't happy to see him. He had ruined his romantic moment. "How did you know I was here?"

"Yuan invited me," he replied, sitting next to him on the bench.

He sighed. She should have told him he was coming. "That's good! I wonder why she hasn't shown up yet."

"I'm sure she'll be here soon." Bo smiled. Of the three, he was the most patient.

"Are you giving her a gift?" Shao asked worriedly. Bo's parents were richer than his parents. He could afford to buy a more expensive gift.

"Of course. Here she comes."

Yuan trudged toward them. Her head was down and she wasn't wearing the new, beautiful pink dress she'd been talking about for months, the one her mother was sewing for her sixteenth birthday. Although she had no siblings, her parents were very poor.

"Let me say happy birthday first, please," Shao pleaded with Bo.

"Okay, Liang Shanbo." Bo teased with a slight elbow nudge.

"Can I talk to Shao in private?" Yuan asked, approaching them, her eyes still cast down.

"Happy birthday to you. Happy—" Shao began singing.

"I need to talk to you in private."

The boys exchanged a puzzled look. Something was wrong. She had never come to the park with wrinkled clothes and tangled hair. Her dark silky hair was always tied neatly behind her slim back.

"I'll be back soon. You can have your privacy," said Bo.

"That was a little rude, don't you think?" Shao said, watching Bo walk toward the nearby tree. If someone had asked him to leave, he would probably have been home by now. He wasn't as refined as Bo. "What happened? Never seen you like this."

"I needed to talk to you alone." She raised her head. Her eyes were red and swollen. She stared at him and then broke down in tears.

He moved forward to hug her but she pushed him away. "What's wrong?"

"I'm pregnant." She covered her face.

"Wha..wha..What?" His eyes widened in terror.

"I am pregnant!"

"Shhh! Not so loud!"

Bo turned back, amused, before leaving the park.

"It's your fault. I told you not to do it. You ruined my life. My parents will kill me."

Shao stood there in shock, speechless. It had never occurred to him that something like this could happen. His head was spinning.

"Say something," she sobbed. "You have to help me."

"What do you want me to do?"

"We should get married." She wiped her tears. "You always said you'd marry me." She tried to take his hand but he pulled it back.

"Are you crazy? It's not the right time."

"It is for me." She looked into his eyes. "You don't want to marry me?"

"I do love you. But I have many dreams to fulfill. Why can't you understand?"

"I understand now." She shook her head and turned away. All she had dreamed was to marry him one day. In her mind, he was the first and the last man in her life. Walking to the park, she was sure Shao would take her in his arms and ask her to marry him. Why wouldn't he? He was a man of honor and dignity, as he had told her numerous times. Now, hearing him talk, she felt as if her heart were being ripped out of her chest. He wasn't a man. He was just a scared boy who had taken away her most valuable possession. She had picked the wrong tree to shelter her from capricious weather, and now the whirlwind was looming.

"Wait! I didn't give you your birthday gift yet." He reached for his pocket.

"You already did, Shao!" She said hysterically and raced from the park. Nobody had noticed her bare feet.

He didn't try to run after her. "I'm too young to be a father. I don't even have a regular job. I can't marry her," he said aloud, walking slowly toward the exit. A week later, he left his childhood town unannounced, just like his teacher, Chao Chang.

"Master! What should I tell the man?" Hu asked, clearing his throat.

Shao raced to the door, shouting, "Bo Wang! My friend! Where have you been all these years?" He surveyed his stocky friend from head to foot.

The men hugged each other with teary eyes.

"You look strong," Bo said, loosening his tight hug. He remembered Shao as a skinny young man, his rib cage sticking out prominently against his pallid skin. In those days, he'd never hug Bo or any boy in the neighborhood. He was touchy about his weight.

"So do you. I can't believe I haven't seen you in so long! Come inside, please. Hu, bring us some tea. My best friend is here."

"I'm already making it," Hu replied from the kitchen.

"Thank you." Hu always knew what to do without asking him. "I felt awful leaving town without saying goodbye to you. Hope you've forgiven me."

"Don't worry. I'm as guilty as you are. I've read about you in the newspapers but couldn't summon the courage to meet you."

"Courage? What do you mean?" Shao asked, sitting on the bench.

"You know! You're an important man."

"I'm just a humble man trying to help our country. Nothing more."

"You're very kind. How is your family? Any kids?"

Momentarily, Shao fell silent. Talking about family wasn't his favorite subject. He had often changed topic when someone asked him about his personal life. To deter people from asking him such private questions, he never subjected anyone, friend or foe, to them. Similar rules couldn't be applied to this guest. He had come from the era Shao wished had never existed. Over the years he had trained his mind not to go back in time, but today he failed. Bo was here and so was Yuan's last image, running toward the park exit.

"I didn't mean to be intrusive."

"Oh no, Bo. Sorry. I was just thinking about our old days. We had so many good times together. As to your question, well, I never married. My parents died a few years ago, and my siblings are scattered all over the country. How about you? You marry anyone?"

"Yes, I did," he replied quietly.

"Lucky girl."

"Please forgive my rudeness for showing up at your door unannounced. I'm desperate. I need help." He leaned forward.

"Bo Wang, speak and I'll do anything. You are like a brother to me. Tell me what's on your mind."

"I need to find my son."

"Your son? What happened to him?"

"One day he became upset with me and left the house. Some people say he joined the CPC. But no one has seen him. I'm worried about him. I shouldn't have let him leave home."

"I'm so sorry to hear that. How many kids do you have?" Shao asked, fearing the worst. Japanese soldiers had rounded up as many young men as they could find and then either executed them or sent them to prison camps. One third of the youth he had recruited were now at the mercy of Japanese prison guards.

"Just one."

"Don't worry. If he works for our party, I will find him for you in no time. What is his name?"

Hu walked in with tea. "Master, Li Kenong is at the door."

"Oh, I completely forgot about him. Bring him in," he said, rising and turning to Bo. "I'm sorry. Why don't you wait here so we can continue our discussion?"

"Please, go and attend to your guest. I'll come back tomorrow."

"That's what I've always admired about you: you're so caring about others. Let's have dinner tomorrow."

"That will be great."

"Let me walk you to the door. I'll introduce you to my friend Li."

Bo nodded and they joined Hu in welcoming the guest.

"Li! We were just talking about you," Shao smiled. "This is my childhood friend, Bo Wang."

Li smiled, bowing his head and then shaking hands. He had known Shao the longest time and had never heard him talk about his friends. "I hope I didn't interrupt your meeting."

"No, no. I was just leaving. See you tomorrow, Shao."

"He looks like a good man," Li said, as they eased into a room.

"Oh wait! I forgot—" Shao Peng sprinted back to the door and called after his friend. "Bo Wang!"

Bo hadn't gone too far. He looked over his shoulder.

"What's your son's name?"

"Peter Chang! His name is Peter Chang," he shouted, waving goodbye and disappearing into a thin crowd.

Shao's heart sank and his stomach churned. *No! No! Maybe it's a different Peter Chang!* He'd never felt so weak.

"He's probably already home. How long are you going to stand there?" Li gently stroked his shoulder.

Shao closed the door quietly. His hands were shaking.

"What's wrong? Are you okay? You look like you've seen a ghost." Li grabbed his elbow. "Hu! Bring some water."

"I'll be fine. I'm a little dizzy," Shao said, looking around for a place to sit. Li helped him to a wooden stool.

Hu hurried in with the water. "Drink water. You will feel better, master."

"What happened?" Li asked worriedly, searching Hu's face for answers.

"Master, you work too much. You don't rest."

"I'm fine, Hu. Could you leave us alone? I need to talk to Li."

"Yes, master. I'll go make you some Darjeeling. It will soothe your stomach." He ran to the kitchen. He could barely write his own name, but he was good at finding natural home remedies for common illnesses. Most of Shao's friends preferred his medical opinion over a doctor's, especially for sexual problems. Hu was discreet and free.

"What's the matter, Shao?"

"I don't know what to do. I'm so ashamed of myself."

"Could you explain?" Li asked with a hint of frustration.

"Bo Wang came to ask me to find his lost son."

"That's not a problem. I can help you," Li assured him with a soft pat on his shoulder. It wasn't the first time someone had come looking for his children. When Japanese forces attacked Nanjing thousands of displaced families asked him to help find their family members. He never refused anyone and was able to assist most of them with the help of his guerrilla task force.

"Can you?" He fixed him with an enigmatic stare. "His name is Peter Chang."

Li's jaw dropped. He sat down. "Maybe it's a different Peter Chang."

Shao rubbed his forehead nervously. "What if it's not?"

"That would be dreadful. What are you going to do?"

"I don't know. If I tell him his son's whereabouts, I betray my party. But if I don't tell him, I betray my childhood friend. There's no easy answer."

"I'm sure you'll make the right decision, especially when party loyalty is involved," Li said with an unusually sharp tone.

Shao understood.

"I think we should postpone our meeting to another time. You seem to have enough issues to resolve." Li rose.

"I'll see you in a couple of days."

"I hope you make a good decision!" Li shook his hand hurriedly and left.

At three in the morning, Shao was still trying to fall asleep. His anxiety grew by the hour as he thought of his best friend coming to dinner, hoping to find his son. "I wish I knew, I wish I knew," he muttered, thinking about his last meeting with Mao Zedong.

"I hear you have much influence over Peter Chang," Mao had said from behind his desk, beckoning him to sit. The lonely chair was placed directly across from the slightly overweight man in his late forties.

"He's a good young man. He's obedient to his officers'

commands," he answered, somewhat baffled. He hadn't known the meeting would be about Peter Chang.

"You have been great to our country and to our party. I am hoping that you will be able to join our head council soon."

"I am honored," he said. His lifelong dream was about to materialize. He was ecstatic.

"You deserve every ounce of praise, and now our party has decided to bestow upon you the most important assignment of your loyal career." Every word from the oval face was enunciated carefully.

"I am grateful that you find me worthy of your confidence. I will never fail to accomplish my duties."

"I never heard a better answer." Mao smiled. He rubbed the small bump on his square chin. "Our party feels that a few tough men, who certainly helped us a great deal to fight the guerrilla war against the Japanese, are now becoming belligerent and burdensome."

"I did not realize the situation had gotten so bad," Shao Peng said. His heart rhythm was abnormal. His sixth sense sounded an alarm. Someone had vilified Peter Chang.

"Our informers tell us that some are even talking about starting their own political party."

"That will be terrible for our country." Shao knew most of the tough guys Mao was referring to. He had hired them and never thought they were any more a threat to the Party than any other Chinese man walking down the street. Not everybody believed in the CPC manifesto.

"I know! That is why the Party has decided to get rid of these insurgents as soon as possible."

"Get rid of—"

"You heard right! We cannot afford to fight them, so we must find a way to eliminate the threat," Mao declared, then asked Shao to bring his chair closer to the desk.

A soft knock at the door woke Shao. Outside the window the sun shone in its full glory. "I'm coming," he said groggily, and shuffled over to his door, where Hu waited on the other side.

"Sorry I didn't wake you earlier. I thought you should rest, but you still look tired."

"Could you make me some tea?" He went out in the courtyard to sit in the sun.

Shao spent most of the day fabricating the story he would tell his friend about his son's whereabouts. *How can I tell him that I'm responsible for sending his son away? No one understands that I sent him to survive and not get killed,* he agonized, remembering Mao's final chilling words: "Make sure none of these men ever come back to China to threaten our party's stability. We like you and don't want you to fail in this mission. Our party has no room for unsuccessful leaders and commanders."

It was still daylight when Hu announced, "Your friend from yesterday is here."

"Bring him in," he said, sweating and looking around his sitting room nervously. This was where he'd said farewell to Peter Chang only a few months before.

"How are you?" Bo asked.

"I am so glad you came. Come sit next to me." Shao scooted to his left and patted the bench.

"Thank you. Are you feeling well? You look a little pale."

"I'm fine. I worked late last night trying to find out about your son."

"Any news?" Bo asked excitedly.

"Unfortunately not. But don't be disheartened. I will keep looking until I find him."

"Thanks," Bo said, closing his eyes a few seconds. "I lied to you yesterday."

"About what?"

"I knew my son came with you from Nanjing."

"How did you know?" Shao's eyes bulged.

"I wrote you that anonymous letter about my son. His life was in danger there. You were the only person who could have helped him."

"Oh, Bo!" Shao wiped his face. "I wish you had told me all this earlier."

"What happened to him? I heard he became a big war hero."

"You heard right. But a few months ago he decided to quit our party. Nobody has seen him since." Shao felt his airways tightening.

"Oh," Bo sighed. "You know I named him after our teacher."

"Chao Chang?"

Bo nodded.

"Come on. Don't make a sad face. I will find your son. Tell his mother not to worry," Shao said, squeezing his shoulder gently. A few years ago he had run into his old teacher at the Beijing train station. After successfully recruiting more members for the Party, he was about to embark on the Shanghai-bound train when he saw Chao Chang walking on the same platform. He was old and walked with a limp.

When Shao approached him, he didn't recognize him, but he was glad to see him once he told him who he was. Chao said he had left town because some men came to his house in the dark and told him to leave or be killed. He chose to run.

Bo sighed, lowering his head. "His mother is dead."

"How awful! I am so sad to hear this. Was she sick?"

"No." Bo shook his head. "She was murdered."

"What? Damn Japanese?" His face distorted with anger.

"No. Peter had a fight with a girl. Her brother and his friends came to my factory, beat us up, and burnt down my factory. My wife didn't survive her injuries."

"You knew where I was. Why didn't you come to me? I will destroy your enemies!" Shao threw a fist in the air. His face was red.

"I wanted to ask you for help but she said no." Tears rolled down his cheeks.

"Why? Who …?"

"Yuan!" he mumbled, stooping his head.

Shao's face went white and his mouth fell open. He had avoided her name for so many years. He was so ashamed of what he did to her that he never tried to find out her plight. The only way to survive the guilt was to bury it deep inside. "Yuan?" he mumbled, feeling as if the Huangshan Mountain had just collapsed on his chest.

Outside Hu was talking to someone. "Master is meeting with his friend."

"Peter isn't just my son, Shao…you left her but I couldn't…..she still loved…" Bo wailed. How could he describe the feelings he'd been carrying since he had stopped Yuan from jumping into the Huangpu River? She'd been crying. Her parents had wished her dead. Her neighbors had called her a whore. Everybody had abandoned her. Even though she avoided him as if he were accountable for her misfortune, he didn't give up. He wasn't a man who could surrender his friends to calamity. He followed her secretly. He knew she was vulnerable and might do something unimaginable. His instincts paid off. He saved her and the life she was carrying inside her. Against his parents' consent he married her before she became a mother. Her son wasn't fatherless. "Shao! Why are you holding your chest? Hu! Hu!"

Hu came running. Kang Sheng was following him. "Master, what happened?"

Shao was breathing abnormally and mumbling, "He…. mm…s…"

"Shao! Shao! Talk to me! What's wrong?" Kang Sheng grabbed his arms.

Shao Peng lifted his head and whispered something in Kang Sheng's ear, visibly shocking him. He squeezed Shao's hand and nodded in short bursts, "You will be fine. I will!"

"Yo… prom…." Shao couldn't finish his words.

CHAPTER EIGHT

Peter Chang was cautiously happy about what went on in his bedroom every afternoon. Kim Suk came to him almost every weekday. On weekends she had to go with Kim Sung to political parties, most of which began before noon and ended around midnight. Peter hated the weekends and always stayed up to watch Kim Suk drag her intoxicated husband to the bedroom.

Lately Peter was surprised to see that Kim Sung had stopped bringing girls home at night. "Maybe he's becoming a better person," he told Kim Suk one afternoon, but she shot him down.

"Of course not! One of the Soviet generals' wives told me he spends most of his evenings in an army-run brothel with her husband."

"You don't need him when you have this." He puffed his chest out.

She smiled affectionately. He looked good without a shirt, especially with that red bruise on his right chest. She had been too wild that day. "I missed my monthly. I might be pregnant."

The news hit him like a brick. Despite day after day of uninhibited sexual bouts, he hadn't considered this outcome. He began to feel guilty. He wasn't as careful with her as he was with other girls. He walked over to her, concealing his trepidation. "Are you sure?"

"I am," she said, as if it were nothing. She showed no sign of worry. In fact, her face was euphoric. "Why are you so pale?"

Peter smiled to conceal his discomfort. He was a little surprised by her deportment. Pregnancy wasn't a trivial matter. "Aren't you worried?"

"'No!'" she rolled her eyes. "But I know he is." She flopped his limp penis and laughed.

Peter gave her an angry stare and told her to stop.

"Don't be such a baby!" She pushed his hands away and was ready to put him inside her when they heard Kim Sung's voice outside the room.

"Kim Suk! Where are you?"

Horrified, Peter jumped off the bed and ran to the door to peek through a small crack in his wooden door. Kim Sung was walking to his room. For the first time in months he'd come home before midnight. Already dressed in her pink chiffon *hanbok,* Kim Suk mouthed him to stay put and tiptoed out of his room. That was a close call.

Peter shut the door silently and, on his knees, looked through the crack. This was the first time he had ever felt fear and it was directed toward Kim Suk. He was sure she didn't suspect that all their hours of intimacy had sewn a seed of love in his heart. He had never felt that about a woman before and was sure Kim Suk probably didn't share his feelings. His heart raced when he saw Kim Sung coming out of his room and Kim Suk walking toward him.

"Where were you? I looked for you all over the house," Kim Sung howled like a hungry wolf. They were standing in the middle of courtyard, his back toward the bedrooms and hers toward the kitchen. The sun was gone for the day but enough light lingered for Peter to see.

Kim Suk's response was inaudible. Peter stuck his ear to the crack.

"What were you doing in the kitchen? Where is Peter Chang?" His hands were behind his back and he looked completely spent.

Peter was sweating. Had they aroused his suspicion? That's why he had come home early—to catch them in the act?

"Peter wasn't feeling well this afternoon. I sent him to rest in his room. I didn't want him to spread his germs, since…"

"Since what?"

"I think I'm pregnant."

You stupid woman! Peter Chang felt his heart in his throat. What he witnessed next was unbelievable. Kim Sung lifted Kim Suk off her feet and spun her around in utter jubilation. Peter thumped his head against the door.

"Oh, Kim Suk, you did really well. Now make sure it's a boy. It's important the first child is a boy! You will have the best medical care. I will get you the best Soviet doctors. You understand?"

"I understand. Now put me down. My back hurts. Why are you home early?"

Kim Sung put his hand on her shoulder and murmured something.

Peter couldn't make out the words but he saw Kim Suk's face turn white. She shook her head repeatedly, her hands on her cheeks, her shoulders slightly dipped. He got to his feet and opened the door, only to see Kim Suk following her husband to their bedroom. The couple didn't bother to look back at him, even though he'd rattled the door hard.

Realizing, he was out of the woods, a deep sigh of relief escaped his lips as he moved toward the kitchen, thinking about cooking rice while he pictured Kim Suk's unforgettable face. He stared at two bags sitting next to each other, one almost full and the other almost empty. "I hate cleaning rice!" he muttered, reaching for the full bag. It had been two weeks since he'd spent most of his day separating the rice from the impurities. He hated Soviet shopkeepers for adulterating rice bags with sawdust and flour in addition to the ubiquitous small pebbles and mouse droppings. Usually he didn't run out of clean rice, but because the majority of his afternoons were tied up with Kim Suk, he had three fewer hours to do all his chores.

"Let's clean you," he mumbled, placing a ten-kilo bag of rice on the table. Apart from the cleaning, Peter loved the kitchen. It was bigger than his apartment in Shanghai and had plenty of storage cabinets. There was a four-foot-high T-shaped counter across from the entry door. Four stoves and Cajun spice canisters occupied the first half of the counter. The other half was used for food preparation. A small, barred window a few feet above the stoves ventilated the room. One cracked sink was affixed to the wall on the left and numerous built-in cabinets were on the right-hand wall. The counter itself was almost three feet deep and there was plenty of open space underneath it. Peter stored his rice, potatoes, onions, and *kimchi* there.

He untied the bag and was scooping the rice with his hands when he heard whispers behind him. He didn't turn his head. It was considered bad manners and would have given rise to suspicion that he was nosing around his masters.

A few minutes later, he heard Kim Suk's clunky house slippers, which had wooden bottoms and produced lots of undesirable noise on hard surfaces. Peter had begged her to get new leather slippers like her husband but she was stubborn.

"He's gone back," she announced, walking in.

Peter Chang turned his face to her. "Something wrong? Have you been crying?"

She didn't answer but pulled out a chair from the dining table where he was working and collapsed. Kim Suk and Peter were the only ones who used the four-chair wooden table. When Kim Sung was home, Peter served their meals in a more formal setting in the dining room.

"I can't believe it." She was looking down at the table, eyes filled with tears.

Peter pushed the bamboo rice sorter aside and placed his hand on her shoulder. "Tell me what happened."

"Shao Peng passed away," she said, raising her head. Her eyes were wet.

"What are you saying?"

"He is dead," she squeezed her eyes. Tears flooded her cheeks.

"How did he die?" He tried to look unaffected by the news, but deep down he was genuinely sad. Even though Shao had deliberately sent him on an impossible mission, in his heart he'd already forgiven his mentor and wondered if he had actually done him a favor by sending him to Kim Sung's house instead of some other place. Shao had gotten him closer to the woman of his dreams.

"I don't know. Kim Sung said he was talking to an old friend and suddenly fell to the floor."

"Just like that?" he asked, sitting down next to her. "I left him in good health."

She ran her fingers through his neatly combed dark hair as if she understood he was holding back tears. "Kim Sung went to Shanghai to pay his respects."

Peter kept his head down. Shao had never mentioned he knew Kim Sung personally. He was a secretive man. What else had he kept hidden?

"What are you thinking?"

"Nothing." He looked up at her face. Her hands felt so comforting against his scalp. "Let's run away from this place. I'll take you away from this miserable life."

"Run away! Where?" She remained calm. The idea wasn't novel. She had thought about it several times before he'd arrived at her house. It wasn't possible, she had concluded. The potential backlash of such a daring enterprise had chilled her bones. The subject had actually come up during the course of a fight with Kim Sung. He told her if she ever tried to leave him, he would feed her to the dogs. Though death didn't scare her, she was afraid that her actions would mortify the CPC.

"We can go back to China or head south!" He grabbed her hands. "We can do this."

"Don't be naive!" She rose, her hands across her chest, "I'm the wife of the future leader of Korea. Look outside the house! There are guards and spies everywhere. But…"

"But what?"

"I may be able to help *you* escape to the south," she whispered.

"Are you crazy? I can't leave you here in this condition." He narrowed his eyes and looked at her stomach.

She put her hands around his neck and reached for his thin lips. He was a real man. Not like her father. Not like her husband.

Time was moving more quickly than Peter had hoped. Kim Suk's protruding belly made him jittery. Eating at him by the hour was the fear that Kim Sung's aunt had articulated the first day she came to visit. "In our family the first child always looks like the father." Peter almost dropped the tea tray on her feet, but Kim Suk responded with a smile and politely cautioned him to be careful with hot tea. Was she carrying his baby? He thought of this when going to bed, when waking up, when cooking, when cleaning, and when he saw her prancing around the house. He wished she would say something about the paternity. There was no way he could ask her the question. How would one go about asking a married woman if the child in her womb belonged to him or her husband? He was in a quandary.

Late one afternoon after Kim Suk, who was in her eighth month, stopped coming to his room, Peter heard Kim Sung's loud, livid voice. He'd been coming home earlier than usual for a month. Peter sprang from his bed and raced out the door. Kim Suk, a few feet from her husband, leaned against the wall. Peter grabbed a broom to sweep the courtyard in order to listen. Kim Sung seemed not to care he was nearby.

"You ungrateful bitch! These people gave me everything we have," he berated her.

"I won't give my child a Soviet name! There are other ways to appreciate people."

Oh! Kim Suk, please calm down, Peter thought, sweeping harder. He'd seen the end of most of their quarrels. Kim Sung would yell and curse, slug her in the face, then either storm out of the house or to his room.

"Shut up, you stupid woman!" Kim Sung lunged forward and slapped her. "You're not worthy of me. Low-life peasant!" After several more insults he left the house, raging. Kim Suk hid her face behind her hands and went to her room.

Peter watched sadly, then dragged himself to his own room, regretting his helplessness. He used to go after her to console her, but she would scream at him, as if he were to blame for her grievances, and throw him out. Her anger never lasted more than a day and she always came back to him in tears, followed by passionate lovemaking. Peter had deliberately followed her because he loved the outcome of her rage, but as her delivery date neared, he resolved not to aggravate her further. He knew she couldn't show up the next day to compensate him.

~

Peter had heard stories of Soviet winters but never thought that one day he would experience such bone-chilling temperatures. At the beginning of autumn, Kim Suk warned him about the cold months to come, but he didn't take her seriously. During winter in Shanghai, his parents used to beg him to wear warm clothes. He would laugh and make fun of their old bones. He wore the same clothes year-round and never felt the need to bundle up in a bulky outfit like his peers. One December he and a few other Chinese guerrillas had followed some Japanese soldiers into Korea, where the weather was so cold more than half his men complained. That was the only time in his life he'd worn an extra layer.

December 1940 was brutally cold in *Vyatskoye*. Kim Suk gave him her husband's old winter clothes, but despite the two pairs of gloves, three wool sweaters, winter hat, knee-length overcoat, heavy wool socks, and sturdy Red army boots, he was still cold.

His cleaning routine had changed. He didn't use a broom to clean the courtyard, but a shovel to clear the snow every morning, sometimes two or three times a day. His room was warmed with a generous-sized Soviet heater, but he hated spending half an hour every morning swaddling in Kim Sung's old clothes, which still smelled of the strong perfume he wore every day. The smell was so pungent that the first day Peter had checked all his pockets twice to make sure Kim Sung hadn't left his bottle of perfume in some hidden pocket. Once outside his cozy quarters, the extreme weather numbed his olfactory nerves on contact and he went about his business without smelling anything.

~

As the end of January 1941 approached, Soviet doctors limited Kim Suk to her room and advised her to stay in bed as much as possible. Kim Sung was back to his old routine and didn't come home until midnight, or sometimes not at all. Kim Suk didn't care if he came home or not and was now sleeping in a different room than her husband. Kim Sung seemed happy with her decision.

I should make her favorite soup today, Peter thought as he piled up the fresh snow in one corner of the courtyard. He needed to clear the passage between his room and the kitchen and then the passage between the kitchen and Kim Suk's room. It had been snowing continuously for the past six hours. When he'd gone out earlier to buy some meat and other kitchen supplies, people in the town were talking about a blizzard heading their way.

Peter's cooking had gotten much better, at least according to Kim Suk, and he prepared her food carefully, especially since her pregnancy. On the other hand, Kim Sung hardly ate at home.

The two hours of shoveling were a total failure. The new snow came down faster than he could clear it, and after seeing that the two-foot-wide pathway he'd cleared to the kitchen was already filled again with the fresh snow, he slammed the shovel against the wall and went to the kitchen. No point fighting Mother Nature, he told himself, stamping his feet at the kitchen doorway.

Just over an hour later, he came out of the kitchen holding a covered tray. It was still snowing. He looked up at the grey clouds and then across the snow-covered courtyard. The evidence of his two hours of hard labor was already buried under new powder. He tightened his grip on the tray handles and headed toward Kim Suk's room. Each step felt heavier than the last. "Oh, oh, damn!" he shouted in panic as he almost tripped over the shovel he'd thrown down earlier, now hidden under the white blanket.

"Kim Suk!" he called through the closed wooden door.

After they started sleeping together, she had told him to call her by her name. She didn't answer.

"Kim Suk!" He rapped the door with his foot.

"Push it harder! It's not latched," her muffled voice answered.

Peter turned his back against it and stamped his feet, then struck it with his buttocks. It opened with a dull thud. The moisture had warped it.

"Why did you go to so much trouble to cook in this weather?"

He closed the door behind him so the heat wouldn't escape and walked to her bed. "You need to eat something." He settled the tray on the bedside table and stood over her. The room was warm and she was lying under a thick, quilted, handmade blanket. Her cheeks were puffy and pink and her hair was spread over both shoulders. She was at least twenty pounds heavier than the last time they had made love. He craved her every night.

"What did you make me?" She smiled, pushing away her blanket. He helped her sit up and propped her up with pillows behind her back.

"I made you something special," he said smiling, looking at the door and then kissing her cheek bravely. Her cheeks turned one shade darker. "I cooked you *galbitang*." She'd told him how her mother used to make her favorite soup, a delicate broth of pork ribs, diced onions, minced garlic, sesame oil, sesame seeds, and peppers. Some people loved it with plain white rice, but he remembered she preferred it alone.

"I didn't know you could make it."

"I hope you like it." He took off his gloves and uncovered the tray, revealing a dark-colored clay pot and two small matching bowls with two white ladles. "Let me get you a lap table." He glanced around the room but couldn't resist staring down at her cleavage. Her blue gown's top two buttons were open. Her breasts appeared two sizes larger. She noticed him looking.

"You think I'm hiding the tray in here?" She pulled her top down and laughed. She wasn't wearing a bra and one of her breasts spilled out. Peter chuckled and tried to move away from her side, but she grabbed his overcoat and slipped her hand inside. He was hard.

"You feel ignored, huh?" She touched his crotch and began unbuttoning his fly.

He didn't move and grabbed her exposed breast and began squeezing it. She moaned softly as she stroked his cock. The pleasure was too intense. He closed his eyes. He was almost at the climax when he noticed her grip around his penis was getting tighter and rougher. He opened his eyes. She was sweating profusely and biting her lips.

"What's wrong?" He grabbed her hand.

"I think the baby is coming," she panted. Peter hesitated, and then dashed to the door.

"Don't go! I'm fine now," she groaned. "It was a cramp."

He looked back, confusion and nervousness all over his face. "You're sure?" This was the first time he'd been around a pregnant woman, and even though the Soviet doctor who checked on her four times a week had told him what to expect, as she got closer to her due date he was still fidgety.

"Yes. Let me have my soup," she smiled.

⁓

A few false alarms later, on February 4, 1941, Kim Suk was

taken to the nearby Soviet army hospital, where she gave birth to a boy. Kim Sung begged the doctors to delay the birth. "Four is a very bad number for the Korean people. It's bad luck," he argued. They looked at each other and smiled. Three hours later, they placed the baby in his arms.

"Peter! Come here," Kim Sung called.

Peter had gone to the hospital with a fresh batch of soup.

"You hold the baby. I need to talk to the Soviet general." Kim Sung transferred the baby to his arms and ran out. Peter felt his knees buckling and his heartbeat quickening. He had spent months preparing for this outcome. But nothing was working at the moment. His hands were shaking with nervousness. Was he holding his own son?

"Give him to me! Before you drop him on the floor," a heavyset nurse came to his rescue. She had been watching him from a distance.

Peter turned over the baby to her as fast as he could and collapsed on the nearby lobby bench. In a state of panic, he had forgotten to check if the newborn bore his resemblance. He thought about getting up and running after the nurse.

"Where's the baby?"

Peter looked over his shoulder. Kim Sung approached. "A nurse took him back."

"Good! Listen, Peter Chang. You are like my family. I'm going to trust you with a very important job." He put a hand on each shoulder. "Can I trust you?"

"Yes, master. You can trust me." Peter looked down at his boots. They were wet from walking to the hospital in two inches of snow.

"The baby is not born yet," Kim Sung said. "You know how stupid people are. I talked to the general and he will make sure that the baby's birth certificate shows a different date and birthplace. I am thinking about February sixteenth, a good day to be born. What do you think?"

"Mmm. You always know best," Peter mumbled. He knew Chinese and Koreans believed in numerology but had never heard of someone going so far as to hide a birthdate. For the most part, the Koreans and Chinese loved having boys and took great pride in announcing their births.

"Good. Now go home and don't tell anyone where we are. I am going to find somewhere to stay while Kim Suk and the baby rest here. If anyone asks you about us, especially my aunt, tell them I took Kim Suk to Paekdu Mountain."

In this weather, Peter thought. Divided between China and Korea, Paekdu Mountain was considered a holy place by many Koreans and Chinese. Some superstitious visitors considered the lake surrounded by the vast mountain a passage to heaven. In winter, nobody traveled there. The treacherous road was buried deep under snow. "Yes, master."

"Very good. Now leave and don't forget our conversation." Kim Sung squeezed his shoulders and slowly walked away, nodding his head.

~

Peter Chang had a hard time controlling his temper when Ko Hee insulted him and accused him of lying.

"Tell me the truth, China boy. Where are my nephew and his wife?" She rolled her beady brown eyes. This was her fifth visit in three days.

"Ma'am, master has taken his family to Paekdu Mountain," Peter told her for the fifth time.

"In this weather?" She looked outside the kitchen door

and stared at the falling snow. It was early afternoon and he regretted leaving the front door open after coming back from the fish market. She hadn't felt the need to knock or, even if she had, he hadn't heard it. He was busy in the kitchen when she snuck up and scared the hell out of him.

"I don't know, ma'am. I'm just a servant," he replied, staring at her back. She was well under five feet tall and had a pudgy, round face, as if the honeybees had feasted on it. Her extremities were covered with layers of gloves and snowshoes.

"Listen, China boy—"

"My name is Peter Chang." He despised her implied insult. His father had told him of the remaining old Korean bigots who considered the Chinese inferior to their race.

"Hey! I am your master's aunt. You interrupt me again, I'll slap you."

You bitch! I'll never forget to close the door again, he thought, grinding his teeth.

"It's getting late. I am leaving." She gave him a final scornful glare and left the house. Peter cursed, closing the door behind her, and went to his room. The woman had ruined his appetite.

—

On February fifteenth, Peter woke up an hour early to start cleaning the house. *Tomorrow is a big day,* he smiled, remembering the conversation he'd had with Kim Sung at the hospital and hoping to see Kim Suk soon. The past few days had been hard without her. He missed her presence and felt lonely.

He began his cleaning in the kitchen and a few hours later ended it with mopping Kim Suk's room for the second time. Her room was spacious. It had a big bed in the center, two waist-high wooden chests of drawers pushed against the wall, a vanity mirror with a small matching stool, and a small window, which she never allowed him to open.

Should I clean his room, too? He stared at Kim Sung's door, latched from the outside. Kim Suk was the only person allowed to go in and clean it. Even before they separated their rooms, Peter wasn't allowed to enter his for any reason. *Maybe cleaning it would piss him off... but why am I not supposed to enter it?* He put the mop bucket aside and looked around guiltily, then unlatched the door. It opened inwardly.

Place smelled like a rotten fish. He held his nose and walked in gingerly. The room was in chaos. Half the floor was covered with his discarded clothes, shoes, socks, and coats, and the other half was buried under newspapers, magazines, handwritten notes, and crumpled papers. No wonder he didn't want anyone to come in here. He glanced at the bed. A white quilt was bunched up beside two red satin pillows. The bed sheet was also red and deeply wrinkled. He drew nearer but immediately jumped back. The bed sheet wasn't wrinkled—it was covered in a glue-like substance. Peter knew it well. His own sheet had been covered with it after Kim Suk had stopped sleeping with him and he was forced to take matters into his own hands, so to speak. The only difference was he washed the seminal fluids off his bed sheet regularly.

What do we have here? He smiled, noticing one of the two bedside tables. He circled the bed and scooped up a magazine. He gasped at the cover photo, a nude, voluptuous, blond European woman. Peter couldn't read the name of the magazine or any of the writing inside. He guessed the language to be French or German. He looked through the pages with keen interest. He'd never seen naked blond women. After leering at each page, he put the magazine back and reached for the top drawer. "Wow!" The drawer was full of similar magazines. He pulled the whole stack out and placed it on top of the table. "What the hell?"

One magazine at the bottom slipped through his fingers. He reached for it. The cover didn't picture a raw girl. It had an image of a swastika. With his brow creased, he began turning the pages. "Shit!" He was horrified. It wasn't a magazine at all; it was a torture manual. He counted more than fifty hand-drawn pictures of a man wearing a Gestapo uniform torturing a man, a woman, and a child. Each picture was gruesome and had writing underneath. He shook his head in disgust. His earlier arousal, from seeing all those naked women, had turned into nauseating apprehension and revulsion. Why did he need this type of book? He put everything back in the drawer and left the room.

At twenty past seven, Peter gave the kitchen a final look. Everything was nice and clean. All the dishes were washed and dried, the tile floor was scrubbed to a shine, and the cabinets and the kitchen counter were clutter-free. Kim Suk was fussy if he wasn't careful about cleaning after cooking. He shrugged and turned his focus to the snow-covered courtyard. It was hardly visible, notwithstanding three of the six light bulbs hanging on a wire running over the courtyard were functioning. He'd never seen all six working at one time. He'd asked Kim Suk to replace the burned-out bulbs but she'd rejoined with, "What's there to see?"

When the snow stopped, he looked at the dark sky, then squinted straight ahead until his retinas adjusted to the dim light and he was finally able to see the courtyard parameters. He wished for no more snow. He knew the odds were against him. Kim Sung's aunt, after seeing him shivering, had warned him the weather was going to get worse. He began walking back to his room. His previous deep footprints leading up to Kim Sung's room were already filled in.

Three hours passed since he'd gone to bed. His light was still on. He hardly ever felt the need to turn it off because it was a low-voltage bulb and the light barely reached his bed. Although his room was small and poorly ventilated—it had no window—he still liked it. It was better than all the other places he'd lived after leaving his father. This room had everything he wanted: a comfortable, wide bed (Kim Suk had replaced his original bed), a small table, a chair, a transistor radio, a single-door closet, some cast-iron hooks on the wall to hang his clothes, and a small bookshelf. He wasn't a reader so he used the shelves to store his shoes.

Unable to sleep, he got out of bed and went to the closet to get the radio. He never enjoyed the radio in *Vyatskoye* as much as he had in Nanjing. The reason was obvious: all the programs were in either Russian or some other language he didn't understand. He dragged the chair to his bed, put the radio on it, and turned the knob to find desirable music. After a few minutes, he finally found a station he could listen to. He clapped his hands upon hearing Brahms's lullaby. He'd heard the piece when he was little. His father loved classical music.

He was sprawled on his bed enjoying the music when the nude images he'd seen earlier started clouding his mind. Suddenly a loud noise startled him. He jumped out of bed, recognizing the source. Someone was pounding on the front door. It was almost one in the morning. He cursed, thinking about the frigid temperature outside and reaching for his overcoat. The knocking stopped. He drew his hand back from the coat and waited to hear another knock. Maybe the person got tired and left. He stood by the wall a few minutes. The radio had stopped playing music and a monotonous voice was speaking in Russian. He assumed it was a news hour.

Good! He sighed with relief. Whoever was stupid enough to knock at this hour has gone. He stretched out his arms, then abruptly rotated on his heel and stared at the radio. The announcer was saying something about Kim Sung. "What was that?" He ran to the radio and scooped it up. But the news was over and the music resumed. He shook the radio as if doing so would bring back the news, and then played with the tuning knob to find another news station. Most of the other numbers on the dial were either silent or static. "Shit! Nothing!"

He was too anxious to sleep. He began pacing the warm room. *What the heck! It's almost morning.* His outerwear was hanging on the wall pegs. He quickly dressed, leaving off gloves and shoes, and sat down on his bed.

A loud noise rent the silence. Peter woke with a start. He had fallen asleep sitting up and rolled onto his side, leaving the lower half of his body dangling out of bed. He fumbled to his feet. The noise came from the front door. He hastily put on his socks and shoes. He stuck his hands in his gloves and almost ran to open it. A cold gust of wind smacked him alert. *Damn!* He shivered. He looked to his right at the front gate. It was shaking. He checked the ground. *I don't think it snowed last night.* "I'm coming. I'm coming," he shouted.

"You damn fool! I'm freezing out here!" A voice howled.

"The witch is back," he mumbled. It was ten past six when he opened the door.

Ko Hee stood before him with red eyes. "What is wrong with you? I came last night but you refused to open the door. I am going to ask my nephew to kick you out of this house, you lazy bum!" She screamed, pushing him aside and marching in. With all her extra layers of clothes, she looked like a bag of rice.

"I'm sorry. I didn't hear the door." He closed the door and followed her to the living room. Few people used this room because Kim Sung conducted his political business outside the house.

"Were you drunk?" She peeled off her brown overcoat and moved within sniffing distance.

"No, ma'am." He never drank alcohol.

"Did you hear the great news?" She asked, removing her gloves. He didn't answer and gave her a vacant look. "Kim Sung is blessed with a son. What a great day to be born," she said, spreading her arms. "February sixteen is a sign of greatness."

"That is great news!" He smiled. How did she find out?

"I know, stupid! That's why I ran here last night when I heard it on the radio." She slapped his wrist. "Hey! What are you standing for? Go make some tea and start cleaning. I am going to visit my nephew."

"Where? Paekdu Mountain?"

"No stupid, the baby was born at the army hospital. I don't know why they traveled so far in her condition. Makes no sense," she said, rubbing her saggy chin.

"I will go make tea," Peter said, looking down at his

snow-covered boots. She hadn't bothered to clean her boots either and now the wooden floor needed a good mop.

"Go. I will come to the kitchen. This room isn't as warm." She picked up her coat and followed him. She was right. The living room was the biggest room in the house and even though it had a large heater, which stayed on every day of the winter, it still needed more heat. Its giant fireplace could provide further warmth, but since the room was hardly used, Peter never lit a fire.

"You make bad tea," she frowned, taking the first sip. She sat at the kitchen table.

Someone was battering the door. "I'll go check." Peter cringed and ran to the door, almost falling to the ground. Kim Sung was standing there, a Soviet army vehicle behind him.

"What took you so long? Go help Kim Suk and the baby out of the truck." He frowned and strode inside.

"Yes, master," Peter said nervously and galloped forward. Kim Suk sat on the back seat, holding a sleeping bundle in her arms. He opened the door. She smiled broadly and handed the baby to him, then carefully got out. The driver nodded and drove away.

"I wasn't expecting you for another two days." His heart was pounding hard.

"Ask Kim Sung!" she said, fumbling toward her room.

"Kim Suk!" Ko Hee came running from the kitchen. Kim Sung was behind her, looking displeased.

"Give me the baby!" Ko Hee said, throwing her arms wide. "Go make soup for her."

Peter handed her the baby and went to the kitchen. Kim Sung was blocking the entrance. He wore a black Soviet *ushanka* hat with earflaps, just like his wife, but the color of his overcoat and gloves was grey. Kim Suk wore red.

"Damn idiots!" Kim Sung said, moving aside.

Peter bowed his head and went straight to the stove. *Who are the idiots?*

"Some son of a bitch announced on the radio that the baby was born today at the hospital. I had to bring him home. I don't want people to know my son was born on Soviet land. He was born on *Korean* land!" He punched his hands together. "You understand, right?"

"Yes, master," Peter turned to reply.

"Make me some rice. I am hungry," he ordered, strolling out to the quadrangle.

"Yes, master." Peter reached under the kitchen counter. Good thing he'd already cleaned a whole bag in their absence.

It took Peter just over ninety minutes to prepare the food. Unsure if he was supposed to take the food to them or if they would come to the kitchen, he went to Kim Suk's room. The door was open. She was sitting on her bed. Ko Hee was cradling the baby while talking to Kim Sung. They all had taken off their outerwear.

"Look at him—my firstborn son. The boy who will carry my name."

"Why did you name him Yuri Ir–seno–*vich*?" Ko Hee had a hard time pronouncing the name, despite her limited knowledge of Russian. "The baby should have a Korean name like you."

"Don't worry about his name. It's just a political thing. You don't know how happy the Soviet commanders were after

I told them my boy's name. His real name is Kim Jong-Il," he said, pushing out his chest.

Ko Hee smiled. "That's a great name, the people of Korea are blessed with this great gift." She turned her attention to the door. "Hey! You are listening to our conversation?" She screamed at Peter, standing at the door waiting for them to notice him. He wasn't able to interrupt. That was considered rude.

"The food is ready. Should I serve it here or in the dining room?" he asked without raising his head.

"Use your brain, it's freezing outside. Bring the soup here," Ko Hee said.

"Yes, ma'am," Peter replied, moving away. He smiled when he heard Kim Suk's sharp voice say, "You shouldn't disrespect our servant."

A few more loud words were exchanged. Peter wasn't able to understand, but it was about him and it wasn't pleasant.

Five minutes later Peter returned. This time he didn't have to wait or speak. Kim Suk asked him to come in and put the food on her bedside table.

Kim Sung was talking to his aunt and sounded a little worried. "He is so special, but don't you think he looks more Chinese than Korean?"

"I have never seen a baby with a more Korean face than this baby. He looks like you," Ko Hee said. "If I didn't know better, I would say this baby is older than a day. Look at his wide eyes. He already loves me."

Suddenly, Peter was relieved. The baby not looking like him meant he wasn't the father. A great burden had lifted off his shoulders. He felt lighter and happier. Kim Sung was telling his aunt, "I should make Kim's birth something special, so people will revere him when he grows up to be their leader."

"That is a great idea. I know, nephew, nobody makes better stories than you," she smiled.

"Don't say I make up stories!" He protested. "I don't enjoy your careless remarks."

Embarrassed, Ko Hee turned to Peter. "You already put the food on the table. Now you want to feed us, too?"

Without a word, Peter hurried from the room.

CHAPTER NINE

By 1941 the Second World War, which officially began when Britain and France declared war on Germany for invading Poland in 1939, was in full swing. A few months after Kim Jong's birth, Germany and its Axis Powers attacked the Soviet Union. During this time, Kim Sung was extremely agitated and spent most days locked in his room. Peter Chang wasn't happy with the situation inside or outside the home. He wished he were part of the war instead of caretaker for a woman who didn't seem to be in any present danger.

On December 7, 1941, Kim Sung came out of his room shouting and dancing. "This is the best thing that ever happened." He wasn't wearing any outerwear and the temperature was below zero.

"What happened?" Kim Suk, still sleeping across from his room with the baby, emerged bundled in warm clothes, as if planning to go out. In fact, after giving birth she hadn't left the house except to take the baby to the doctor. Peter Chang watched Kim Sung's jubilation from the kitchen. He'd never seen him this happy.

"Those stupid Japanese attacked the U.S. at Pearl Harbor! Now they're going to pay," he beamed.

"You're sure? Americans don't like to fight. They've been sitting out the war while so many innocent people are dying. Look what Hitler has been doing to the poor Jews—eliminating them one by one."

"Who cares about Jews? Let them die." Kim Sung waved his arm. "Japan is our enemy. I want them destroyed and kicked out of my Korea."

Kim Suk confronted him. "You know the Germans, Italians, and Japanese are in this together."

They argued until the baby cried and she returned to attend to him.

What a self-serving bastard. Peter remembered the torture magazine with disgust and began slicing onions. Dinner was three hours away.

~

As the war entered its final phase Kim Sung was hardly ever home during the day, and many nights he didn't come home at all. He didn't care to tell his wife his whereabouts. She didn't care, and Peter was happy with the situation. He spent his mornings playing with Kim Jong and his afternoons making love to Kim Suk. Contrary to what he'd heard from one of his former guerrilla friends—that after the birth of a child women don't like sex—Kim Suk's libido was in overdrive, and she wasn't shy about demanding that Peter copulate with her every afternoon. He was always ready to perform no matter how tired he felt after cleaning and cooking, and now babysitting.

Late in the summer of 1943, Peter had finished his daily chores and was lying on his bed thinking about his father. He didn't know why he should suddenly think of him. Peter hadn't heard anything since the day he left his house with the garment bag on his shoulder.

I sure miss him. He dabbed at his wet eyes with the back of his thumb.

Something in the doorway distracted him. Provocatively dressed in a see-through navy blue gown, Kim Suk entered. She'd never come to his room this late. He jumped out of bed.

"Everything okay?" When she was halfway to his bed, he closed the door.

"Yes." She smiled. The dim light made her look sexy and desirable. Her puffy lips were covered with a new shade of red and she wasn't wearing any undergarments.

"Where's Kim Jong? What if Kim Sung comes home?" He said without shifting his gaze.

"You like it?" She smiled, looking down. "Don't worry! Kim Jong is sleeping and Kim Sung isn't coming home."

"In that case, why are you still wearing a gown?" He put his tongue in her mouth and squeezed her breasts. It had been over two months since he was able to fondle her breasts without milking her. She had breastfed Kim Jong until he turned eighteen months.

"I thought that was your job." She slipped her hand in his pajama pants. He was harder than he'd been in the afternoon.

He smiled and pulled her gown down to her ankles. She stepped out of it and kicked it aside. He stooped and his arms encircled her curvy buttocks, lifting her off her feet. His pulsating penis hanging over his pants, he dropped her on the bed and scrambled out of his clothes.

"You worked hard this afternoon. Let me do the work now." She motioned him to lie down. He obliged with an enthusiastic smile. She pushed his penis upward, lay on top of him, and began slithering. Her body was slippery and she smelled good. "You like it?"

"Oh shit!" He howled, tossing her to the side.

"Ouch!" She squealed, feeling his nails dig into her ribs. "What happened?"

Peter didn't answer but, his hands covering his genitals, he rushed to the door. It was ajar. He discreetly stuck out his head.

"What's the problem? Peter!" Kim Suk came after him, naked.

He raised his arm to stop her getting any closer.

"You're making me nervous. What is it?"

Peter pulled his head back in and pushed the door closed. He looked as if he were fighting the urge to vomit. His lips were white. "I think little Kim was watching us. I saw his face."

"Are you sure?" She asked, frantically putting her gown back on. "Maybe the wind opened the door."

"There's no wind." He got dressed. "Hurry up! Please. Go check on him."

"Don't make me panic, he's only two." She ran out of his room.

That two-year-old is a devil, he thought, pacing his room, waiting for her. Lately he'd been concerned about Kim Jong's odd behavior and was wondering if he should talk to her. He would tonight. An hour later, she came back with a smile.

"Did he see anything? What did he say?" he asked, pulling her by the wrist.

"Easy! You almost twisted my arm."

"I'm sorry." He released it and held her by the shoulders.

"Calm down, he's sleeping." She massaged her wrist.

Bug-eyed, Peter shook her. "I saw his eyes staring at us. He was here!"

"I don't know what opened the door, but I assure you it wasn't him. He's sound asleep."

Peter cast her a dubious glance. *Maybe she's right. But... I swear I saw his face.*

She saw his uncertainty. "What?"

He looked into her eyes. "I must tell you something."

"Go on." She looked amused.

"He scares me sometimes."

"Who?"

"Kim Jong." He dropped his hands from her shoulders and sat on his bed.

"You're scared of a baby?" She furrowed her brow.

"Don't look at me like that. I'm not crazy. I know what I'm talking about."

"Go ahead, tell me how a two-year-old boy frightens you." She sucked in her lips to keep from laughing.

"I've never seen a child who enjoys watching others get hurt. A couple of times I've nicked my finger cutting vegetables, and each time little Kim has laughed at seeing my blood. You remember on Tuesday when Kim Sung slipped in the courtyard?"

"Yes, I remember."

"Kim was so happy that he clapped and asked him to fall again."

"All children are like that."

"Not all children. What do you think happened to the little birds Kim Sung bought for his birthday?"

She looked frightened. "What? You told me you forgot to close the cage and they flew away."

"I lied. I didn't want him to get into any trouble. When I went to check on the birds they were already dead. He had twisted their necks. I told him not to say anything," said Peter, continuing, "You remember the cat that used to come to our house?"

Kim Suk nodded. She hadn't seen the stray cat in weeks. It used to jump over the wall and wander around the courtyard.

"He drowned it in the water canister."

Kim Suk stared at him in disbelief. "Why didn't you tell me all of this before?"

"At first I thought it was one of those things kids do at this age."

"What changed your mind?"

"Just now, before running away from the door, I think he gave me a thumbs up. I'm telling you, he was watching us!"

She laughed with relief. "You're going crazy! He's too young to stick up his thumbs at you, Peter. Stop imagining things! He never came to this room."

He sighed. "I hope you're right."

She looked at her watch. "I'm going now. It's getting late."

He nodded.

"Hey, Peter! Make sure he doesn't *strangle* me tonight," she jeered, leaving the room.

Peter smiled halfheartedly in return and waved his hand.

The unsettling change in Kim Jong's behavior happened when he turned two. Even though Kim Suk told him Kim Sung wasn't happy about his son spending most of his time with the domestic help, Peter was undeterred and took every opportunity to play with him. One day when Peter was seeking him out, he noticed Kim Sung's door wasn't closed properly. He was about to latch it when he saw Kim Jong sitting on his father's bed. He was flipping through the dirty magazines. Peter ran in, lifted him off the bed, and took him to Kim Suk's room, where she was crocheting a colorful doily. He put him on the floor mat with his toys and went back to put the magazines away.

Where did that torture magazine go? He scratched his head and scanned the room. All the nude magazines were there, but that was missing. Maybe Kim Sung took it out of the house to show his friends. How did that boy open this latch? It was almost four feet off the ground. Maybe his father forgot to close it properly.

Two days later Peter was dismayed to find the torture magazine in little Kim's toy box. God damn it! Those pictures must have terrified him. Even young children were pictured being tortured by the Gestapo. He mechanically turned the cover page and gasped. "What the hell?" Kim Jong had added to the black and white drawings with a red pencil. Now the blood oozing from the victims was red. He stared at the boy, asleep on his mother's bed. Kim Suk had gone for a bath. He returned the magazine to Kim Sung's bedside table and wondered what his reaction would be to his son's defacement.

A week passed and, to his surprise, Kim Sung never

mentioned it. Peter promised himself he'd never tell anyone unless asked.

~

Kim Jong's behavior worsened as he approached his third birthday. He had a violent temper. He would throw his toys and cry for hours if he didn't get his way. At times, Peter seriously considered smacking him across the face when he threw his food at him.

"This boy needs a good beating," Peter said to Kim Suk after Kim Jong bit her on the arm. She was trying to quiet him down so she could take a nap. Peter was in the kitchen when he heard her scream. He ran to her room and saw little Kim sitting on the floor crying. She was holding her wrist in pain.

"Take this damn monster from my sight," Kim Suk said. Peter nodded and took the boy to his room. He put him in the chair. It was time to talk to him.

"Why did you hurt your mother? That wasn't a very nice thing to do. How would you like it if she bit you?"

"I didn't bite too hard," the boy sobbed. "No one can hurt me!"

"What do you mean nobody can hurt you?"

"My dad told me I am very special and if anyone doesn't listen to me or hurts me he will punish them."

"Remember! You can catch a lot more flies with honey than with a flyswatter."

"I hate honey." Kim Jong jumped off the chair and ran out of the room.

Peter didn't follow him but sat on the chair wondering if he had been as bad a child as Kim Jong. *There's no way I was ever like him*, he thought, trying to recall his own childhood. The sound of falling dishes brought him up short. He raced to the kitchen and saw Kim Jong standing on the table, holding a porcelain soup bowl.

"What are you doing?" Peter asked, seeing the shards of broken dishes everywhere.

"I am doing this!" Kim Jong threw the bowl to the floor.

"That is it! You little piece of—" Peter roared, lifting him off the table. Kim Jong's eyes were wide with fright and astonishment.

"You will go play with your toys." Peter squeezed his shoulders. "You understand me?"

"You're bad. You sleep on my mommy," he yelled.

Peter's hands fell from Kim Jong's shoulders. His face was white and beads of sweat shone on his forehead. What if the boy repeated those words? Two days ago, Kim Suk told him she might be pregnant again. Peter gathered his strength.

"That was a very bad thing you said about your mother. You know that if your dad finds out you said something bad about your mother, he will never ever speak to you again and might even send you far away to school and then you will never see your mommy again."

"I don't want to leave my mommy." The child sniffled.

Relieved his arguments had the desired effect, Peter kept scaring him until he was sure the boy would never say anything.

~

After Kim Jong's third birthday, Kim Suk announced her pregnancy. Ecstatic Kim Sung sent Peter to Aunt Ko Hee's house to deliver the news. Although she lived only three miles away, it had been months since she'd last visited. One day Peter heard Kim Sung tell his wife how upset Ko Hee was that a crippled knee forced her to remain housebound, and that she missed Kim Jong so much. Peter chuckled inwardly. He knew why she'd stopped coming. After Kim Jong poured hot tea on her expensive boots and spat on her face when she tried to lecture him about his misbehavior, she stormed out of the house declaring she would never return.

Peter wandered through the tree-lined streets and soon arrived at Ko Hee's boxy brown house. No windows or vents faced the street. Its trees and shrubs foreshadowed a prominent spring—he could smell the vegetation. *My beautiful day is about to be ruined.* He slumped as he passed through the iron gate and knocked at the door. He wouldn't give her an opportunity to insult him. He was glad she'd stopped coming and wished her knee story were true.

I hope she's home, he thought, and began counting in his head. When he was a child, after hours of playing with friends he would come home and pound on his front door nonstop until his out-of-breath mother answered. She told him he must always give a person a chance to get to the door before breaking it down. "How much time?" he'd asked. She closed her eyes in thought. "Fifty! Count to fifty before you knock again."

He was up to thirty-nine when Ko opened the door and grunted. "Oh, it's you. Come in. I was thinking about you."

Thinking about me? He decided to withhold the news he'd come to deliver and followed her into the house. He was more interested in knowing why she was thinking about him.

"Let's go in here," she said, pointing at a green door.

Peter nodded, admiring her house. It was larger than Kim Sung's, he estimated by the size of her courtyard. There were five rooms, all next to each other and facing the courtyard.

"Come!" She pushed the door.

She doesn't look sick, Peter thought, entering the ornate room. His eyes popped. *Now I know why Kim Sung likes her! She's rich!* He looked at the expensive furniture, huge framed paintings on the wall, and wall-to-wall rug with its picture of a dragon. She ordered him to sit.

Peter gave her a puzzled look. He had never sat in front of her or Kim Sung.

"I said sit." She pointed to a chair across from her divan. She wore a long, blue one-piece dress with wide, flowery sleeves. He thought it was a Western dress.

"Yes, ma'am." He sat on the absolute edge, ready to run away. He never felt comfortable around her.

She noticed. "Relax! You're not my servant." He responded by sliding back in the chair.

"Master is having another baby," he blurted out.

"Huh." She said vacantly, staring behind him.

Surprised by her tepid reaction, he turned around. She was staring at a man-size framed painting of a pack of hungry coyotes encircling a lion.

"Nice painting," he said, facing her. "Kim Suk is *pregnant.*"

"I heard you the first time." She rose and walked to the painting. "When is she due?"

"I'm not sure. In a few months."

"You should know!" She said, moving away from the wall and strolling toward him. Her hands were behind her back and her shoulders were hunched.

An alarm sounded in Peter's head. "I don't know her delivery date."

"Isn't it your baby, too?" She asked, standing over him.

"*What?*" He swallowed hard. His face had turned grey and he could hear his heartbeat.

"You fooled my nephew, but not me. I know what's going on between you and Kim Suk."

Engulfed in sweat and fear, he looked into her gauging eyes. "It's not true. You shouldn't make such accusations."

"I'm not accusing you. I'm telling you the truth." She snickered. "Kim Jong looks just like you. An evil boy like him couldn't have come from our family. He has filthy Chinese blood in his body. You and that whore—"

"You bitch!" Peter shouted, jumping on her back and knocking her to the ground. She tried to scream but he quickly turned her over and climbed on her chest, grabbing her neck. Her eyes protruded in fear. "I'll break your neck if you make a sound. Do you understand me?"

She tried to nod but couldn't lift her head. He put his knees on her spread-out arms.

"Who told you I was sleeping with her?" He was breathing hard. She should have been the last person on the planet to know about all this.

"Kim Jong! Let me go. I can't breathe," she moaned, twitching.

"Did you tell anyone else? If you lie I will snap your neck." He tightened his grip.

"No. I didn't tell anybody. I told Kim Jong not to tell anybody. Let me go."

"Why, bitch? Why didn't you tell Kim Sung? You hate

me." He ignored her choking. He was sure she was faking it. He wasn't using all his force.

"Because… because…" she gasped for air, "it would ruin his—" She was turning white.

"His what?" He removed his hands from her neck and got off her chest. "Talk!" He ordered, grabbing her collar and lifting her up.

It was too late. Ko Hee was lifeless.

For the first time since he'd started working at Kim Sung's house Peter asked Kim Suk if he could go to his room before making dinner. She was in her room, busy with knitting needles, while little Kim tortured the toys he'd received on his third birthday. She gave Peter a surprised look and asked if he was feeling all right. He told her he was a little under the weather and needed to rest. She nodded and told him to take the evening off. She would make dinner. He thanked her, went to his room, and shut the door. Kim Sung wasn't home, and Kim Suk didn't know that her husband had sent him to Ko Hee's house.

He jammed his head in his hands. *What have I done?* It was only a matter of time before someone discovered her body, which he'd put on the divan before escaping her house unnoticed. He knew so little about the woman. She'd been married four or five times, had no children, and all of her husbands were dead. Peter never understood how such an ugly woman with bad posture and a horrible attitude could attract so many men. She must knew how to do a man properly, was his conclusion after he exhausted all other plausible reasons.

What if someone saw me going in or coming out? So what! Nobody knows me outside this house. Plenty of Chinese and Koreans live in this Soviet village. What if Kim Jong tells his father what he told Ko Hee? He pulled his hair. *I have to keep a close eye on that little devil and encourage his father to send him to a boarding school.* He'd heard Kim Sung arguing with his wife about Kim Jong's future schooling. He wanted his son to study at an elite boarding school in Switzerland, but Kim Suk wanted him to study in local schools like other children.

He couldn't sleep or rest. When he heard a knock, Peter got up from his bed to open the door. Kim Suk stood there with a large bowl of soup.

"I don't remember you ever closing your door before. How are you feeling?" She came inside. He only latched the door when she was in the room with him.

"I'm fine. But I have a terrible headache," he said, squeezing his forehead. "You shouldn't come to my room anymore."

"*Why?*" She put the bowl down on the table. "Peter, what's wrong? You've been acting strange since you came in. Where were you? I didn't see you come back with a shopping bag."

"I went to buy fish but the fishermen were already gone."

"At noon?" she asked, surprised. Normally he bought fish early, out of the boats instead of at the market. He said the fish were fresher and tasted better. She'd agreed. "And why don't you want me to come to your room? I'm not so pregnant that you can't make love to me."

He raised his face to her. She was standing a step away. "Kim Jong is getting older. If he sees us together all hell will break lose. We'll both end up dead. You now have two kids to think of and, honestly, I'm not worthy of you. You have a bright future ahead of you and I'm just a servant." He put his hands on her shoulders. She squirmed.

"Oh, I see! You don't want to see me anymore." She had tears in her eyes.

"No! It's not like that. You know I love you and would do anything for you. But you must think about the future. You're the wife of the future leader of Korea. Look around you. The Japanese are losing everywhere. It's a matter of months before they leave Korea." She turned her back. "I'll never leave you, Kim Suk. I'll stay as long as you need me."

"That's enough, Peter! I admire your honesty. You don't need to worry about me. I can take care of myself. You can leave whenever you want."

"Don't say that. I love you. I'm not going to leave you." He moved closer to her.

"I won't force you to leave, but it will be easier for me if I never see you again," she sobbed. He tried to reach out to her but she had already unlatched the door. "Good night."

"Kim Suk! Don't be upset! I'm only doing this for you. Look! I made you a gift out of seashells." He hurriedly opened his closet to retrieve a bracelet. He'd been making it for the last week or so. She loved seashells.

"No! I can't accept any more gifts." She looked at her stomach and opened the door.

"Wait!" He chased after her to the courtyard. The front door clanked. Kim Sung was entering. *Shit! I forgot to lock it!*

"Why the hell was this open? How many times have I told you to keep the door locked on the inside?" It was the first time Kim Sung was angry with Peter.

"He was ill. He forgot to close the door," Kim Suk hastened to Peter's defense.

"Well, don't stand there! Go and close the door!"

"You look upset. Is everything okay?" Kim Suk asked.

"Ko Hee is dead," he mumbled, dropping his shoulders.

"*What? How?*" Kim Suk was holding her cheeks.

"I don't know." He collapsed in a chair. "I thought instead of sending Peter to give her the news about your pregnancy I should have gone myself. I got to her house and knocked, but the door wasn't closed. I knew something was wrong. She would never leave it open. I ran in. She was on the couch. I thought she was sleeping so I called out, but she didn't move. When I drew near, her eyes were wide open—she was dead."

"I'm so sorry! Little Kim will be so upset. He loved her," Kim Suk said, sitting next to him and placing her hand on his knee.

"No need to tell Kim Jong. I don't want him to hear any bad news," he almost whispered. "You should have seen her… how she was lying there… her hands on her chest and her feet straight. I think she died praying. My poor aunt! I am going to give her a big funeral."

Kim Jong wailed like a siren.

"What's happened to him now?" Kim Suk said. She ran out of the room, glancing over her shoulder at Peter.

"Go make me some tea and bring it to my room." Kim Sung said.

Peter went to the kitchen wondering why Kim Suk gave him that look. Kim Sung lingered in his chair a few more minutes, staring at the dark sky, then slowly walked to his room.

Kim Jong had stopped crying.

Kim Sung invited all his close friends to Ko Hee's funeral at the local church. She was his mother's younger sister. Initially, Peter was assigned to take care of Kim Jong at the ceremony, but at the last moment, Kim Sung changed his mind and told Peter to stay home with the boy. Peter was relieved and terrified at the same time. Taking care of Kim Jong wasn't an easy task, especially for more than eight hours. Kim Sung had planned a lunch reception after the service. The church had a big auditorium in the back, which served as a reception area for services like funerals and weddings.

Just after seven that evening Kim Sung and Kim Suk returned home. Peter opened the door and asked if he should set the table for dinner. Kim Suk said yes; Kim Sung said no. Peter went to the kitchen, wondering why Kim Sung was in a foul mood. It didn't take long to find out.

"So what if all that stuff wasn't hers?" said Kim Suk. Dressed in black hanbok and no makeup, she looked elegant. Pregnancy had brought a glow to her skin.

"I thought she owned the place and was rich! I didn't know she was living there as an old Soviet general's mistress. Don't you think she was a little old for that?" He paced around.

Peter moved closer to the door.

"We don't know what forced her to live like that."

"The worst part was when I went to her house today. The general was already there and kicked me out like I was nobody. Son of a bitch!"

"Don't be upset. He's an old man. I'm sure if he knew

you, he wouldn't have done that. You should eat something. You didn't touch anything at the reception."

"I'm not hungry! I don't *ever* want to hear that bitch's name in my house again! Do you understand?"

"Your aunt?"

"What kind of a stupid question is that? Who else? That damn woman is dead to me."

Kim Suk couldn't hold in her laugh. "She *is* dead."

"You're stupid!" He'd lost his temper, but instead of demonstrating it any further he went to his room.

Peter heard the footsteps and quickly moved to the stove. Kim Suk was coming in.

"Listen! I changed my mind. I'm not hungry either," she said. "How was Kim Jong? Did he give you any trouble?"

"No, he was good. He's sleeping." Peter's day hadn't been as bad as he'd expected. Kim Jong did misbehave for an hour or so, but when Peter began telling stories about karate the boy grew interested and insisted on a demonstration. After years without practice, Peter was surprised he was still quick on his feet. The rest of the day, Kim Jong followed him around, insisting on learning Kung Fu. Peter agreed, on one condition: Kim Jong had to obey him.

"That's good. You can go and rest, too." She walked away without looking at him.

I will always love you, Kim Suk, Peter thought sadly and headed to his room.

⁓

By the eighth month of her pregnancy, Kim Suk had given up most of her routine—visiting friends, going to parties on weekends with her husband, and crocheting—and confined herself to her room. The doctors didn't see any medical need for it and tried to convince her to stay active, but she rebuffed their advice and stayed in. Kim Sung didn't offer any opinion on the matter and kept busy with outside politics and war-related activities.

On the other hand, Peter's life had gotten busier. His afternoons, which had been the highlight of his day when he and Kim Suk explored each other's naked bodies, now revolved around teaching Kim Jong karate. Since he had told her to stop coming to his room, she hardly spoke to him directly and now used Kim Jong to communicate with him. Every morning the boy came to the kitchen with a handwritten list of chores and instructions on how she wanted her food served. Peter followed the list faithfully. She now forbade him to enter her room and had placed a small table outside where Peter was to leave the food and pick up the dirty dishes. If it weren't for her frequent visits to the latrine, no one would believe she lived in the house.

~

It was still daylight when Kim Sung arrived home. Tired of exercising and playing, Kim Jong had gone to his mother's room while the indefatigable Peter was busy in the kitchen. All the Kung Fu practice was making him feel better and stronger.

"Where is Kim Jong?"

"He went to his mother's room, master."

"That boy spends too much time with her." Kim Sung looked toward his wife's room. "I heard you're a good karate teacher."

Peter remained quiet. He didn't like, or need, to brag.

"Is it hot in here?" Kim Sung asked, unbuttoning his white shirt. His long sleeves were rolled up to his elbows and his black pants were wrinkled behind the knees.

Peter looked at the sky. It had rained two hours earlier. "I will get you some water," was the only response he could come up with. When he returned with a clear pitcher of water and an empty glass, Kim Sung was sitting in the court-yard, sweating heavily.

"Water, master." Peter put the pitcher on the table and filled the glass to the rim.

His head bowed and one arm resting on his thigh, Kim Sung patted the air to make him put down the glass. Peter was about to when suddenly Kim Sung fell forward.

"Master! " Peter shouted in panic, trying to lift him. Kim Sung was having difficulty breathing. "Wait, master! I will get someone." He made him lie flat on his back on the mat and ran to the door, knowing that two Soviet guards protected the house round the clock.

Seconds later, when he came back with the guards, Kim Suk was standing over her husband and telling him not to move. Kim Sung was holding his stomach, in deep pain. One of the taller guards spoke in Russian to his partner and then bent over and picked up Kim Sung like a child and ran to the door.

Kim Suk asked one of her friends to watch over Kim Jong and went to the hospital with Peter. It was the hospital where Kim Jong had been born.

A nurse directed them to Kim Sung's room. "What happened to him?" Kim Suk asked a doctor leaving it.

"Don't worry... He'll be fine. He's just exhausted. Let him sleep."

"Should we wait here?" She pointed to a wooden bench in the hallway.

"Ma'am, you go home. I'll wait here and let you know when he wakes up."

"*You* go home and take care of Kim Jong. I'll stay here," she insisted, sitting down.

She's gotten so big, Peter thought, wanting to tell her again to go home and rest. But looking at her stern face, he deemed it proper to follow her orders.

When he arrived home, he found Kim Suk's friend screaming in the courtyard.

"What happened? Where is Kim Jong?"

"Tell Kim Suk I will never watch that devil child again!" She left without another word.

Peter searched frantically and found Kim Jong sitting on the floor in Kim Suk's room playing with his toys. "What happened to Lin?" Peter demanded. He didn't know the woman's last name or anything else about her.

"She is stupid. I told her to show me and she started screaming."

"Show you what?"

"This." Kim Jong reached under the bed, pulled out a magazine, and pointed to breasts.

Peter grabbed the magazine, one of Kim Sung's, and hid it behind his back.

"Where did you get it? Your father will be very upset if he finds out you touch his things." He spent an hour or so explaining how he should not look at those dirty magazines if he wanted to be a true karate master. Kim Jong promised to stay away from his father's room and went to sleep after Peter told him that his mother had to stay at the hospital.

The next morning he made a huge breakfast and packed it into a wicker basket. With the basket in one hand and Kim Jong's hand in the other, he walked the boy to the hospital.

A young and attractive lobby nurse sitting behind the counter eyed Peter furtively the moment he came in. When he asked her for information, she told him that Kim Suk was in labor and Kim Sung was still undergoing medical tests.

Someone called his name. A young man in a white coat walked toward him. A stethoscope hung from his neck and he held a clipboard.

"I'm Peter Chang."

"I'm Dr. Vadim," the man smiled. "Is this Kim Sung's son?"

"Yes, sir, this is Kim Jong."

"I'm glad you're both here. We need to test your blood to make sure you're not sick."

"There's nothing wrong with us. We're fine," Peter insisted.

"Come with me. It takes only a minute. We don't want you or this child to end up in hospital." The doctor ushered them to a nearby room.

When Peter and Kim Jong returned to the lobby, an older nurse had replaced the friendly nurse. Peter sighed and approached her.

"Miss, is there any news about Kim Sung or Kim Suk?"

The nurse scowled officiously. "Kim Suk gave birth to a boy five minutes ago and Kim Sung is still having tests."

Peter lifted Kim Jong over his shoulders. "You're so lucky. You have a brother to play with."

"I don't want a brother!" Kim Jong screamed and began kicking.

CHAPTER TEN

D r. Boris Kasparov was one of four senior doctors at the Soviet hospital assigned to important patients, such as high-ranking Red Army generals and their families and high-value politicians, and rarely to patients with grave injuries or incurable diseases.

After a long shift, sixty-two-year-old Kasparov had only just arrived on the doorstep of his government-assigned residence when an army officer came to inform him about an emergency at the hospital. His three senior colleagues were in Moscow, operating on a dying politician.

"Who's the patient?" He asked, knowing it didn't matter. The hospital administrator had categorized the patient as worthy of special treatment.

"I don't know, sir," the officer replied. Although Kasparov was a civilian, he was treated with great respect. He was an authority on hematology and his medical opinion was considered the last word. He had authored several books on human blood and was the most sought-after lecturer in Western universities. But, to his chagrin, since the inception of the Second World War he was confined to the Soviet Union.

"Okay, I'll be there shortly," he informed the officer and went inside the house. He lived alone. His wife of thirty-two years had died three years ago. Several young nurses would have loved to date him, but he shunned them. He wasn't ready for a new woman in his life.

Twenty-three minutes later, he arrived at the hospital. Ariel Kukes was standing by the front entrance, staring at his watch. As long as he could remember, he'd never seen the administrator outside his office. He hastened toward him.

"I'm so sorry to drag you back here, Dr. Kasparov. My humble apologies."

"What happened? I thought I left everything fine." Boris's voice lacked any hint of friendliness as he stood in front of the man twice his size.

"It's an urgent matter. We need to discuss it inside. I hope you don't mind, General Grigory Mekler is on his way to discuss the matter with you as well."

"*Grigory Mekler?*" Boris looked confused but nodded and accompanied him. It would have yielded nothing to inquire why one of the most influential Soviet commanders was coming there. The administrator was tight-lipped—a good trait when you ran a hospital.

"I think my office will be the best."

"Why?" Boris asked, standing before a door that bore his name and titles. Ariel didn't respond but marched down the hallway. Boris clinched his jaw and strode after him. Not many people at the hospital liked him, Boris included. He considered him too authoritative and meddlesome. Ariel required each doctor consult with him before any medical intervention involving a high-profile patient. He had fired several staff members for not following his orders. Boris had once told him that he wasn't going to wait around for his permission to help his patients, and Ariel had threatened him with administrative discipline if he continued his defiant behavior. However, Boris refused to fall in line. So far, Ariel hadn't made good his threats. Boris wondered if his medical stature had something to do with it.

"Come, please," Ariel said.

Boris smiled courteously and walked inside a spacious, windowless room twice the size of his own office. Maybe his giant bulk needed a giant office. Six dark-colored chairs were lined up opposite his own cozy chair and imposing wooden desk. The walls were all painted glossy white like the rest of the hospital. In the far right corner of the room, a brown leather couch and a coffee table sat in front of three more chairs on an orange area rug.

"Have a seat, doctor." Ariel closed the door and took his seat behind the desk.

Boris waited. For the past two years, he'd been hoping that, after the end of the war, he might retire. He wanted to spend his twilight years writing his memoirs and traveling.

"Doctor Kasparov, do you know Kim Sung?"

"Not personally. I ordered his blood tests this morning." Last night Boris had been ready to go home when one of Ariel's assistants asked him to help Kim Sung. He examined him and didn't find him in any imminent danger. He told one of the doctors on duty to run blood tests to make sure he was healthy.

"Why did you order blood tests? Did you think he was in serious condition?"

"Wait a minute! Did you drag me here because I didn't consult with you about his treatment?" Boris asked angrily.

"No, not for that." His jaw tightened. "I just want to know what's wrong with him."

"He's fine. I thought it was fatigue, but to rule out anything else I asked for blood tests. A standard procedure."

"His blood report is here." Ariel bent to open a drawer. Boris wondered if Kim Sung's blood was positive for something more serious than he'd anticipated. "Here it is." He removed four brown folders and slid one of them in Boris's direction, holding on to the other three.

Boris began reading it. Unlike his peers, he was able to read without eyeglasses.

"So?" Ariel asked after a short interval.

"So the man has sexual diseases. I thought that was a pre-requisite for a politician." Boris laughed and tossed the file back on the desk. "There's no life-threatening disease in here."

Ariel lifted an eyebrow. "I thought you didn't know him. How'd you know he's a politician?"

"I guessed it. Am I wrong?"

Without warning, the door flew open and a tall man dressed in an army uniform strode in. Both men jumped out of their seats. "Sorry to barge in like this, but I'm in a hurry."

"I'm glad you could come, General." Ariel shook Grigory Mekler's hand. Boris did as well. He knew the general. He'd diagnosed and treated his anemia years ago.

The three men stood around Ariel's desk.

"Dr. Kasparov," Grigory began. "Did you see Kim Sung's blood report? Is it possible?"

"The question is no longer whether it is possible. The report is clear. The question is whether we can treat him."

"What? Treat him?" The general turned to Ariel. "What's he talking about?"

"I was in the middle of telling him."

"Where are the reports?"

"Here, sir." Ariel scooped up the folders and handed them to the general, who gave them to Boris, requesting he read them carefully. They watched Kasparov go through each one.

"What do you say, doctor?" Grigory Mekler asked impatiently when Boris had finished.

"Well! According to the blood results, Kim Sung is not the father of these two boys."

The general looked defeated and crumpled into a chair.

"But—"

"But what?" Mekler lifted his head in hope.

"This Peter Chang could be the father of both."

"Huh!" The general shook his head repeatedly and paced the room. Boris and Ariel watched him until he suddenly stopped and turned to them with an inscrutable smile. "I know it isn't your field, but can you stop a woman from having babies? And I don't mean condoms."

"Yes, there are ways. However, none of them are fool-proof. Why?"

"Never mind. Thank you so much for your help. You can go home now. And please keep this matter to yourself." The general patted his arm.

"Of course!" Boris smiled. He'd been reminded before of the oath of secrecy he'd taken fifteen years ago when he agreed to work for the Red Army. "Good night." He shook hands and left the administrator's office. He was completely drained.

A short drive later he was back home, cursing himself for leaving the front door open. This wasn't the first time. He admonished himself by slapping his forehead. He'd left some lights on before leaving for the hospital, but wasn't sure the living room light had been among them. He looked around carefully, a habit he'd developed after repeatedly forgetting to lock the front door. He lived in a safe area but remained cautious.

Everything looked okay, he thought, closing the door and going to his living room. The half bottle of vodka and an empty glass still sat on his coffee table. He filled one third of his glass and slumped into his chair taking a deep sip. He raised his glass in front of his eyes. His vision was blurry. He rapidly shook his head and put the glass down, then stood up. *What's wrong with me?*

He grabbed his throat, convulsed violently, and collapsed to the floor.

~

At the hospital Ariel Kukes walked General Mekler to his car and asked him again, "Do I need to do anything else?"

"No. I'm glad you called me. Make sure this news doesn't go beyond you."

"You know me. My outside is like a T-34 tank and my inside, like a vault." He thumped his chest. "Nothing gets out of here."

The general laughed. "Be careful. Our tanks aren't doing too well."

Ariel examined his office carefully. He'd locked up all the important files, and locked the door. He walked all the way to the stairs, then turned back to see if he'd left any files on the table and if his office door was shut properly. This had been his routine every day for the past six years that he'd administrated this military hospital. His late wife had told him that he kept checking doors, cabinets, closets, and faucets because he was a perfectionist. He agreed, but sometimes his obsession aggravated him. One day he'd driven all the way to the hospital when he realized he'd forgotten to recheck the stove, and returned home. It was off. Meanwhile an important politician had left the hospital angry. He later went to the politician's home to apologize. He didn't want to lose his job. The politician and Stalin had gone to school together.

Ariel arrived home exhausted and went straight to take a bath. He attributed his sound health to ice-cold baths, which he'd learned about when supervising a Siberian prison camp. One day on patrol he noticed that a prisoner a decade older than he was looked younger and sharper. He discovered that he took ice baths every day. A year later, he was promoted and became a hospital administrator in *Vyatskoye*. He thanked two retired generals for his promotion and continued to take frigid baths.

He dipped his head under the water. When he tried to raise it, he couldn't. Four gloved hands pinned him to the bottom of the bathtub. He struggled to release himself but failed.

Two hours later, a man reported to General Grigory Mekler. "It's done."

"Good." He'd read their files. Both men had a tendency to spill secrets while drunk, and both loved their vodka.

CHAPTER ELEVEN

Although Kim Sung wasn't able to change the date or venue of his second son's birth because of his own confinement, he was still happy to give the boy a Russian name to appease his Soviet friends. "We will call him Shura," he announced as soon as Kim Suk returned home from the hospital. She didn't oppose her new baby's Russian name as much as she had her first son's. No one ever called him Yuri.

"You can call him whatever you like. For me he is Kim Man-il," she said, waddling to her room to nurse the baby.

Kim Sung bent over Kim Jong and waved his finger. "Never marry a stupid woman."

Kim Jong solemnly nodded, as if he understood his father's comments, and ran after his mother. Kim Sung turned to Peter, who was collecting Kim Jong's abandoned toys in the courtyard. "Consider yourself fortunate that you're not tied to one of those."

"Should I get you tea, master?" It was wise to stay on the sidelines during these husband-and-wife quarrels.

"No. I need to go out and take care of some business."

"Master, the doctors said you should rest."

"Doctors are stupid. They kept me two days in the hospital," he said, "And ran all kinds of stupid tests to tell me I was okay. Bastards! I wish you hadn't panicked and had those stupid guards take me to those butchers."

Peter stood through the diatribe until Kim Sung had discharged his grievance, "Should I bring your overcoat? It will get cold."

"That's a good idea. Peter, what happened to your arm?"

"Oh!" A round, red spot on his right arm was visible below the long sleeve he'd rolled above his elbow. "I think I got an infection from that needle. I'm glad Kim Jong is fine."

"What are you talking about? Something happened to Kim Jong?" He asked worriedly.

"When we went to the hospital to visit you, the doctor told us we had to take blood tests to make sure we were healthy. I got this spot because I've been scratching my arm. Don't worry, master. Kim Jong didn't have a mark on him. I checked it myself."

Kim Sung was furious. "Those bastards! Who told them they could do that? I'm going to talk to the administrator. He's my good friend...." He bellowed all the way to his room.

I shouldn't have let them take Kim Jong's blood. He's too young to get a disease, Peter thought. He'd wondered if Kim Jong would be scared when the doctor pricked his arm without warning. It was a big needle and Peter thought the doctor was too aggressive. He'd considered asking him to be gentle with the toddler when an old nurse came in and drew

Kim Jong's blood with the utmost care and tenderness. The boy actually smiled the whole time.

"Are you going to stand there or close the door after me?" Kim Sung asked. He had on a knee-length blue coat and white scarf. Despite his filthy room, the man knew how to dress.

Peter ran after him to close the door.

A scream came from Kim Suk's room.

CHAPTER TWELVE

The streets teemed with military trucks, UAZ-469 off-roaders, and soldiers carrying heavy duffle bags on their shoulders, and the sidewalks teemed with civilians. Most of the civilians were women and children, who stood in front of the sprawling shops to watch the men pass. Some women with painted lips and revealing clothes tried to get the soldiers' attention, but only a handful, the young ones, were able to. "You're wasting your time!" an older woman with a saggy chest and thick makeup advised. She was right. These men were going back to the war after a week with their families, wives, and girlfriends.

"The whole herd is out today." A man leaned forward and looked outside his military vehicle at the streetwalkers.

The driver sat bolt upright without comment. His job was to maneuver his vehicle skillfully through the crowded street and get the general to his destination on time. He'd have taken a different route but the general insisted on this street. He wanted to see his young soldiers leave for the battle; knowing most of them wouldn't come back alive. They were just the fuel of war.

"We're late," the general said softly. It wasn't normal. Most men of his rank weren't polite.

"I'm sorry, sir. Do you want me to take a side street?" The street he was thinking of was only a block away, and he knew if he moved his automobile to the far right, he could squeeze past the fuming green truck ahead. He could hardly breathe, but his lone passenger in the back seat seemed fine. That's what was important. A general's sanction could galvanize his career. It wasn't a dream. It happened more times than people realized. He personally knew two men who drove one-star generals and were promoted. His general wore three stars.

"Go ahead! Take the side street!"

Although it was less crowded, it was narrow and wobbly. The road was paved with red bricks but many were missing. Rumor had it people stole them to fix their homes, but they never caught anybody doing it. At one point, the driver almost lost control of his vehicle and drove into a house. Thanks to ten years of off-road driving training, he veered just in time. Unfortunately, the front end of the UAZ-469 was scraped and the general was massaging the corner of his forehead.

They stopped in front of a heavily barricaded orange building. Two armed men approached. The general opened the door and got out. The men stiffened and saluted. The general returned the salute with the same vigor. He wore all his pins, stars, and stripes. He was ready for a formal meeting. This meeting could ensure his future or pitch him into the gallows of the disconnected proletariat, a fate he had feared and loathed growing up.

The general examined his uniform for any last-minute adjustment and marched toward the building. A tall soldier with a thick chest and wide shoulders saluted him and held the door open. He answered the salute and went inside. The door behind him closed with a bang. He was standing in a small lobby. He looked to his right and left. Both passageways were empty. He removed his hat, stuck it in his armpit, and strode down the hallway on his left. He couldn't suppress his shoe noise. The marble floor was squeaky clean. He was able to see his fogged image on it. Forty-nine steps later, the general stopped before a white door. He fixed his collar, wiggled his shoulders, knocked, and without waiting went into the room.

"Good afternoon, gentlemen. Sorry for the delay," he announced, standing before a large desk. Three men dressed in dark suits and ties sat behind it, looking as if they'd been there too long and had either run out of conversation or were tired of each other's company.

Foreign Minister Vyacheslav Molotov greeted him. "Good to see you, General Mekler." The minister, in his mid-fifties, had dark hair, a long face, and an extended forehead due to hair loss. He sat on the far left.

The general inclined his head. "Thank you for seeing me on such short notice."

"Let's hear it," the youngest of the three men, sitting on the far right, said. He was in his early thirties and had rounded shoulders. Grigory had never seen him before. Supposedly he was a politician he'd met back in the days when he was a colonel. He looked to be of medium height, and his face should have been unforgettable.

The man sitting in the middle introduced the one who'd just spoken. "This is Yuri Andropov. He's filling in for Anton Gormykin. As you might know Mr. Gormykin is very ill."

The center man had thick hair but a hairless face. He was political commissioner of the Red Army. His name was Leonid Brezhnev.

"Please send my warm regards to him. I hope he gets well." Grigory spoke the truth. Anton was the head of Army Affairs and a pleasant fellow to be around. He turned to his replacement. "It's a pleasure meeting you." The man's name sounded familiar but nothing more. He wondered if Anton was to be permanently replaced.

"I read the file you sent me. What should we make of it?" Molotov asked, lowering his eyeglasses.

Grigory cleared his throat. "Since this committee has assigned me the duty of keeping track of Kim Sung, I felt obligated to inform you that he didn't father his children. I think it will destroy his political career if news gets out that his servant is their real father."

Brezhnev leaned forward. "We understand! We have much invested in Sung. That's why we asked you to monitor him instead of fighting those bastard Germans and their filth on the border. Sung is the only man who can give us full access to Korea after the Japanese leave."

"I understand, sir," Grigory said. He hadn't been offered a chair; though more than a dozen were lined up against the wall.

"If he were a European leader, his servant screwing his wife would actually earn him sympathy. Orientals are different. Kim Sung would be a laughingstock and no one would respect him again. His days would be over. You need to make sure that doesn't happen." Molotov said, shifting his glance between the general and the men sitting next to him.

"I can assure this committee that I have already taken

the necessary precautions to keep the matter secret." Grigory straightened to his full six feet and thrust out his chest. He was in his late forties and a little overweight, but his face was thin.

".I have full confidence in your capabilities, and I think I speak for everyone on this panel." Molotov consulted his peers. Leonid nodded with a generous smile. Andropov was staring down at his lap.

Unfriendly, Grigory thought and smiled. "Thank you, sir." The meeting was going better than he'd expected. He'd been concerned that the committee might rebuke him for his tardiness in finding out this information. In truth, if he hadn't asked his old, retired, flamboyant friend to court Kim Sung's deceased aunt, he'd never have suspected anything of this nature. She was lonely and vulnerable, and the only person who visited Kim Sung regularly. Grigory needed to know what was going on in his house.

Molotov looked at his watch. "I must leave, so unless there are questions, let's adjourn."

"I have one." Andropov lifted his head. All eyes focused on him. "What will you do to ensure there are no leaks or other collateral damage?"

Grigory's face tensed. "I do not discuss my strategies or plans."

"That's not what I asked you," Yuri said confrontationally, sitting ramrod straight.

Brezhnev came to his defense. "General Mekler is right! This committee has no jurisdiction over his methods of operation. His job is to accomplish his assignment at any cost. You may leave, General! We admire your service and loyalty to the Soviet Union."

"Thank you for your kind words, sir." Grigory pursed his thin lips. Andropov didn't look pleased. His face was red and his prominent jaw throbbed. "I will not fail to deserve your confidence," he asserted, pulling his cap from his underarm and donning it.

The men rose from their chairs. Grigory left the room with a sense of pride and sudden urgency. The door guard saluted him vigorously as he opened the door. Grigory admired the soldier's quick response with a smile and a salute. He probably hadn't expected him to leave the building so soon. He approached his vehicle from the rear. His driver and two other soldiers were laughing and smoking. Grigory wished he could let the men enjoy a peaceful moment, which was hard to come by in wartime, but he was in a hurry. There were things he had to do and instructions that needed to be delivered. He cleared his throat. The men dropped their cigarettes and tensed their postures. Grigory moved closer and directed the driver to get behind the wheel.

"Yes, *sir.*" The driver was needlessly loud, as if compensating for his inattention.

Grigory wore a smile until he settled into the back seat and ordered the driver to go. The two soldiers were still saluting, hands stuck to foreheads. He knew from his own experience that as soon as his vehicle was gone they'd pick up their cigarettes and go about their routine. Grigory had done that numerous times himself as a young soldier of low rank.

"We'll stop at my residence first," the general said, noticing their speed had slowed, the driver unsure of the destination.

"Yes, *sir,*" the driver replied with enthusiasm, pushing the accelerator.

Forty-five minutes later, the vehicle pulled into his driveway. He didn't wait for the driver to open his door. If it weren't for military protocol, he'd have driven his own transportation. He got out.

"Wait here, I won't be long." He went inside. As he headed to his bedroom, one of his two servants informed him his wife wasn't home. He wasn't surprised. She loved to attend parties. They'd been married twenty years and her social life didn't always include him. He actually preferred it that way. With all the war news hammering inside his head, he had little appetite for entertainment. Before the war, he used to think about the children his wife couldn't have, but now he was happy her medical condition had prevented it. The world was full of trouble and he wasn't going to leave any children behind to suffer.

After changing into civilian clothes, he wrote a note for his wife. Not that it mattered—he knew most of her late-night parties ended the same way. She drank until she couldn't hold a glass between her fingers, then came home and slept until late afternoon or until he got home. But he always wrote a note if he'd be out late, a habit he'd learned from his janitor father who died years ago… the same month as his mother. He had no other siblings or relatives.

"I hope I wasn't gone too long," the general smiled. He wore a dark suit and a long overcoat. The driver spotted him coming out of the house and was holding the UAZ-469 door open.

"No, sir."

"Good! I want you to drop me at the Arbat Street and leave."

"Yes, sir."

The clock ticked five after five when he asked the driver to stop.

"What time should I pick you up, sir?"

"You don't need to. Go!" He slapped the side of the vehicle.

The driver looked around nervously before driving away. Grigory stood at the side of the street and lit a cigarette. Few people knew about his habit since he never smoked in uniform and only a handful of close friends and associates ever saw him in civilian clothes. He savored his cigarette and watched the people walk by on one of the most famous streets of Moscow. This street housed several important government buildings and the people who held the key jobs in those buildings. Luxury shops, like the one behind him, were full of women with fur coats, stiletto heels, and purses made of exotic animal skin.

He twisted the cigarette under his black moccasin and ran his eyes along the shops. Ten stores out of fifteen were still open, selling luxury items like watches, jewelry, furs, and fashionable women's clothing. He walked past the stores and turned left into a small, poorly lit passage that smelled of urine. The last time he was here, he'd seen a couple of wealthy men urinating on the wall. He thought they might be too proud or shy to ask for the proper toilet. He covered his nose.

The dingy passageway led to a door unworthy of its ritzy neighborhood—not only old and rusty but badly dented. The doorman had told him last time that it got that way because of some men with the patience of five-year-olds. "I guess when your dick is as hard as a gun barrel you can't think much," he told Grigory after pointing him to one of the rooms.

Grigory regretted knocking so loudly, but it was too late. The echo, which made him feel worse, was followed by a distressed grunt on the other side. He wondered if the noise had caught a urinating dignitary by surprise. The door opened to the sound of rusty hinges and eroded door pivots. A diminutive man, by all Soviet standards, looked him in the eye and asked, "You have an appointment?"

"Don't need one!" He pushed the man aside and walked up the stairs.

"Hey, you can't go in like that!" The man followed him.

Grigory sensed his build intimidated the man. "Go ahead. Call the police."

"What's going on?" A female voice asked.

Grigory turned to see a woman standing at the head of the stairs. She was either Korean or Chinese and couldn't have been more than five feet tall. "I need to see Chin Ho."

"We don't have boys to fuck, only ladies. You fuck ladies?" She asked boldly.

Hit by a sudden urge to strangle her, Grigory swallowed hard. "He's a friend of mine. Go tell him to come down."

"Oh! You client friend. Go wait outside. Let him enjoy. Go now!" She waved her hand.

"I guess I have to get him out of here myself." Grigory bounded up the stairs. The doorman chased him but stopped short of touching him.

"Sir, please go downstairs and wait." The woman changed her tone to polite. Up close, he looked menacing. A man you didn't want to mess around with.

"Chin Ho! Chin Ho!" He cried, tearing down the narrow hallway.

"General!" A door behind him opened and an out-of-breath lanky man stuck out his head.

"Put on your damn clothes and meet me outside."

General Grigory Mekler consulted his watch. He'd been pacing outside the building over seventeen minutes, waiting for Chin Ho.

I should rip his balls, he thought, noticing a woman staring at him. *What does she want?*

He threw her a friendly smile and turned his back. Women often flirted with him. He got coquettish looks every time he bumped into his wife's friends or went to his office. He had numerous female officers under his command. Unlike his fellow generals, he was handsome and soft spoken. His wife laughed when he complained about one of her friends. "Hey, if I weren't your wife I'd look at you, too. You have that animal charm."

I'll give him five more minutes before I drag his ass out of that whorehouse. He reached in his pocket for a cigarette. Rarely did he feel the need for a second cigarette so fast. Three to four hours might pass before he felt the urge.

"I'm so sorry, General."

"What the hell took you so long?" Grigory sneered, pulling his empty hand from his pocket. He had little patience for people who made him wait, especially when he had something urgent to accomplish.

"Again, I'm sorry. I didn't think it would take this long." He rubbed his hands together briskly. The weather was getting cooler and he wasn't wearing much. No gloves, no scarf, no head covering, just a plain blue sweater and dark pants. In his twenty-plus years of life, he hardly ever felt the need to cover his slim physique with heavy winter clothes. On a few occasions, however, the glacial weather forced him to dress properly and cover his dark hair under an aviator fur hat. He hated the look. It made his long, well-balanced face look longer and his brown eyes smaller.

"What would take this long?" He frowned. "Don't tell me you…"

Chin Ho grinned. "Well, she was young, and I just couldn't leave her."

Grigory glared.

"I had blue balls. It's been—"

"What? Two days since you fucked a whore? Why don't you get a girlfriend?"

"Sorry. I'll never do it again," he said, lowering his head. He was telling himself to shut up and not to offer any further excuse. The general didn't speak so colloquially with everybody. He had seen him in action, tearing into people who hadn't complied quickly enough with his orders. Some of his peers suggested he had more starch in his neck than in his army uniform.

Grigory laughed. "You can't keep it in your pants. Your fly is open."

"Oh, sorry," Chin said shyly, buttoning. "If you don't mind my asking, how did you know I was here?"

"It wasn't difficult. I know where to find you in the evenings. There isn't another Oriental brothel in the city. Anyway, enough of that. I'm here for something far more important. So shape up!"

Chin Ho recognized the sudden shift in the general's tone and became tense. One could gauge the importance of a message by paying close attention to his voice, which changed from normal to deep to a hoarse whisper, and not always in the same order.

"I need information on a man. I need to know everything about him." Grigory said, looking around. More stores had shuttered their doors and the foot traffic was lighter. "His name is Peter Chang."

"Chinese?"

The general confirmed it with a gentle nod. "He works in Kim Sung's house."

"That shouldn't be a problem." Chin searched his pocket. "Eh, left my *Papriosa* somewhere."

"Try *Belomorkanal*," Grigory said, offering his own cigarette pack.

"Thanks. I didn't know you smoked."

"I do occasionally." Grigory waited for him to light up. "I want you to get on this assignment right away."

"Should I know anything else about this Chang?" He asked, blowing smoke clouds. In his mind, he was wondering why the general had picked him for such an easy job. Any man with a little spying experience could do it.

"Drive me home. I'll tell you the rest on the way."

Driving to the general's house didn't take more than half an hour. The Moscow streets were dead and Chin Ho was a fast driver. The general told him twice to slow down. He almost ran over a pack of stray dogs.

General got out of the UAZ-469 massaging his back. He was sure Chin had hit a pothole on the way. "I hope all is clear. Don't take this task lightly. It's not as simple as it seems. Now, you're more than welcome to join me for a drink."

Chin declined politely. He preferred not to drive after a drink. A few months ago, he had almost lost control of a car and plunged into the Moskva River. Nobody would have known what had happened to him. Soviets ridiculed men who couldn't handle their vodka. After all, the drink was their national pride. Therefore, Chin offered a different explanation. "If your assignment wasn't so urgent I would have loved to take a few shots."

"I guess you are right. See you in a week. I need his complete report."

"Of course. You know my work is immaculate."

"I know, Colonel," Grigory smiled. "Good luck. I'll be waiting."

The Arbat Street was dark and deserted when Chin Ho pulled up in front of a five-story building. He read the "no parking" sign and parked under it. *Why not? I'm not blocking anyone.* He measured the street's width in his head, knowing he wouldn't see any traffic. Army vehicles weren't allowed to drive here and the wealthy residents stayed indoors after the shops closed.

He walked through the dim passage and knocked on the iron door.

"Wait!"

"It's me!" he shouted.

"Ivan?" The voice sounded surprised.

"Open the damn door! The smell is killing me!"

"Sorry!" the voice stuttered and opened the door.

"What the hell is wrong with you? Move!" He pushed the man aside, climbed the stairs, and stared at the five-foot-wide, intentionally dimly lit hallway covered with its red oriental rug. He passed the four closed doors, a sign that all the girls were busy with clients or sleeping, and went straight to the door marked "office." He knocked.

"You're back?" asked the Chinese woman with puffy eyes and a thick layer of makeup. "That girl is busy right now."

"I'm here for you." He barged in, ignoring the look on her face.

"Oh!" She shut the door in a hurry. "I won't even charge you." She began pulling down her top.

"Keep your clothes on!" He frowned. "I'm not here for that." He looked around the drab room. In one corner were the chair and desk where she ran her office, and in the other were her bed and a small vanity mirror. A small metal chest sat at the foot of the bed. A bathroom and kitchen, shared among all the girls, were on a different floor.

"Oh, you like me to …..?" She bent her thick fingers as if she were holding a glass of water and began jerking them back and forth toward her chapped lips.

"No!" He raised his arm. She was too vulgar for his taste. He liked his whores shy and submissive. Dirty talk was fine but dirty sign language was a turn-off. "I'm here for a different reason."

"What?" She asked, grabbing her fatty waistline. The smile on her face was replaced by scorn. She would have cursed him out of the building if he weren't such a good tipper. She kept all the tips. The girls were paid a flat fee.

"I remember you saying you ran a house like this in *Vyatskoye*. Why'd you leave?" She'd taken charge of the brothel about a year ago. A Korean woman ran it before that.

"Why you ask me? I don't tell you." She raised her eyebrows. "You go now!"

"Listen, Flower!" Nobody knew her name, so that's what everybody called her. He towered over her threateningly. "Answer my questions or else."

"My boss will be very upset if I talk to you." She looked scared.

Chin gave her a long, cold look. He knew the man behind all these brothels. He was the brother-in-law of an influential Soviet politician and considered above the law. "No need to be afraid. This conversation will be our little secret."

She eyed him cagily. "You already know we don't stay at one place more than a year. Clients get bored with the same girls. They want new and fresh girls."

Chin knew she was right. He didn't like to visit the same girl twice. "I know, but they don't change the person in charge every year." The Korean woman had stayed almost three years.

"Listen, we don't have choice. We move when we are told to move. Why are you asking me all this?"

He locked eyes with her. "Do you keep a diary of all the clients?"

"No!"

"So if I look around your room, I won't find any list?"

"Even if I have a list, it's just for accounting. Nobody tells his real name. You said your name was Ivan but your friend called you Chin Ho." She rolled her eyes.

Chin laughed. "Maybe you can fool someone else, but not me. You know my real name." The man running these brothels wasn't just in the pleasure business. He gathered personal client information to help his brother-in-law collect rich donations and political favors. The genteel men who secretly visited such places would be horrified if their depravity became known.

"You came to check if I have your name on the list?" She was nervous.

"No. I want to see a list of your clients in *Vyatskoye.*"

"I don't have that list. Our boss …"

Chin read her face carefully and asked if she knew Kim Sung and if he was her regular client. The question surprised her. She tried to change the subject by offering him a free visit to a new girl who had just arrived that night. But he kept pushing her until she yielded.

"Yes! Yes! He came almost every night," she said, throwing her arms out. "Now leave me alone!"

"How about a man named Peter Chang? Did he visit your place? Do you know him?"

"No, I don't remember that name."

"Are you sure?"

"I am. Now go home! I need to rest."

"Come here then." He took her hand. "So this visit isn't a complete waste of time…"

"What you doing?" she asked.

"Taking you up on your offer."

CHAPTER THIRTEEN

"I hate my mother!" Kim Jong screamed. "I hate her baby!"

"How many times have I told you to control your anger? You can never be a karate master if you don't know how to think properly," Peter said.

The boy sat on the kitchen table and Peter wiped his face with a wet cloth. Minutes ago he had rescued him from his mother's wrath after he dropped his younger brother. Peter wasn't sure he'd done it deliberately, but Kim Suk insisted she saw him throw the baby on the hard floor when she refused to let him hold him. Peter was relieved Kim Sung had already left. He would have raised hell if he'd seen his wife's handprint on Kim Jong's puffy cheek.

"I hate them. They are ugly."

"Don't say that! Nobody hates their mother. And the baby is your brother. You're going to have fun playing with him. You're lucky to have a brother. Did I ever tell you I wanted a brother so bad but my mommy couldn't have another baby?"

Kim Jong slumped his head down and didn't reply.

Peter gave him some cookies he had bought for himself earlier. Since the arrival of a new baby, Kim Suk hadn't been too involved with Kim Jong. The baby kept her awake nights and in the morning, she was too tired to pay attention to her older son. Feeling neglected, Kim Jong had become more irritable and hostile. Peter told himself the situation was temporary and that when the baby got a little older, everything would go back to normal. He wouldn't admit to himself they had never been normal.

Weeks passed without further incident. Kim Jong avoided his brother. Peter thought it was an unfavorable development, but before he could voice his opinion over lunch with Kim Suk, she told him she was happy the boy wasn't hounding the baby. He wished he hadn't alarmed her about Kim Jong's behavior. Even though she'd dismissed his previous concerns entirely, Peter noticed she was overprotective of her new baby and wouldn't allow Kim Jong to be alone with him. Kim Sung was hardly home to notice anything.

Peter was cutting up bok choy when Kim Suk called him. He wiped his hands on the kitchen towel and went outside. She was looking up at the sky.

"The weather doesn't look good." It had been raining on and off for days. "Can you take care of Kim Man for a couple of hours? I need to attend a funeral."

"Of course," he replied. Since their relationship ended, she spoke to him only when necessary. At times, he missed her and thought of sweeping her off her feet and throwing her on his bed to make wild love to her, but thinking about the consequences of his lust sent a chill up his spine. The memory of Ko Hee's lifeless body and glaring eyes was emblazoned on his mind. He thought of her almost every day.

"I'll go get ready."

Peter returned to the kitchen, guessing it would take her more than an hour to dress. He hadn't seen Kim Jong since breakfast, when he had run away to play with his toys. Kim Sung hadn't come home last night. Half an hour later, he was adding the pile of vegetables to the boiling water when he heard her call him again. *That was quick!* Perhaps dressing for a funeral required little time. During the course of his employment, he had witnessed numerous husband-and-wife arguments because she took too long to get ready. Kim Sung wasn't the type of a man who cared how well his wife dressed or looked. Of course, that wasn't the case with other women. Peter had heard him use all kinds of unfriendly adjectives to describe women he met. Some of his comments were so crude they even made Peter blush.

She was holding Kim Jong's hand. "Hold him tight, make sure he doesn't go to the baby's room. I put him to sleep, and if nobody bothers him," she stared pointedly at her son, "he'll sleep for a couple of hours or so."

Peter took control of Kim Jong. The boy looked sullen and his stiff arm suggested he didn't want to be restrained.

She bent over Kim Jong. "You be a good boy and do *not* go near your brother. Okay?" She was pointing at her room. Kim Jong nodded and took shelter behind Peter.

"Let's go to the kitchen and make you a very special treat," Peter said, swinging Kim Jong's hand.

"See you soon. Be good now," Kim Suk yelled from across the courtyard. She lingered at the front door.

Peter instructed the boy to stand still so he could close the door. Latching the door he shouted from a distance, "You know, on Chinese New Year my mother used to make me *Nian Gao*. Today I'm going to make you the same dessert.

You'll love it." He turned. Kim Jong was gone. "Oh, no!" He raced to Kim Suk's room. Her door was wide open.

~

"Please, let me see the baby!" Peter Chang entreated the pudgy nurse sitting behind the reception desk. Kim Jong was standing next to his leg.

"How many times have I told you to go over there and sit down? Go sit!" she barked.

Peter shuffled back to the bench. What a bitch! He then turned his attention back to frightened Kim Jong who was holding his finger tightly. "See what you did? Didn't I tell you to be nice to your brother?"

The boy didn't lift his head or make any sound.

Peter squirmed, looking down at his bloody shirt. He could hardly believe that Kim Jong had used karate on his brother and slammed him to the floor. While he was closing the door after Kim Suk, Kim Jong had sneaked into her room and injured Kim Man. The baby suffered a huge gash on the back of his head and was bleeding profusely when he brought him to the hospital half an hour ago.

"Hi, Natasha."

Peter's head swiveled. The pretty nurse he'd seen when he brought the soup for Kim Suk was walking toward the reception desk.

"I don't know how you keep a smile on your face when working behind this desk. So many stupid people come here asking the same stupid questions over and over," the pudgy nurse wailed.

Peter assumed the nurse was referring to him. *Go to hell!*

He thought. He had a lot more on his mind than a rude nurse who wouldn't let him see the baby.

"That bad?" The pretty nurse smiled, taking her place behind the desk.

"You deal with the insane. I'm out of here." Pudgy collected her belongings.

Kim Suk will be furious! Peter thought uneasily, and then wondered how Kim Sung would react to his favorite son harming his younger son. *I know he'll blame me. It was my job to keep an eye on the boys.* He glanced furtively at the reception desk. The pudgy nurse was leaning over the desk, still babbling. The pretty nurse seemed to be smiling, but Peter sensed she was faking it to look polite. *Maybe she's her supervisor. She can't be her best friend. I bet she has no friends, and no one has ever done her either. Who would? She's so ugly, I wouldn't do her if she were the last woman on earth.*

He forced a grin when Pudgy gave him an annoyed look while walking away. *Eat shit!*

"Are you doing okay over there?" The pretty nurse waved.

"We're fine, thanks." Peter raised his arm. He was going to give her a few minutes to settle into her shift before he asked her about the baby's condition. He had no doubt in his mind that the departing nurse had badmouthed him. She reminded him of Ko Hee: snippety, crude, and xenophobic.

Still smiling, she pushed back her shoulder-length, light-brown hair and began scribbling on the clipboard. Peter couldn't resist giving her a second glance. She had huge ocean-blue eyes, a long neck, a round face, and a smile worth every gaze. He looked to his side. Kim Jong was dozing off.

"Hello, pretty face!" a low-pitched voice said.

He turned to see a tall man with a strong, sallow face

coming down the corridor. He was dressed in hospital scrubs and holding a brown clipboard under his thick arm. The nurse looked in his direction and put down her pen. She was smiling.

Peter looked down at his feet at his worn-out brown slippers. He hadn't had much time to put on shoes, even though one of the guards had insisted on taking the baby to the hospital in his truck. But he was so panicked that he pushed the guard aside—a man twice his size—and ran to the hospital. It was only a quarter of a mile.

"I said no!" the nurse shouted.

Peter saw the man leaning over the desk. The nurse sat bolt upright, her face tense.

"Come on!" he laughed. "How long are you going to mourn your dead husband? It's been three years."

"Peter! Peter!" Everyone turned to the source of the piercing shout. A frazzled Kim Sung trotted through the entrance.

CHAPTER FOURTEEN

Peter cringed behind the kitchen stove. Outside Kim Sung was berating his wife for leaving the baby alone at home.

"You'll wake the baby. The doctor said to let him sleep," she reminded him.

Peter had been holding the baby in his arms and Kim Sung was talking to the doctor when a distraught Kim Suk rushed into the hospital. Apparently, the same house guard who informed Kim Sung about the baby had told her, too.

"*Now* you're thinking about him. Where were you when he fell off the bed and split open his head? *Thank god* my Kim Jong was there to save his life. He could have bled to death." He looked at his son playing with his new toys. Peter had hidden the facts and told him that he was in the kitchen when Kim Jong came to tell him his younger brother had fallen off the bed. Proud Kim Sung sent his driver to buy toys for his brave son.

"I went to a funeral," she said, tears trickling down her cheeks. "I care about my sons as much as you do."

Knowing what was coming next, Peter bit his lip.

Whenever Kim Sung ran out of words to say to his wife, he let his hand do the talking. A few years ago Peter didn't think striking a woman was as bad as his mother had described to him. Now watching a man hit a woman made his blood boil. Some days he wished he could grab Kim Sung's hand and break it beyond fixing. A man who struck a woman was a coward. It still bothered him that he himself took Ko Hee's life. But there was no other choice. Her poisonous words could have destroyed the life of the woman he loved. He wasn't afraid for himself.

"I'll deal with you later," Kim Sung warned. "Peter! Close the door. I can't stand this mindless woman."

Peter breathed a deep sigh of relief, closed the door, and went to the kitchen.

"You lied to him, didn't you?"

Startled, he turned to see Kim Suk standing close to him, her eyes still wet.

"I'm sorry, ma'am. I don't understand you."

"Don't give this 'ma'am' bullshit! Tell me the damn truth! Did Kim Jong hurt his brother?"

"Kim Jong didn't harm the baby."

"You lying son of a bitch! There—"

"*Kim Suk!* Don't you dare call my mother a bad word. I will—"

"What? That baby could not have fallen off the bed. I put huge pillows on the edges. You're a lying son of a bitch!"

"Find yourself another servant!" He kicked the table leg and stormed out of the kitchen. *That's it! I'm leaving this bullshit. Go to hell!*

"She doesn't need me. I'm ruining my life serving this ingrate." Peter vented his anger while stuffing his clothes in a tiny suitcase and dressing in his nicest clothes. He hadn't planned to lie about the baby falling from the bed until Kim Jong pleaded with him on their way to the hospital. "Don't tell my mommy."

"Why not? You don't listen to me. How many times have I told you to stay away from the baby?" Peter admonished while running with the bleeding baby in his arms. Surprisingly, Kim Jong was running as fast as he was. "Don't tell my mommy."

Without thinking, just to quiet the boy he promised not to say anything to his parents.

As he lifted his suitcase and gave his room a final glance, the front door rattled.

He put the case down and waited to see if Kim Suk would answer. The door clattered again. When he opened it, he was surprised to see Kim Sung, who wasn't expected back for hours.

"Oh good! You're dressed up. I need to send you out."

"Master, may I talk you?" Kim Suk and Kim Jong weren't in sight.

"Of course. After you come back. My aunt's friend sent a message that he wanted to send some of Ko Hee's effects to me. I want you to go with the driver and bring them to me. You know where she lived?"

"Yes, master," said Peter, dropping his head. He didn't know how to tell Kim Sung that he was done serving him and his dysfunctional family and wanted to leave.

~

It was five minutes before eight when the truck pulled in front of Koo Hee's house.

"I'll be back," Peter said. The driver gave him a dismissive look and nodded.

Peter looked at the house. His heart beat fast, remembering what had taken place during his last visit. The temperature was chilly but he could feel the sweat on the back of his neck. He took a deep breath to calm his nerves and knocked at the door. An elderly Soviet man, bundled head to toe in warm clothes opened it.

"Mr. Kim Sung sent me to get some items."

"Of course. You must be his servant. Come inside," he said politely.

Peter felt his heart trying to escape his chest as the man led him to the room where he had ended Ko Hee's life. The room looked the same except that a young man now sat on the divan, where he'd put her lifeless body, and was staring at him.

"This is Kim Sung's servant," the old man said. The young man smiled and rose to his feet. "Nice to meet you."

Nice to meet me? Who says that to a servant? Peter nodded but avoided speaking. Standing here made him uncomfortable and the old man sensed it.

"A black trunk is by the wall. You can take it. If the darn thing weren't so heavy I would have brought it to the door myself."

"No problem." He almost ran to the trunk. He wanted to get out of there as quickly as possible. Ko Hee's strong perfume still lingered in the room.

"Your name is Peter Chang, right? Ko Hee said many good things about you."

Peter knew the man was being mendacious. She hated him.

"She was a kind person," he mumbled, feeling a lump in his throat. She was a bitch! That's how he would remember her.

"Let me give you hand." The young man came over and grabbed the other handle.

Peter thanked him as they loaded the trunk onto the truck. The driver offered no help. He was too busy enjoying his cigarette.

"You're welcome," he replied, holding out his hand. "I'm in town for a few days. I would love to have someone show me around."

Peter accepted his hand. "I'll ask master if he can spare me a day off. I wouldn't mind showing you around. It's a beautiful village."

"Great! But ... don't tell Kim Sung you met me. He hates my family. That's why Ko Hee didn't want me to visit her here."

"I understand. I won't say anything."

"Thanks. Hope to see you again."

"I didn't get your name."

"I'm so sorry," he laughed. "I'm Chin Ho."

CHAPTER FIFTEEN

When Peter returned he noticed Kim Sung's shadow at the door, smoking and pacing. "Did he give you anything?" He asked, running toward the truck.

Peter told him about the trunk.

The trunk didn't please Kim Sung. His frown suggested that he was expecting a lot more. Why else would he send a giant truck to fetch his deceased aunt's belongings? "That's all?"

Peter nodded. It amused him to see Kim Sung control his anger in front of the Soviet driver. He probably wanted to scream "What the fuck! That's all that bitch left me?!" But then his master wasn't the same man to the outside world. He was polite and thoughtful. Only a handful of people recognized his duplicity. Shao Peng was one of them.

"Grab the other end. It needs to go to my room."

The driver jumped out of his seat to help. Kim Sung told him to stay in the truck and to keep the engine running. He had an important meeting.

After they stored the trunk, out-of-breath Kim Sung

straightened his back, "I'm very happy you and Kim Jong get along so well."

"He's a good kid," said Peter.

"Tell my stupid wife. She doesn't treat him properly. I want you to keep an eye on him. Kim Jong is the future of Korea."

Peter closed the door and examined the courtyard. He picked up two empty rice bowls from the table and went to the kitchen. All the dishes were washed. He wondered why Kim Suk had done it. Perhaps she was accustoming herself to doing the chores while her husband found a new servant. Kim Sung would have no problem replacing him. He had money and resources.

He went to his room and was equally surprised. Clothes he knew he'd packed were hanging on wall hooks. He opened the closet and found his empty suitcase. His clothes and sundries were put back in their original places.

"May I come in?" Kim Suk was at the door.

"It's your house," he replied coldly. She entered, the baby in her arms.

"It's getting cold. You shouldn't be carrying the baby out of the room." He peeked at Kim Man, fast asleep. His head was wrapped in a white bandage. "Did you unpack my suitcase?"

"Listen, I came to apologize for calling you names. I was very upset. You don't know how hard it is to believe that your son is trying to hurt your other son. I'm so terrified by all this and can't even talk to my husband about it. You're the only one who understands the situation. I know you're angry with me and want to leave. Please don't leave. I need you." She sat down on his bed and broke down in tears.

"Don't cry!" He placed his hand on her shoulder. Her tears were melting him. "You can find somebody better than me. You don't need me. I'm a clumsy servant."

"You want to leave these kids and walk away?" She stared at his face.

"I…." He searched for something to say.

"Don't you love your own—"

"Can I be alone a minute?" He turned his back on her. She rose, weeping, and walked out. Peter sat on his bed and closed his eyes to concentrate. Though he hadn't let her complete her sentence, he knew what she was going to tell him. Her words weren't safe to be spoken in the open, and he wasn't ready to hear them. In a moment of rage, he had forgotten that Kim Suk was tied to him forever. After taking a few minutes to gather his thoughts and emotions, he resolutely strode out and found Kim Suk in the courtyard. "I'm not leaving."

The next morning he fed Kim Jong breakfast and sent him off to play. Kim Sung hadn't come home. Kim Suk didn't usually eat until ten. It was only nine when she entered the kitchen.

"You're early today," Peter observed. "Where's the baby?"

"Sleeping in my room." She sat down facing the courtyard. Kim Jong played outside. "As long as he's out there, the other one is safe here!"

He noticed her red eyes and tired face. "You didn't sleep well?"

"The baby was fussy. I had to keep his head still." She yawned, fixing her tangled hair.

"Does he need a checkup?"

"Tomorrow. His bandage needs changing. Will you be angry if I repeat my question?"

"Please don't."

"So I was right! You're a good man, Peter." She echoed his sigh. "I don't know what to do about Kim Jong. How can I keep those two apart?"

"Don't worry, they'll be fine. I went to Ko Hee's house," he said to distract her.

"I forgot to ask you about it. What did you bring?"

"A trunk!' He put a steamy teacup in front of her. She preferred her tea before food.

"Trunk? What was in it?" she asked. Her hands encircled the cup.

"I don't know."

"Um. So you finally met her lover. How was he?"

"Lover?" He feigned ignorance. After the funeral, he'd overheard Kim Sung's diatribe.

"Yes," she smiled mischievously. "None of us knew she had a man in her life. Her house actually belonged to her boyfriend. So what was he like?"

"Old," Peter said, focused on the stove. "But I met a young man there."

"Who?" She put the cup down.

"Uh, maybe I shouldn't. He told me not to tell Kim Sung."

"What are you talking about?"

"The old man said he was Ko Hee's distant relative."

"She didn't have any other relatives."

"Maybe she did and you didn't know about them. You

didn't know everything about her. You didn't even know she had a lover."

"I guess you're right," she conceded. "She was private about her own affairs."

"So this young man asked me if I could show him the town."

"Did he say where he was from?"

"No, and I didn't ask. He's staying at her house."

"Why don't you take a few hours off and show him around?"

"Not today. I haven't done any cleaning yet."

"Don't worry about the house. You need to get out and breathe fresh air, too. Go!"

"On one condition."

"What?"

"I take Kim Jong with me."

"I don't know what I'd do without you." She smiled. "Take him. Take him."

CHAPTER SIXTEEN

General Grigory Mekler was sitting in front of a slow-burning fireplace when one of his servants approached cautiously to inform him about a visitor. He looked at his watch: ten o'clock. His wife wasn't home and he wasn't expecting her back before midnight.

"Who is it?" he inquired lazily. The vodka, the reclining chair, and the fireplace had drained his vitality and he was thinking about bed.

"Mr. Chin Ho."

"Send him to the library," he ordered, thinking he was back so soon.

When the general entered the room, Chin was standing over one of many bookshelves, browsing through a book. Grigory was an avid reader of Mark Twain, Khalil Gibran, Dostoyevsky, Proust, and many other authors represented in his collection.

"I didn't know you liked poetry." Chin looked fresh and energetic.

"Sometimes. I wasn't expecting you this early. Would you like a drink?"

"I wouldn't mind."

The general reached behind his desk and took out a clear bottle of vodka and a glass.

"You're not drinking?"

"I've had enough." He handed Chin a drink and sat down. "So did you find anything?"

"Yes and no." Chin sat across from him on a wooden chair and took a sip. "I saw Peter Chang. Your friend was a great help in setting up the meeting. Unfortunately, even after spending half a day with him walking around the village, he was reticent about his personal life. Wouldn't say a damn thing about himself. I tried to bait him with my own personal stories but that man didn't budge. The only thing he said that seemed to slip from his tongue was that his father owned a small textile factory in Nanjing."

"That's it?"

"So far."

"It's not enough."

"I know. That's why I came to tell you I'm leaving for China in the morning."

"You think he's worth pursuing?"

"If I hadn't met him, I would have concluded that Kim Sung's wife is just having an affair with her servant, which isn't that usual. But this guy's deeper than he looks. He has me curious. Even if you aren't interested in him, I am."

"Okay. Let's see what's in his closet." Grigory smiled. "I think I'll have another drink after all."

CHAPTER SEVENTEEN

Kim Suk interrupted Kim Jong's afternoon karate lesson. "I was thinking about what you told me yesterday."

"Keep your arms straight! Head up! Don't look at your feet! You need to look your opponent in the eye!" Peter instructed. "Now stay horse ready and count to twenty," he ordered and turned to Kim Suk. She wasn't supposed to be talking to him while he was teaching. "I'm sorry, what did you say?"

"I said I was thinking about what you told me the other day about Ko Hee's relative."

"Bend your knees... What did I say?"

"That he asked you too many personal questions."

"I think he was just being polite... Okay, Kim Jong. You're done for the day. Now go sit on the mat and stretch."

"Maybe," she mumbled. "Would you mind watching Kim Jong? I need to visit my friend."

It was the third time this week she'd asked him to look after Kim Jong while she visited her friend. He thought it was a good idea for her to get out of the house and socialize. She looked a lot happier. "Of course."

"Thanks," she said, strolling back to her room.

Peter was showing the boy how to stretch properly when she came out of her room with the baby. She was covered in a heavy layer of makeup and wore a new dress. He wondered why she needed to be dolled up to visit a friend. She had a Soviet driver at her disposal to take her wherever she wanted, but most of the time she preferred to walk. "If Kim Sung comes home early, tell him I took the baby for a walk," she reminded him, and departed.

Two hours later, she returned with dancing eyes and a smile on her face. Peter was in the kitchen trying to plan dinner. He wished she still told him what to cook. A few months before she'd asked him not to bother her about the menu and to cook whatever he wanted, as long as it wasn't sweet. She hated sweets and desserts but loved rice and noodles.

She came into the kitchen. "Do you think I should have him examined?"

He dropped the ladle in alarm. "What happened to the baby?"

"Nothing! I was talking about Kim Jong. Don't you think he's ... out of proportion?" she whispered, looking over her shoulder. The boy was busy playing in the courtyard.

"I don't understand."

"Haven't you noticed that his head is too big for his body? You don't think he'll grow up to be a dwarf?"

"No!" he chuckled. "There's nothing wrong with him. When the nurse who drew Kim Jong's blood told Peter the boy wasn't normal size, he kept it to himself, dismissing it. Any six-foot-tall woman would say that about a small child.

"Are you sure?"

Peter nodded and turned back to the stove.

The weather turned cooler the next day. It drizzled on and off. Peter had closed himself in his room to sew his underwear. He'd stretched a little too far when Kim Jong egged him on to do a split. When Kim Suk knocked he smiled at her inconsistent door manners. Sometimes she just pushed it open, and sometimes she knocked when it was wide open.

"One second please," he said, stowing his sewing kit and underwear under the bed. He opened the door. "I'll have lunch ready soon."

"I'm invited out for lunch. Will you take care of Kim Jong?"

In this weather? Her face was painted with layers of makeup and her hair was neatly coiled on top of her head. She wore an elegant black coat that fell to her slender calves. "I'll take care of him. Should I ask one of the guards to drive you? The weather is awful!"

"No. No. I like it. It's perfect for a walk," she smiled.

"The baby might get wet if—"

"Don't worry. I'll take the umbrella."

There sure is something fishy going on here, he thought uncomfortably.

Kim Sung came home early that night. Peter served the family dinner—it had been a long time since husband and wife ate a meal together—and went to his room. Tonight he didn't have to tell Kim bedtime stories; his father was there and nobody told stories like he did. Once Peter had eavesdropped and nearly choked trying not to laugh when Kim Sung told his son that Hercules was Korean.

Why can't I fall asleep like I did in Nanjing? He wondered, tossing on his bed. *Maybe if I stopped thinking about Kim Suk I could.* He laced his fingers behind his neck and stared at the ceiling. *Is she seeing someone else? Why not? She's young and pretty. Who wouldn't want her? But the baby... it's disgusting! She has no shame.* He got up, panting, his ears red. *What's wrong with me? I can't prove she's fucking someone. What if she's telling the truth?* He paced. *I need to find out. I'm supposed to protect her... I should stop her if she's seeing someone.* He hugged himself and went to bed, feeling he'd made peace with himself.

~

"What do you say we go to the park to practice?" he asked Kim Jong, sitting at the kitchen table eating his breakfast. Kim Sung had left the house before six. Peter insisted on making him something but he refused. These days Kim Sung looked happier and was friendlier. Peter knew why: the global war was going in favor of the Allied forces. The Germans and Japanese suffered defeat after defeat and, according to the latest rumors on the streets of *Vyatskoye*, it was only a matter of time before Hitler gave up and ran like a rat.

"Park?" the boy asked, playing with his food.

"Yes! Didn't I tell you I used to practice in the park for hours? Now finish your food and go play. I'll do my chores and we'll go to the park after that."

By two o'clock Peter had finished his work and was donning his shoes when Kim Suk sought him out. "Kim Jong said you're taking him to the park."

"Yes, I told him we'd go. The weather is so nice today." The sky was deep blue, the sun bright, and the air unusually warm for winter. The villagers were concerned. By this time, there should be mountains of snow. Old people were blaming the Nazis.

"It's a wonderful idea. I'm going out, too."

I bet you are. You're going to visit your friend. He grinned.

"Why are you smiling?"

"Oh, nothing. I was thinking it'll be a fun day."

She tried to read the thoughts behind his smile. But nobody could. His face and brain rarely communicated. He knew how to prevent his thoughts from inhabiting his face, a technique he'd mastered practicing *Qigong*.

The walk to the park should have taken five minutes, but with little Kim, it took ten.

"I don't like this place," the boy protested. The village residents called it a park; in reality, it was an open space with a patch of grass and overgrown weeds. "Let's go to the park with the slide and swing."

"It's a little too far. Why don't we practice here and go to the other park afterward?"

"No! I want to go there now!" Kim Jong stomped his feet.

"You behave like this and I'll take you home," Peter said sternly, grabbing his shoulders.

The threat worked. Kim Jong stopped throwing his tantrum, but he looked angry. Peter didn't care. Coming to the park was an excuse to get out of the house. The park was on the same side of the street where he'd seen Kim Suk walk to her friend's house. Peter's eyes darted between the boy and the street. *I'm sure she'll pass by soon,* he thought, and instructed the boy to start jumping up and down to warm up.

"What kind of jumping is that? Your feet are still on the ground." He stifled a smile.

"My clothes are too heavy," he complained.

"You're right." The boy's mother had made him wear too many layers. Normally, he taught him in his cotton shirt and pants and no shoes. '"Maybe we—"

Peter saw Kim Suk walking down the street carrying the baby. He wondered why she didn't use a baby carriage, which would have been much easier. Kim Jong tugged his sleeve.

"Huh? I was saying…" Kim Suk was in front of a house. The boy yanked his sleeve harder. "I was…" He looked at the boy, then back. She was gone. "Let's go home to practice."

Kim Jong wasn't happy, but Peter promised him cookies so he agreed. After an hour of Kung Fu, they went to the kitchen.

"How was the park?" Kim Suk was home.

Oh, I didn't close the door. He ran outside. She was standing over Kim Jong, who was ignoring her and playing with his toy car.

"How was the park?" she repeated, seeing him head for the front door. "I closed it."

"It was good. I'm sorry I forgot to close the door."

"Don't worry. Kim Sung makes too much fuss over an open door."

He followed her to her room.

"You want something?"

"I need to buy rice. We're almost out."

"Then go buy some," she laughed, cuddling the baby in her arms. "I've told you many times you don't need my permission to buy house supplies. Just go to the store and get whatever you need." The Soviet government owned the grocery store and all Peter had to do was fill his grocery bag and sign a piece of paper with Kim Sung's name on it. He wondered if Kim Sung had a charge account or if the Soviets were just generous. Either way it wasn't normal. Everybody else paid cash.

"How about Kim Jong?"

"You want to take him?"

"Can I leave him with you?" Late afternoons, when she wanted to rest or nap, she would ask him to watch the boy.

"Yes," she replied. "Kim Jong! Come to my room. I'll tell you a story."

Who was the friend who put her in such a good mood? He pondered on his way out. Kim Suk closed the door behind him. He stood staring at the two guards, their backs against the house. Judging by the cloud of smoke hovering over them, they were smoking. No wonder Kim Sung wanted to keep the door closed. With those two idiots on duty, anybody could walk in and they wouldn't know it. Good thing they replaced the guards every week.

Five minutes later, he stood in front of the house where he'd seen Kim Suk disappear. From here, it was difficult to tell how big the house might be inside; tall cinderblock walls surrounded it. *Okay! I'm here. Should I knock?* He pictured getting yelled at or chased by an angry stranger. *I have to have a plausible excuse for knocking.* Suddenly his face lit up. He smiled and struck the door brazenly.

The door squeaked and opened. Peter turned white.

"Come inside, Peter."

CHAPTER EIGHTEEN

Chin Ho opened his eyes and blinked rapidly to clear his vision. He didn't know who had nudged his shoulder to wake him. The train compartment was empty, and strewn about was the trash his fellow passengers had left behind. He looked outside the window. The platform was jammed with people. Some were smiling, some scared, some sad and worried, and some looked as if they weren't there by choice. For a moment, he considered to which category he belonged. Nobody had forced him to come to Shanghai. His curiosity was the sole reason he was here. Some folks might consider it borderline insanity to travel to another country in time of war, but he wasn't too worried about those kinds of people either.

He removed his briefcase from the overhead compartment and looked out the window. The crowd was thinning. Time to go. He tightened his grip on the handle and stepped out onto the platform. The stench of misery and hard labor wafted from inadequately dressed coolies whose livelihood depended on train schedules and passengers. Buttoning his warm overcoat, he felt sorry for them. He could do nothing to help them except bring a larger suitcase so they could assist him in return for compensation. He had no problem paying them. He had enough money in his briefcase to pay them all.

"Sorry I'm late, master."

"Don't worry! I just got here," he said to his sixty-two-year-old servant.

"How was your business trip, master?" The man reached for his briefcase.

"Let me hold onto it." Chin Ho smiled. "The trip was good."

When they'd arrived at a small, well-furnished house in the suburbs of Shanghai, he asked his servant to make him his favorite duck soup and wake him around seven p.m. Sleeping upright on an uncomfortable wooden bench in a noisy train was no substitute for a nap on his own cozy bed. No matter how few days a year he spent in this house, the bed made him feel at home. During his prolonged absences, his servant lived there and took care of the house. Chin Ho liked and trusted him. He was a man of few words. Most of his family members were dead.

He kicked off his shoes and climbed into bed. *I should spend more time here,* he thought and instantly shook his head. *No, I can't. I just can't.* He fought off a sudden sense of anguish and drifted into his past.

~

He had been only four years old when his parents decided he wasn't normal like his brothers and sisters or the other neighborhood children, who spent most of their time playing or loitering aimlessly on street corners. "Look at my son, reading a book like a real scholar," Chin Ho's mother bragged to anyone who showed up at their door: the milkman, a friendly neighbor, a street peddler, or the street barber who often went to homes to cut hair.

"Your son will make you very proud one day," his father's friends would say every time they came for dinner. His father worked at the local garment factory and hardly earned enough to make ends meet.

"You hear this, Chin Ho? You're going to make me a very proud father."

"I hope you're not saying this to get free food," his mother would joke with them. She was a patient and caring woman. Chin Ho never saw her rest during the day. Rain or shine, she was always busy working around the house.

Chin Ho loved all the attention he got, but in truth, he didn't know how to read, and his illiterate parents didn't know that their youngest son was only interested in the illustrations, not the words. He was too young to understand printed words. Nevertheless, his parents, who had immigrated to China like many other Korean families during the Japanese occupation, were excited to see at least one of their seven children interested in books. His older brothers and sisters had no inclination for education. His bothers wanted to grow up and start a pig farm, whereas his four sisters preferred learning sewing and cooking from their mother.

Chin Ho rode his father piggyback to school on his first day. He was too young to understand why the older kids, who were gathered outside waiting, laughed at him. He smiled at them bravely. His father didn't leave him alone, like all those other children whose parents were too busy to wait with them; he stayed until the groundskeeper opened the gate.

A few hours later Chin Ho emerged from the school proudly, and full of confidence. He was the only child in class who'd answered all the questions right.

"Here's my boy," he heard his father's elated voice, and before he knew what was happening he had scooped him up and landed him perfectly on his broad shoulders.

"My teacher said I was the smartest in the class," he babbled, wrapping his little arms around his father's forehead.

"I'm not surprised. I know you're smarter than anybody in the whole world," his father replied affectionately. Chin giggled. That was what he wanted to hear.

"Son, can you move your arms a bit higher? I can't see if you cover my eyes," he laughed, stopping on a busy street corner. Their house was only a few blocks from the school, but the children had to cross the busy street and it was dangerous for pedestrians. Most of the day it was jammed with trucks, rickshaws, and bicycles. There were no stop signs or traffic sentries to control the unruly traffic. In the last two years alone more than eleven people had died on the five-mile-long road. The neighbors appropriately called it a death road.

"Hold on tight! We have to cross this street exactly like we did this morning." His father proceeded cautiously. "I can't take you to school like this for the rest of your life," he said, trying to see through his son's tight grip, which had slipped down from his forehead and impaired his vision, forcing him to step in a pothole. "Chin Ho!" he shouted in panic as he tripped and fell flat on his face. The violent fall catapulted the boy from his shoulders and through the air. He landed in the middle of the street, unharmed.

"Chin Ho! Don't move! Stay still!" his father moaned as

he stood and dusted off his clothes. His scraped knees bled through his black shredded pants, his hands and elbows were bruised, and his forehead was covered with dust and blood, but the sight of his little boy unhurt gave him the strength to rise. He shouted his thanks to the people who had blocked traffic to protect his son. "See, I'm coming," he smiled encouragingly and limped heavily toward Chin Ho. But he failed to see a big military truck, transporting soldiers, break loose from the stalled traffic and head straight for him. He looked at his son wretchedly before the truck struck him hard, tossing his body like a rag doll on the same sidewalk where they'd stood minutes ago, carrying his son on his shoulders, smiling.

Chin Ho never talked to anyone about his father's death. He spent countless nights in bed awake and crying, blaming himself. His mother turned out to be much stronger than anyone suspected. Two weeks after cremating her husband, she assembled the children into one room and talked to them. "I know how much you loved your father and how much you miss him. But we have to live like your father wanted us to live. You must work hard to make a good future for yourself. Your father's boss has agreed to hire me in his position."

"Who will take Chin Ho to school?" his oldest sister asked. She was the chubby one his brothers always made fun of.

"Uncle Kwan," his mother announced, waiting to see his reaction. Kwan was her older brother. He still lived with his parents a few miles away.

"But I thought Dad didn't like him," his sister said.

"No, he didn't dislike him. He just didn't get along with him, that's all. Children, we have to stick together like a good family and appreciate that your Uncle Kwan has decided to come here and live with us. He will be a great help." She spoke passionately, as if proselytizing nonbelievers.

"But, Mom—" his sister began, but she gestured for her to be quiet.

Only a few months ago Chin Ho had seen his parents argue. "Your brother is in his thirties with no job, no wife, and no brain. He's a leech on your poor parents. Why the hell should I invite him over?"

"I'm his only sister. This is my house, too! Shouldn't I be able to invite my relatives?"

"Listen! I didn't want to tell you this, but I've heard unsettling rumors about him and I don't want him around my kids."

"What rumors?"

"You really don't know?"

"No! Tell me what rumors!"

"Some people say he touches children," his father whispered, but Chin Ho, who was sitting nearby staring at his book, heard it perfectly and wondered why his father would dislike a person who hugged and played with kids.

"He likes to play with kids. There's nothing wrong with it."

"You're naïve! Just don't invite your brother when I am not home."

"So we all agree about Uncle Kwan?" Chin Ho's mother asked, staring at her children for their approval. They all knew she'd already made up her mind. Three days later Kwan moved in with them, lock, stock, and barrel. Unlike Chin Ho's siblings, the boy had never met him. His father had barred him from the house before he was born.

"So you're the one who took care of my brother-in-law?" he asked Chin, smiling.

Even though he didn't understand his uncle's comment, Chin Ho thought he could see something sinister in his smile. "You shouldn't smile."

"Why not?" he frowned.

"Yes, Chin Ho. Why did you say that?" shouted his mom through the kitchen door. She was making her brother's favorite rice soup.

"Nothing!" he replied, and escaped from the room.

The house, built on a very small plot, had only three rooms. All the girls slept in one and the boys in another. The third room had belonged to his parents, but after his father's death his mother gave the room to her brother and moved in with the girls. All the rooms opened onto a small courtyard, where they ate most of their meals on a comfortable mat, unless it was raining or sweltering hot. On those days they ate in their rooms. The kitchen and the latrine were located on the other side of the courtyard, and next to the front door was a big pile of logs, a couple of axes laid carelessly on top of them. His mother still used wood to cook their meals, even though the kerosene oil stoves were popular.

"What happened? What did you say?" his middle sister asked him as soon as he walked into her room. She sat on a bamboo floor mat, legs crossed, a yellow piece of cloth on her lap. She was hand-sewing a tunic for their older brother who was turning fifteen on Thursday.

"Nothing really," he said, sitting beside her. She was so focused on her needlework that she didn't even look up.

"You must have said something, otherwise why is Uncle Kwan talking like that?"

"Like what?"

"Shhh… just listen!" Her hands stopped moving.

"You need to discipline these kids. They don't respect their elders like we did," Kwan complained. He sounded like he was chewing. His mother didn't say anything.

"I just told him not to smile," Chin Ho whispered in her ear.

"Why?" she whispered back. She was almost thirteen and petite, with long black hair, a long neck, pretty dimples on both cheeks, and she always sat straight like a needle.

"He was saying mean things and smiling, so I told him not to smile."

"His teeth are really yellow and crooked," his sister laughed and patted his shoulder, as if he'd done something useful. "Why don't you smile anymore, little brother?" She put away her sewing and hugged him, knowing the answer was painful.

After the death of their father nobody saw the once-jolly Chin Ho smile. He took his father's demise the hardest, becoming isolated and distant. His older brothers and sisters, at the urging of their mother, tried to cheer him up, but they all gave up one by one. He wasn't interested in talking to any of them. He spent most of his time staring at his books, the scene of his father's accident playing repeatedly in his mind, until he burst into tears.

I wish I was dead, too, he sometimes thought, especially when walking to school with his uncle, who always woke him late and trailed him slowly, like a somnambulist.

"Hurry up! We'll be late again," he told his uncle one day when he was walking more sluggishly than usual.

"Be quiet!" Kwan yelled. He caught up to him and

slapped him on the back of his head. An unsuspecting Chin Ho keeled over, hitting his head on the pavement.

Kwan saw the walnut-sized red bump on his forehead. "Don't tell anybody or I'll kill you." He yanked the boy off the ground and dusted him off, paying particular attention to his bottom and genital area, and smiling strangely. "You're so good. Why can't we be good friends?" He tickled his scalp, but the little boy jerked his hand away and ran to school.

That night, while pretending to be asleep, he watched his two brothers sleeping a few feet away, snoring as if after a day of hard labor. But they weren't the hardworking type. His older brother was almost fifteen but not even close to maturity. Like other boys his age he still played marbles, ran after loose kites, and talked trash. His younger brother, twelve, was worse. He hung out with worthless boys who stole and beat up people for money.

"Be quiet," Chin Ho said grumpily, raising his head above his pillow, but the snoring continued. "I should go and sleep in the courtyard," he grumbled, rising from the floor.

The dark room smelled like sweat. The door was latched from the inside. He gathered his pillow and a small blanket his sister had sewn him for his fifth birthday and walked carefully to the door, not wanting to step on his brothers. One night he'd needed to go to the bathroom and accidentally stepped on his oldest brother's face. He howled like he'd been stabbed and punched him hard in the stomach, shouting all kinds of profanities, then went back to sleep. But Chin Ho had stayed up all night massaging his tummy.

He pushed the door gently, but it squeaked. His father used to grease the doors so the rusty hinges wouldn't make so much noise, but nobody bothered any more. He stood outside the room a few seconds, afraid to close the door because of the awful sound. He put his pillow and blanket on the floor mat. It wasn't a very dark night, even though the moon was less than half full. He lay on the mat with his knees pulled to his chest and both hands clasped behind his neck and looked at the sky. He thought he saw more than the unusual number of stars and gently reached his right arm toward the sky to touch the glimmering dots, they looked so close.

While admiring the sky he heard the familiar squeaky sound. He lowered his arm and waited to be discovered in the courtyard and asked why was he sleeping outside. His mom told him once, "Don't sleep outside. Bad spirits fly around after midnight. They can get inside you and turn you evil." He'd almost believed her until his father winked at him and smiled.

He was lifting his head to see who had come out of their room when Uncle came out of nowhere and stood over him. He tried to get up but Kwan sat on his chest and put a small knife to his neck, "You make a sound and I'll slash you like a pig—then your brothers and sisters."

"You're too heavy. I can't breathe," Chin Ho moaned. His face was white with terror.

"Don't move or speak. Let me do this or I will kill you all." He got off his chest and, with a rough jerk, flipped him over like a coin.

"What are you doing?" He resisted and tried to kick, but Kwan was too strong to fight off.

"For the last time, don't move or talk!" He squeezed his neck hard against the mat and climbed on his back.

"Get off my son, you bastard!"

Chin Ho heard his mother scream and then felt warm and wet. He turned over as fast as he could and saw her hitting her half-naked brother with an axe. He was begging for mercy, growling like a pig being slaughtered, covered in blood. His mother didn't stop, even after he'd stopped moving. She kept swinging until one of his older sisters came running out and hugged her away. His other sisters came to investigate the commotion, but his brothers slept on.

"What happened, Mother? Why did you do this?" his sister cried frantically, her arms wrapped around her mother's waist tightly so she couldn't escape and start swinging her axe again. She stood panting, her face covered with Kwan's blood.

"Come here, Chin Ho. Let me change you!" Another sister pulled him from a corner, where he was standing naked, shuddering in horror, his body also covered with blood.

"I don't want you to go to prison, Mom!" he heard his sister crying as his other sister scrubbed him hard with a wet cloth, rubbing off the evil. She helped him put on one of her shifts and asked him to lie down beside her on the floor mat. He obeyed and wanted to snuggle her tightly, but she covered him with a blanket and left the room at a reckless pace.

The warmth of the sunbeam made him open his eyes, but he moved his head to the right to avoid looking at it directly. The door was wide open. He didn't know what time it was or how long he had been sleeping. There was no one in the room. His sisters' blankets were neatly folded and piled on a pillow in one corner. His head hurt badly but he was too scared to get up and walk out of the room. His face was more red than white, and he felt terribly hot under the blanket, but he didn't want to let it go. It was the first time he'd felt so scared and lonely in his own home. *Where is everybody?* He thought, remembering the previous night's horror.

"Are you awake, little brother?" asked his oldest sister, sticking her head in the room.

"I'm awake." He gathered his strength and sat up.

"Come outside, then. I'll make you something to eat," she said, and disappeared.

He looked at the door carefully and then tiptoed out of the room. *Why, everything seems so normal,* he thought, looking around the courtyard. It was clean and orderly. There was no dead body and no bloodstains on the mat where he had tried to sleep last night.

"Where is Mom?"

"What do you mean, silly? You know she always goes to work at this time," she yelled from the kitchen.

"Where is everybody else?"

"They all went out, as they always do!" She came out of the kitchen holding a small soup bowl. "Here. Drink this. It'll make you stronger."

"I'm not hungry," he said, looking around cautiously.

"You need to eat more. An empty stomach can give you nightmares." She pecked his cheeks. "You're so hot. Go back to my room and lie down. You need to rest."

"But, but…" he kept looking around.

"But what? Why do you keep staring at everything? Did you have a bad dream?" She took his hand and walked him to her room. "Look at me, Chin Ho. Everything is fine. Mom is at work, the kids are playing outside, and…" She hesitated a brief moment. "…Uncle Kwan wasn't happy here, so he moved out early this morning."

"But I saw—"

His sister covered his mouth. "You had a nightmare. Rest and make sure you never talk about your bad dream. Mom says if you talk about scary dreams they come true. Okay?"

"No! No! It wasn't a dream! It wasn't a dream!"

~

"Master! Master! Are you okay?" Chin Ho opened his eyes. His servant stood over him, worried.

"I'm fine." He wiped his sweaty face.

"Duck soup is ready, master."

"Go. I'll be there," he said, holding his head between his hands. *I hate this city.*

CHAPTER NINETEEN

"Don't stand there. Come inside!"

Peter stared at Li Kenong's chubby wife in disbelief. She had trained him to be Kim Sung's servant. He remembered how she'd treated him. "What are you doing here?"

"The question is, why are you here? Did anyone see you?" She closed the door and gestured for him to follow.

Perplexed and flustered, Peter looked around the house. The layout was similar to Kim Sung's home but it was much smaller.

"Who are you talking to?" A young Chinese woman appeared holding a wooden spoon.

"An old friend."

"Is he staying for dinner?" the girl asked, observing him.

Peter kept his eyes on the older woman. She was connected to those who had concocted a scheme to eliminate him. Killing her probably would please her husband. She was still unattractive but twice as large as he remembered. The big mole on her upper lip had gotten bigger and darker and the hair growing on it was at least an inch long. And when she smiled, her yellow chipped teeth were lined up crookedly on receding gums.

"No," Li Kenong's wife answered, and then told him to sit on one of the two benches in the courtyard. "Kim Suk warned me you were getting suspicious. How are you, Peter? I heard you are a good housekeeper."

She wants a fucking medal? He knew she was congratulating herself for teaching him. Ignoring her friendly demeanor, which he knew was as fake as her toothy smile, he asked, "How long have you been living here? Where is Commander Li Kenong?"

"Shhhh," she patted the air. "Keep it down!"

"Don't you dare shush me! I'll break your damn hand!" He got up. He'd been wanting to say that since the day he met her. "Now answer me!"

"I am your Commander's wife. You need to respect me," she answered phlegmatically.

"Too bad he isn't here. I would have shown him the respect he and his friends deserve," he snapped, tightening his fists. All the bottled up anger was ready to explode.

"This is my daughter's house."

He wanted to scream that he didn't give a shit but the woman continued.

"I visit her two or three times a year. She's married—"

"I don't care!" He took a step back. "How long have you been coming here?"

"Before you got here," she muttered.

She was the pigeon who'd been transporting information to the CPC. He had thought about it. Li Kenong had portrayed her as a simple housewife who had nothing to do with politics or war. Peter thought it was odd his warrior commander would select such a wife. Now it all made sense. Her wretched appearance made her viable. Though she was draconian during Peter's training, her attitude changed when her husband returned home to check on his progress. With him, she was cravenly submissive.

Someone knocked at the door. "You should leave. It could be my son-in-law." She went to the door and returned with a Red Army soldier. "Tell your ma'am I would love to come to her party," she said to Peter, gently pushing him toward the door.

The soldier smiled at him as his wife came out of the kitchen and began talking to him in Russian. Commander Kenong's daughter married a Soviet?!

"I'm not done with you! I'll be back tomorrow," Peter whispered in the harpy's ear.

She gave him an icy look and closed the door.

Peter began walking home, thinking of the daughter. A Chinese woman marrying a non-Chinese man, considered disreputable, was rare. But a union between a Soviet man and a Chinese woman was unheard-of. He wondered if Shao Peng knew about it. Commander Kenong would have been the butt of all jokes if his comrades knew. Maybe the CPC forced Li to commit his daughter to their cause? All scenarios were possible. They did it to Kim Suk. At least Li's daughter seemed happy. Peter had read that in her ardent eyes when she greeted her husband.

He shook his head free of that and focused on the matter at hand. All this time Kim Suk had been communicating with them under his nose. Was she even trustworthy? He kicked the air in rage and frustration. In the past, he'd asked her if she felt abandoned because the CPC never tried to contact her to check on her welfare. Her answer was always no. He never believed her and thought she was too hurt to admit it. She'd sacrificed her youth to marry a man she didn't love. What else would she do to make her party happy?

He moved to the side of the road to avoid a big army truck passing through the narrow lane. *I need to buy some rice!* He recalled his alibi and turned south.

Peter washed the evening dishes and went to his room. Kim Suk asked why he was so quiet. He blamed a headache. She sympathized and suggested he rest, without offering to help with his chores. He didn't care. She was busy with the kids and Kim Sung was out, as usual.

I should go to her house before Kim Suk ... I'm sure she'll tell her I visited. So what if she tells? I don't care a shit for them or their secret meetings, he thought, stretching out his arms, battling insomnia. Life had become a lot more complicated. He used to fall sleep as soon as he climbed into bed. In those days his mind was free.

He opened his eyes and looked at his watch. Six in the morning. *Did I even sleep?* He rose from his bed. The heater was on but he felt cold. He changed his clothes and cracked the door. Cold air hit his face. The cobbled courtyard was covered with snow. Ugly winter had arrived. He closed the door, hoping it wasn't a storm. He really needed to talk to Li's wife.

It snowed nonstop for three days. He had never seen so much snow fall from the sky. Kim Sung had left the village to attend a meeting. Kim Suk and the kids stayed in her room. The weather had paralyzed his plans. Peter thought about going to visit the woman but he wasn't sure it was a good idea. What if nobody answered the door?

The fourth day he looked up at the sky cheerfully. It was dark, but no snow fell. He hurriedly dressed and left the house, passing an army vehicle with fogged windows parked a few feet away. Its engine was running and its tire tracks on the snowy street looked fresh. Everything else was blanketed. Peter had experienced rough weather before but this blizzard had been a monster. It almost swallowed the whole village. He tottered to his destination and knocked. No one replied. He could feel his heartbeat quickening under his heavy clothing.

He knocked again, this time harder. The door opened slowly. The man in the Red Army uniform gave him a questioning look.

"I'm sorry to bother you this early." Peter swallowed. He hadn't expected him to be home. Most soldiers left home before five.

"Who is it?" A young face peeked from behind the uniform. "Oh, you! Sorry, but my mother is not here. She went home."

Peter thanked them; regretting he'd missed an opportunity to know more about his own life.

As expected, no one was around to ask where he'd been or why he'd left the door open. He went to the kitchen to make himself tea. He wasn't a breakfast person. His first meal of the day was early lunch. The boiling water hissed on the stovetop as he sat on the chair and watched his breath escaping his mouth.

"Can I have a cup, too?" asked Kim Suk, huddled in a warm blanket. The bottom edges of the blanket were wet.

"You left the kids alone together?"

"No!" She smiled, looking down at the baby inside her coverture. "He's been awake since I heard the door. Who was it?"

"It was me... It's cold. Why don't you go back to your room and I'll bring you tea."

"I'm sick of being cooped up in that room." She rocked the cooing baby. "Look, Peter, Kim Man agrees with me."

"Sit here," he said, pointing to a chair close to the stove.

"Did you go out?" She looked down at his snowshoes.

Peter's heart began to race. He hadn't considered confronting her directly about her mysterious visits, at least not until he'd talked to Li's wife. But now the woman was gone and who knew when or if ever she would come back?

"Did I ask you a difficult question?" she teased him.

"I went to see your friend. But she was gone." There! He said it.

"My friend?" she asked, puzzled.

He scrutinized her face. Their eyes locked. "Stop playing games with me. I know all about your secret visits to Li's wife. I trusted you."

She jumped off her chair, her face a mix of emotions. He couldn't tell if she was livid because her secret was out or relieved that a burden of secrecy had been lifted off her shoulders. "You followed me?"

"Yes. Why did you keep me in the dark?"

"Two things." She sat down. "One, you shouldn't have followed me. Two, what difference would it have made if I'd told you?" She paused to look at the baby. "I know you feel betrayed, but don't rush to judge."

"I thought we were together in this. How would you feel if I'd done this to you? What else have you been hiding from me?"

She pursed her lips and closed her eyes. "What I did was for your own good. You need to trust me."

He snorted. "That's what I've been doing since I came here."

"You need to believe in me. I'll never betray you, Peter. Think calmly. It will all make sense."

Is she right? What would I do if I knew she was passing Kim Jong's secrets to the CPC? Wasn't that the reason she was forced to marry him? She's doing her job. "I guess you're right," he said in defeat. There was no other explanation for her secrecy.

"Good! I knew if you thought logically it would make sense to you." She smiled victoriously. "There is one thing I should have told you earlier."

"Mommy! Mommy! I'm cold!" Kim Jong screamed, entering the kitchen.

"Who told you to leave the room without shoes?" She ran to him and took him away.

Peter squeezed his temples and watched the snow start to fall again.

~

In Shanghai, six middle-aged men sat in a meeting room. They all wore the same loose fitting gray tunics with no buttons, round collars, and wide sleeves. The table before them was covered with maps, papers, and freshly filled teacups.

"Don't worry too much. I have my men looking for him," a portly man assured them.

"Who do you think he's working for?"

"We'll find out soon. More tea?"

"Yes. But let's discuss this matter more carefully."

Everybody nodded.

CHAPTER TWENTY

Chin Ho restlessly glanced at his wristwatch and noticed a young boy sitting across from him, staring. He smiled. The boy squirmed and buried his face behind his mother's arm. She tousled his hair and smiled affably. "He's shy," she offered, encouraging conversation.

"How old is he?" He reluctantly took the bait. He guessed the boy was seven or eight.

Her lips moved but he couldn't hear her words over the loud, throbbing noise of a passing train. He pretended to understand her reply and looked out the window. Everything passed so quickly he could hardly focus.

"You live in Nanjing?" She looked a few years younger than him. Her face wasn't pretty, but her loose clothing hinted at a rounded body. Girls with desirable curves in this part of the country commonly hid their bodies under ugly dresses, avoiding unwanted attention.

Chin wished he had kept quiet. He lacked the propensity for small talk. "No," he replied, hoping his curtness would discourage further inquiry.

"You live in Shanghai?" She proved him wrong.

Chin nodded. He'd considered flirting with her, before the young boy called her mother. When it came to bedding a woman, he played it safe. He'd once courted a woman who turned out to be married to a crazy man—who made his life hell until he beat him to a pulp. The man never bothered him again, but Chin Ho stopped pursuing married woman or even women he suspected might be married.

She smiled politely and rested her head on top of her son's.

Silence felt good.

The train was losing speed. He checked the time. They would arrive in Nanjing ahead of schedule. He hadn't experienced such punctuality on Soviet trains, which were notoriously slow and delayed. The passengers began collecting their possessions. His compartment was fully occupied. His valise was on the rack overhead. He preferred to leave last. He hated unnecessary jostling. He never understood why people were in such a hurry to get off.

After a slow crawl and a loud siren blast, the train stopped. As he expected, people ran to the exit shoving and pushing. The woman and her son also stayed in their seats. She stared out the window, searching. Perhaps someone was meeting her. When most of the travelers had left, he rose from his seat and took down his suitcase.

"Are you visiting your family?" the woman asked, slowly standing.

"No!" he snapped. Her smiled disappeared.

He felt guilty. She was just being friendly. He needed to reciprocate her kindness. "I'm here to find someone." He flashed a smile.

"Oh, I'm sorry."

He found her response strange. She was instructing her son to stay close to her after they left the train. "Why are you sorry?"

She held her son's hand. "So many people come to this city to find missing loved ones, but few succeed. The Japs have destroyed our city."

Damn Japs! He hadn't been to Nanjing since the Japanese soldiers had committed one of the worst war crimes in recent history and murdered thousands of innocent Chinese. They were the reason he joined the Soviet Spy Agency. Few people outside the top command of the Red Army knew about its existence. General Grigory Mekler ran the SSA. Although he had never met another agent, he knew they numbered in the hundreds, if not thousands. He'd never received formal spy training, worn a uniform, or attended any secret meetings. His recruitment was based on his linguistic skills: he spoke fluent Chinese, Korean, Japanese, and Russian. He didn't know why General Mekler called him Colonel. Once, when the general seemed friendlier than usual, he tried to find out more, but the general responded with a burst of laughter and sent him away.

He deliberated a second and slowly followed her to the exit. "I'm here to find my childhood friend."

She threw a glance over her shoulder, a muted smile on her round face. "A girl?"

"No!" he exclaimed. "He is not a girl."

The woman laughed at first and then apologized. "Sorry, I didn't mean to be rude."

"Do you think I'm going to stand here all day waiting for you to get off the train?" a man with gray hair and a long gaunt face growled as he stuck his head into the compartment.

Chin Ho glared at him and he glowered back. Her father?

"Sorry, Lee. This man is seeking someone, too," she said, getting off the train.

Not her father. He stood at the exit and watched a mob of haggard coolies run toward him. They'd seen his suitcase but, as in many parts of Nanjing, they weren't allowed to board the train. They had to hawk their services from the platform. He loosened his grip on the handle and let the first hand take his suitcase.

"We should tie his legs so he doesn't run so fast," an aging, out-of-breath coolie said to the others around him.

"Don't blame me if you're old and can't reach the passengers," the young man grinned.

"Just wait a few more years. You'll be running slower than we walk."

"Take me to the rickshaw," Chin Ho ordered, ending the verbal sparring.

"My wife tells me you're searching for your friend."

Chin Ho stopped and looked to his right. The woman's husband stood with his family.

"That's true," he said, motioning the coolie to wait.

"I was a journalist before those pigs burnt down everything," he said sadly. "I've helped many people find friends and relatives. I can help you, too, but it'll cost you."

This man was smart, Chin thought admiringly. He had used his old profession to create a new line of work for himself. The Japanese had damaged his livelihood but not his spirit. The majority of Chinese men acted the same way. Nationalism was at a peak. "Okay. I can afford help." He smiled. The reality was Chin would have no problem finding his target. It was his job and he was very good at it. However, the man before him could use some financial help to feed and clothe his family. The little boy's shoes were torn. He hadn't noticed it before.

The man's tense posture relaxed. "You won't be disappointed hiring me. I still have many connections in the city. Who are you looking for?"

"Peter Chang."

"Peter Chang!" the man repeated loudly, and then began laughing. "He's looking for Peter Chang!"

What the hell? People were laughing all around him. He put his hands on his waist and twisted his mouth. "What's so funny?"

The man suppressed his amusement. "So many come asking for Peter Chang that the name has become a joke. Are you Japanese or just working for them?"

"I am not Japanese!" he insisted. "Maybe people are looking for a different Peter Chang. It's a common name."

The man moved closer, his right elbow resting on his left palm and his hand on his face, and asked with a mock smile, "So your Peter Chang's father didn't own a textile factory in this city?"

Chin swallowed. His impression of Peter Chang had been correct. He knew the man didn't walk or talk like a servant. He walked with his head high and his chest out.

"Listen! You don't have to answer. Your face says it all. Since my wife told me you're a nice person and my son likes you, I'll tell you what I know. You don't need to waste your time here. My information won't do you any good or harm Peter Chang. I'm sure he is either far away or dead. Either way he is better off than the rest of us."

Chin concealed his reaction but his red ears were a

definite giveaway. "He was my best friend. I've been out of the country for several years. I thought he still lived here."

"I've heard that before," the man smiled ambivalently. "Peter Chang lived here with his parents before thugs burnt down their factory and killed his mother. A few months later, he disappeared. Most people believe he killed the boy responsible for his mother's death and ran away. Some thought he was brave to honor her, but some thought he was a coward to run. A few months after he left, we heard rumors that he'd joined the Party."

"What party?"

"The Communist Party! A year or so after his disappearance Japanese dogs began breaking down our doors searching for him. They killed anyone they suspected knew him. My cousin, who was the last person to see Peter Chang in this city, was shot in the mouth and dragged behind an army truck."

"Sorry for your loss," said Chin. The man's eyes were watery. "What about Peter's father? They killed him?"

"He disappeared. Nobody knows if the Japanese took him or he went into hiding."

Chin Ho motioned for his coolie, handed him some bills, and sent him away. He took a few more from his wallet. "Why were they after him?" he asked, handing over the money.

"Rumors say he'd killed so many Japanese soldiers, including the nephew of a Japanese general, the government put a bounty on his head."

Chin Ho bit his lower lip. He'd known there was something special about Peter Chang but had never imagined that the man working as a servant for the next leader of Korea was a Chinese guerrilla fighter. A chill ran down his spine as the man continued his divulgences.

Twenty minutes later Chin Ho thanked him and his wife and smiled at the boy, who looked terribly bored.

"Is there anything else you want know?" the man asked in a gracious tone. He'd earned more money in the last hour than he'd made in the last month.

"No, thanks," Chin Ho replied. He went to the ticket window to return to Shanghai, unaware that a man had followed him.

His servant, Han, was surprised to see him at the door. Chin Ho said he'd finished his work sooner than expected and went straight to bed. His was thinking about Peter Chang. Why would an accomplished guerrilla fighter exchange his weapons and dignity for a broom? It made no sense. Obviously, Kim Sung didn't know, or he'd offer him a more dignified job than carrying his slippers and cleaning his house. What else did servants do? Made love to their masters' wives. Thank goodness, he didn't have a wife. If he did, he'd certainly never hire a servant with a penis....

He opened his eyes. The room was still dark. The two windows were covered with opaque drapes. He blinked rapidly until he could read his watch. *One o'clock!* He put it next to his ear to see if it was still ticking. He slowly rose from his bed, still wearing the same white shirt and black pants he'd worn on the train the day before. It was a bad habit, and he wasn't proud that many nights he went to bed in his clothes because he was either too tired or too lazy to change.

He pushed open the door and closed his eyes against the bright daylight.

"I was thinking about waking you earlier. Lunch is ready," Han said from a distance.

"I wish you had," he said, stretching and yawning. "I'll go freshen up."

Han wasn't a fabulous cook like Chin Ho's mother, who'd died a week after he turned nineteen, but he tried hard.

"Your dumplings are pretty good," Chin said after lunch. "How about tea? I'm not fully awake yet." Han brought a clay teapot and a cup. "Han, have you ever heard of a man named Peter Chang? I heard that the Japanese have a bounty on his head."

"Japs have a bounty on all our heads," he said bitterly. "I don't know why, but this name is familiar."

Chin Ho put down his cup and got to his feet excitedly. "Peter Chang sounds familiar?"

The servant lowered his head, his hand on his chin. "It does. But I can't remember… I'm getting too old. My memory is not what it used to be."

"Here! Drink some of this tea? You know what they say about green tea—it cheers the heart and clears the mind."

"I already had a few cups early in the morning."

"Then do whatever helps you remember things. I'm going out to take care of business."

Han promised to think harder, but didn't ask why his boss was suddenly so interested in the name. He knew his limits.

Chin Ho changed his clothes and headed for the door with his briefcase.

Ninety minutes later, he walked past several dilapidated houses and stopped in front of a particularly timeworn one. Some shirtless, shoeless children were playing marbles next to it. He looked down the street in both directions and then knocked at the door. A woman opened it, screamed, and pulled him in.

Four hours later, the door opened again. He kissed her on the forehead. She was crying. He briskly left the neighborhood before anyone could see his wet eyes.

Just after dusk he arrived back at his house empty-handed and found Han pacing the courtyard. "Master, I remembered where I heard that name."

Chin wasn't tired anymore. "Where?"

"My friend Hu Yaobang talked about him."

"Who's he?"

"He worked for Shao Peng."

Shao Peng. He closed his eyes to try to dig that name out of his memory, but nothing came to mind. He spied almost exclusively on Soviet elites who didn't see Stalin as a good leader and Japanese commanders who spent most of their off-duty hours in bordellos.

"What did he say?"

"I don't remember his words, but I know one day I went to visit him after the death of his master. He was down in the mouth. Hu spent—"

"Where does your friend live now?"

"Same place. His master left the house to him. Shao Peng was a good man."

"Why don't you invite him over? I'd love to know more about Peter Chang."

"I don't think he will come. He has so many health problems. His back—"

"Why don't you visit him then? He would probably love to see you."

"If it's okay with you, I will visit him next week."

"Next week? Why wait? You know what? I'll take you there myself. Now go get me some dinner. I'm starving."

Chin Ho finished his noodle soup and went to his room. *Time sure flies!* His reflection in the mirror smiled back at him. *I'm sure if father were alive he'd be so proud,* he thought, holding back tears and cherishing his visit to the house where he'd been born. His unmarried sisters still lived there, but his older brothers had disappeared without a trace. *My sisters will never live in poverty again.* He smiled and went to bed in peace. Tomorrow he would buy a new briefcase.

The next morning Chin was dismayed to see Han lying sick in bed. *You could have picked a better day,* he thought. "What's wrong?"

"I don't know. I feel weak and dizzy." He tried to get up.

"Stay down. You should rest," he said gently, pushing him back.

"I was looking forward to visit my friend. But now I've made myself sick."

"Don't worry. You can visit him later. Where does he live?"

"Not far. Three streets behind our house. It's a nice house."

"You stay in bed. I'll go get you some medicine."

By searching within the three-street radius, and with the help of a passerby, Chin Ho found Hu Yaobang's residence in less than an hour. A hunched old man answered the door.

"Are you the owner of the house?" Chin asked firmly.

"Um, yes. I am." The man seemed more confused than frail.

"I'm from the city government. I need to see the papers proving you are the rightful owner of this house." People were scared of government officials and would often not ask them for identification for fear of offending someone important. Disobeying a government official was a serious offense and could land a person in jail indefinitely.

"Please come inside. My master, Shao Peng, left this house to me."

"Do you have proof? Where are your property papers?"

"Please, sit here. I will get the papers."

Chin Ho regretted having to scare the old man.

"Here they are," the man said, coming out of a room.

Chin Ho took the stack of crumpled papers out of his hands and began reading them. "I heard good things about your master."

"You knew Shao Peng?" Hu asked. There was a spark in his gloomy brown eyes.

"Not personally." He kept his eyes on the papers. "But one of my best friends used to praise him. Your file is in order. Congratulations on owning this beautiful house."

"Thank you. If you don't find me rude, may I ask your friend's name?"

"Peter Chang. Have you heard of him?"

"Heard of him? I fed him in this house. He was such a great—" He stopped himself.

"Small world." Chin got up. "I haven't heard from him lately. He still comes here?"

"Oh, no. He wasn't my friend. He came to visit my master."

"I wish I could find him. Haven't seen him in ages. You wouldn't know his whereabouts, would you?"

"I'm afraid not. He used to live by that Chuma Garment factory, but not anymore. I think he went to Burma."

"I must leave. I'll make sure no one from the government bothers you about your property again."

"You are very kind."

Chin Ho walked with him toward the door and then turned. "Why Burma?"

"I don't know. During Master Shao Peng's funeral I overheard that Peter wasn't invited because he was out of the country."

Two hours later Hu leaned out the door, checked both sides of the street, locked his door, and walked along the dusty street. Soon he was panting and knocking at another door.

"What are you doing here?"

"Someone came to my house claiming to be a city official."

"What did he ask?"

"He wanted to know about Peter Chang."

"Hmm. Describe him."

"Between twenty and thirty, Korean face, tall and skinny, brown eyes."

"That was him."

"Could I ask you something?"

"Sure. You've been working with us so long you can ask me anything."

"I thought the CPC didn't care about Peter. Why the sudden change of heart?"

"Don't know. I'm following orders just like you. Now go home."

~

The leader of the CPC, Mao Zedong, was having lunch with Kang Sheng.

"I hope you know what you're doing. It might set a bad example."

"I don't care. Shao entrusted me with his last wish and I will fulfill it whether you like it or not. I will protect him at any cost."

"You and your short temper," Mao laughed. "I guess it was kismet you ended up in his house right before his death."

"It wasn't. Li Kenong told me Shao seemed vulnerable and I should visit him before he opened up to his friend."

"What happened to his friend?"

"I don't know. He left the house deeply agitated. Let me ask you a question."

"Go ahead."

"What if I were Shao and you were Kang. Would you do it?"

Mao thought briefly. "Yes, I would protect your son."

CHAPTER TWENTY-ONE

"You're a worthless woman," Kim Sung berated his wife after she refused to leave the children behind with Peter. He wanted her to attend a memorial service with him at the same hospital where she'd given birth. The Soviet government had decided to name the hospital after its two most prominent members, who'd recently died. Renowned hematologist Doctor Boris Kasparov's body had been found in a local lake. Reports suggested he'd been driving too fast when his car skidded off the narrow road. Hospital administrator Ariel Kukes had died of a heart attack while bathing. Security around the village was tighter than normal. No civilian could get near the hospital without a special invitation. All patients were moved to the upper level and the hospital was closed to all new patients.

"I'll be more than happy to go if someone else can watch Kim Man. Peter Chang can't watch both kids and take care of the house at the same time."

"You go and get ready! I will find someone." Kim Sung gave her a boiling glare and stormed out of the house.

Peter stole a glimpse at Kim Suk, in the kitchen holding the baby. Under different circumstances he would have felt offended that she didn't trust him to watch both kids, but he knew she was right. Kim Jong couldn't be trusted alone with his younger brother and no one could convey this to Kim Sung, who believed his older son was an angel in human form.

"What are you thinking, Peter?"

"Something you said earlier."

"About what?"

"I don't know. You were in the middle of a sentence when Kim Jong interrupted."

"Oh, yes, I remember. It's not a good time."

The minutes became hours and the darkness swallowed the daylight, but Kim Sung didn't return. Kim Suk made several trips between the kitchen and her room and finally declared, "He went by himself. Thank goodness!"

Peter agreed and cleared the table.

"Could you come here?"

Too tired to think, he went to her room. The children were sleeping.

"Your father didn't abandon you."

"What do you mean?" He was alert now. The mention of his father was painful but he veiled his expression. He was too proud to let himself drown in a stream of emotions. Not in front of others.

"Li Kenong's wife told me your father went to Shao Peng's house to look for you."

"My father didn't know Shao Peng."

"Commander Li was there when your father visited him.

Li's wife told me Shao introduced your father as his best friend."

Peter looked at her face in disbelief. If she was joking, he wasn't amused. But no! She would never kid about his father. She knew it was a touchy subject. He had told her. "Are you sure about all this? I never heard my father speak about Shao Peng."

"Huh, it's strange…" She approached him, shaking her head, and took his cold hand. "Your father was present when Shao passed away."

Peter felt as if he were caught in a vortex, completely helpless. Nothing made any sense. He was convinced his hidebound traditionalist father wouldn't befriend a communist.

CHAPTER TWENTY-TWO

Chin Ho was standing in front of a rundown garment factory when a man resembling Buddha, round face, round belly, stretched out earlobes, approached him with a frown.

"This is private property."

"I apologize. I've been out of the country for several years. Someone told me my best friend lives here."

"Are you talking about Peter Chang?" The man crossed his arms on his chest.

"Yes. Is he here?"

"Your ungrateful friend doesn't live here anymore." The man gritted his teeth.

Chin Ho sighed. "I was looking forward to seeing him."

"If I were you, I would get better friends."

"Thanks." Chin smiled and wended his way to the street.

"Hey, you!" a melodious voice called behind him.

He spun on his heel and saw a pretty girl waving her arm. "Me?" He pointed at his chest.

She nodded and ran toward him.

Wow! She has some chest on her! He admired her bouncing bosom. He wished she would never stop running.

"Are you friends with Peter?" she said, coming close.

"Yes. A man told me he doesn't live here anymore." He tried not to stare.

"That was my father. He doesn't like Peter," she said sadly.

"Why?"

"Peter left without telling him. My father used to like him a lot."

"That doesn't sound like Peter. Maybe he left because of an emergency. I'm sure he'll come back to apologize to him."

"You think so?" The girl's eyes sparked with hope before becoming gloomy. "I heard him say he was going somewhere to protect some woman."

"He told you?"

"No. I heard him when I was going to his... If you see him, tell him I'm angry with him."

"I will." Chin promised. "What's your name?"

"Cui," she said and ran away. This time faster.

How could someone leave her behind?

It was clear Peter Chang was protecting Kim Sung's wife. But why? She had Red Army protection. The whole village did. No one entered or left without military permission. Who's he protecting her from? It wouldn't be a bad idea to delve into Kim Suk's past. *Maybe she's the one I should be investigating...* Chin fell asleep.

Hard work, bribes, and spying produced the answers. A CPC defector told him that he'd known Kim Suk when she worked in the kitchen for the Chinese guerrillas. Chin Ho dug deeper into her history and confirmed that she had strong ties to the CPC, but he couldn't ascertain for sure if she were still an active member. Peter Chang's presence denoted that she was a valuable asset, and that's the only proof he needed. He sent his findings to General Grigory Mekler through a secret messenger and asked for further instructions.

The next morning he woke up humming. "All work and no play makes Chin Ho a dull man." His servant smiled at him and asked permission to visit his old friend, Hu Yaobang.

"Of course! Go and have fun. I might be out myself," he said with a broad smile.

Cui had excited him and reminded him of Jin, whom he'd met two years ago when sexual desperation led him to Shanghai's red district. After an hour of wandering (most of the prostitutes who approached were not his type), he got lucky when a pretty young woman in a window offered her services. He sprinted upstairs like a charging bull and mauled her all night. At first she wasn't too happy when he overstayed his visit, but when he paid her handsomely she was more than delighted and sent him away after an appreciative fellatio.

Chin Ho put on his best clothes, shaved, sprayed perfume, and went to visit Jin, hoping the extremely cold weather would be a deterrent to other horny men. He was wrong. The district was packed with men of all ages. He controlled his smile at an old codger, at least seventy or eighty, waddling along with walking sticks.

Chin Ho banged on her door. Anticipating her nakedness hardened his penis. He took a step back and called her name. The window opened above and her face appeared. "Ivan?"

"Yes, it's me!"

"I'm not working today. Can you come back in three

days?" She sounded disappointed. Chin couldn't blame her. He hadn't met a woman who didn't desire him again. Knowing how to please a woman in bed was his strong suit. Where some sexual acts were considered taboo among Chinese and Koreans, he preferred them, going the extra mile.

"May I come up and talk to you?" he asked, noticing other men ogling in her direction.

She disappeared and a few seconds later opened the door with a valid complaint. "I haven't seen you in ages. I thought you got married or something."

"I'm not the marrying type. I need my freedom." He followed her upstairs. She wasn't wearing any makeup and was dressed in a somewhat unflattering long, white gown.

"What have you been up to all this time?" she asked, pointing him to a wicker chair next to her bed. The room was a drab and smelled like a sweat lodge, but then he wasn't there to admire her housekeeping.

"I was out of town on a business trip. How come you're not working?"

"I'm having a lady's day," she said coyly.

Damn my luck! He forced a smile. "Oops. I guess I picked the wrong day."

"Or you can stay and we can talk like friends." She smiled, sitting on the edge of her bed. It wasn't the first time she'd tried to strike up a conversation. Chin always had a good excuse to leave. Talking to a whore after sex wasn't something he looked forward to. "Maybe I can come back later."

"I understand. I guess you're busy," she said, shiny brown eyes focused on his face.

Of all the prostitutes, she was Chin's favorite. Unlike the others, her face still looked innocent and trustworthy. If she walked down the street in a respectable neighborhood wearing a silk cheongsam, nobody would ever guess her profession. So how did a face like hers end up here?

"What are you thinking?"

"Nothing. So let's talk and get to know each other better. Why not?"

"You start."

"No, you go first. My life isn't that interesting. How did you end up here?"

She looked at the floor. "Can we talk about something else? It's not a very good story."

Chin was intrigued. Experience taught him girls who worked in brothels and similar places loved to tell their life stories to regular customers. Some hoped that a touching story might win them a husband or a rescuer. Chin didn't fit either category. He thought most of those stories were pure exaggeration. "Oh, go on and tell me."

She closed her eyes for a couple of seconds as if to decide, then said, "I'll tell you my story if you promise…"

"What?"

"Not to get mushy. I don't want sympathy."

He laughed. "I thrive on the misery of others." Girls from many different lifestyles had told him that over the years. He hadn't given it much thought. In his mind, he'd done nothing wrong. He wasn't obligated to relate to every girl he took to bed. Sometimes alcohol did make him say things he didn't mean, but the girls should have known better.

She chuckled and began. "I was born in Shenyang a few weeks after my father died. I was ten when my mother remarried and sent me to live with one of her sisters in Wuhan. My aunt was a nice woman who didn't have kids. She and her husband treated me well at first. Then one night my uncle came to my room and raped me. I was bleeding and wanted to cry out but he covered my mouth and warned me not to make any noise. The next morning, before my aunt woke up, he took me back to my mother and told her I was too difficult to take care of.

"My mother and her husband weren't happy about my being there but had no choice. He constantly picked on me. I obeyed him because I didn't want to go back to my aunt's house, but he still complained and talked about my returning to live with her. Scared and sad, I told my mom what my aunt's husband had done to me. She cried the whole night and blamed me.

"A week later I was home alone with my stepfather when he wrapped his arms around me and asked about my ordeal at my aunt's. My mother had told him! I was too embarrassed to give him details but he kept insisting, then threw me on my mom's bed and climbed on top of me. 'Did your uncle do you like this?' He smiled and tore my clothes. I tried to fight him but he was too big and strong. He raped me several times before my mom came back. I didn't tell her because I had no other place to go. My stepfather raped me almost every day. Sometimes I suspected she knew but didn't want to do anything about it."

"Wow! You had a shitty life." He smiled insensitively.

Her face was dark. "Fourteen years, four months, and five days after my birth I ran away from her house for good, hoping to find a better life. For a week I wandered alone through my crowded city. I met an old man who gave me the money to travel to Shanghai."

"*Gave* you the money? Did he ride you, too?" he asked, hiding a smile.

She gave him an icy stare. "My first years of independence in Shanghai turned out to be the worst of my life. I began servicing men like you to afford food and shelter."

"You tell some story! Phew!" he said, pretending to wipe his forehead. "Where is your lovely family now?"

"They live in the same place." She wiped her tears and laughed. "When you told me you were thick-skinned I didn't believe you. But now I have to admit it, you are a bastard."

He laughed. "I told you I'm no softy. I've heard all kinds of stories."

"Let me wash my face and then you tell me your story. I hope I get to laugh at you."

"Don't take too long. I was hoping for something special after this storytelling session," he called after her.

"You men are animals. I told you I'm not working today," she said from behind a curtain, separating her room from an alcove. "Hey! I hear you moving around my room. You'd better not be snooping!" She threw open the curtain. Ivan was gone.

CHAPTER TWENTY-THREE

At three a.m. Grigory Mekler was wide awake, his wife beside him in the fetal position. He'd kept his eyes closed when she tottered in at two and crashed on the bed, plastered. He was thinking about Chin Ho's message.

"Peter Chang is a former Chinese guerrilla fighter CPC sent to protect Kim Jong's wife, Kim Suk. Not completely certain, but sorry to inform you that Kim Suk might be passing on her husband's secrets to CPC. Waiting for advice. Chin Ho."

This will end my career! He left his bed and went to the library to better contemplate his military future. Kim Sung was already married when he was assigned to him, and it was his duty to monitor the people close to him. *Worst-case scenario, I can say I thought the previous general-in-charge had vetted the wife and servant before retiring.* He poured himself a sip of vodka and sat down. *I can't believe I was so wrong!*

He'd once thought that surveillance on Kim Sung was the easiest thing he'd ever done, given his daily monitoring log:

0600 subject leaves home

0620 subject arrives at Soviet Command Center, 347 Kremlin Street, for morning briefing

0841 subject leaves building, goes to his office in same military compound

1000 group of Korean men visit him [conversation recorded and translated; file attached]

1200 subject goes to officers' mess for lunch

1400 subject leaves military grounds and goes to gentleman's club

2400 subject comes out of club drunk and goes home

From time to time the general wondered if his superiors were punishing him, having him waste his productive years chasing a foreign politician who spent two-thirds of his day drinking and copulating with whores. He got sick of reading the same intelligence report after he discovered that, while Kim Sung was busy whoring, his wife was doing the family servant.

At seven in the morning, his driver dropped him at the front gate of a building he knew too well. The guard saluted and opened the door. He walked down the hallway, took off his hat, and knocked. "Come in, General!"

Grigory adjusted his uniform and entered. Only one man, not three, sat before him.

"You didn't give me enough time to summon the others, but that's fine. We can handle this on our own, can't we?" Yuri Andropov purred.

"I must present my findings to the whole committee," he said firmly. He wished Gormykin were here instead of this locum tenens. Anton was a seasoned politician who understood the underlying complexities of intelligence gathering. After his last visit, Grigory had reviewed Andropov's profile. His parents had died when he was young. During his school years he was active in the Soviet Communist Party and, after finishing his education, he gained access to Stalin's close friends, which resulted in fast-track promotions. Grigory wished he had dug more deeply.

"We're fighting a war with the Germans and can't just drop everything to meet with you. We need at least a week's notice. You're lucky I was in town. My two comrades are busy."

"I'm under no obligation to present my findings to a single member, but given the current war situation I have no problem briefing you alone."

"Very good. Go on," Yuri said eagerly.

He cleared his throat and told him Chin Ho's findings.

Yuri removed his glasses and leaned forward. "You should have known this information years ago. I'm very disappointed. You and your men have been sleeping on the job, General!"

"You are entitled to your opinion. I don't have to agree with you."

"I don't like your smug manners." Yuri scowled.

"I feel the same way." Grigory put on his hat and left the room. He wasn't going to let a civilian get under his skin. In his long military career, he had seen several politicians appear and disappear. Once a retiring general told him, "Politicians are like lawn weeds: you don't notice them until they grow big and unsightly. Remember to pack a weeder when you go to meet one." In the background, Yuri Andropov was threatening him with disciplinary action.

Go to hell! He left the building.

CHAPTER TWENTY-FOUR

Chin Ho checked his pockets for keys and then knocked. Han opened the door with lightning speed.

"Oh, master, I was worried about you," he said, moving to the side and examining him head to toe. "You are well?"

"Very well. Something urgent came up and I didn't have time to notify you," he explained, knowing his servant would worry about his sudden disappearance. He usually informed him when he went away for long periods.

"You were gone three days. I had so many bad thoughts in my head, I couldn't sleep."

Chin Ho patted his shoulder, sorry he'd made Han worry. After his mother died, he didn't think anybody cared about him. "Don't worry about me too much. Go to bed. We'll talk in the morning."

They heard a thud at the door.

"Maybe that man is back." Han said.

"Who?" He checked his watch. "It's nine o'clock."

"He came this morning…"

Chin Ho opened the door. "Oh– I nev–" he stuttered.

"Please come inside." He shook the stranger's hand warmly and led him to a private room. He closed the door behind them. "I can't believe you're here. I didn't even know you knew my house."

"Should I get you some tea?" Han asked from the other side of the door.

Chin looked at Grigory Mekler, who wasn't a tea aficionado, and said, "No, go to your room and sleep. We don't need anything."

Grigory Mekler waited in the chair while Chin fixed him a straight scotch.

"Sorry I don't have vodka."

"This will do." He belted it down. "Is your servant trustworthy?"

"Yes! Very loyal," Chin assured him, taking the seat opposite. He was a little anxious to see him in his house. He didn't want to commingle his private and professional lives. He enjoyed the life of secrecy and anonymity, which suited his personality so well.

"I read the report you sent me. Are you positive about your findings?"

"Absolutely!" He leaned forward. "I confirmed that Peter Chang and Kim Suk are both connected to the CPC."

Grigory ran his hand through his thinning gray hair. The dark circles under his eyes suggested lack of sleep. "These Chinese outplayed us! They had a perfect plan to influence Kim Sung through his wife."

"You think she's influencing him?" asked Chin. He had seen a variety of the general's moods, but it was the first time his strong face displayed worry.

"Doesn't seem that way now, but it could all change once

he gets back to Korea. I think Kim Sung has two personalities. One day he's charming and understanding and the next he's evil incarnate. His conversation tapes with his compatriots aren't pretty. He treats them like dirt."

"Why don't they get rid of him? He isn't running a country yet."

"How can they? We and the Chinese are both supporting him."

"Why?"

"Because we hate the West and the U.S. This man will keep them busy with his stupid ploys while Stalin and Mao expand their economic ideologies around the globe."

"I'm not cut out to absorb this much political talk." Chin grinned. He considered himself a political agnostic, not caring which way the political wind blew. He was in it for the money and that's all that mattered. He wasn't ashamed to admit that his loyalties were open to the highest bidder. So far the Soviets had rewarded him generously. "Tell me what you want me to do."

"*You* can't stand political conversation? Imagine having to live with these mealy-mouthed politicians every day of your life, like I have to."

"Condolences," Chin replied facetiously.

Grigory smiled. "We need to come up with a plan to neutralize the Chinese threat. But more importantly, we need to find Kim Suk's replacement."

"You mean find him another wife?"

"Yes. Otherwise the Chinese will find him one and we're back to square one."

"You have someone in mind?"

"No one specific. We need a Korean woman who is

willing to work for us. You need to find someone who can be trained to accomplish our goal."

"What kind of woman does he like?"

"He has your taste," the general needled him.

Chin Ho blushed. "It might take some time to find the right person."

"I am aware of it. We'll train her and then introduce her to Kim Sung, and at the same time remove his wife and her lover from the scene."

"Sounds like a good plan. I'll begin right away."

The general rose and went to the door. "Excellent! Also, prepare yourself…"

"I'm always prepared." Chin wasn't stretching the truth. Day or night, rain or shine, nothing could ever stop him from executing his mission to perfection. That was why the general favored him among his peers and assigned him to critical missions.

Grigory turned, put his hand on his shoulder, and whispered, "I'm talking about your ultimate mission."

Chin Ho opened his mouth to say something, but the general gestured for him to be quiet and vanished in the darkness.

When Chin was in bed trying to sleep, the general's last words stuck in his head. Ultimate mission? What was he talking about? He considered every possible scenario until the long-awaited sleep robbed him of consciousness.

He awoke refreshed and determined. He ate breakfast under the watchful eyes of his servant, who complained he didn't eat enough and was turning to skin and bone. Chin Ho assured him he was perfectly healthy and left the house. He had one last thing to do before embarking on his mission.

Still nine-thirty! I'm sure she doesn't wake up this early, he thought, entering the red district. The street wasn't as busy as it had been during his last visit—more old men were prowling than young men like him. He passed up the winks and solicitations, and stopped. He knocked at her door. A few seconds later an unknown face opened it with a smile.

He rechecked the numbers on the building. "Where is Jin?"

The woman, though a few years older than Jin, was every bit as pretty. She smiled professionally. "She had to leave for a few days. But don't worry. I promised to take good care of her customers. Do you want to come upstairs?"

"Do you know when she's coming back?" he asked, battling his rock-hard penis and brain. The woman was a little thick. He preferred slender girls.

"No!" Her hospitality was waning, and she was distracted by something behind him.

"I guess I—"

"Told you she isn't here," she said tersely, then smiled. "So nice to see you again."

Before Chin could make out what she meant, a flabby man shoved him out of the way and went inside. The gleeful woman shut the door.

~

Chin Ho spent the next week traveling and searching for Kim Suk's replacement. The job he initially thought would be simple turned out to be arduous. He couldn't find one woman who fit the description "able to marry a man destined to become the leader of Korea." Failure wasn't an option, Chin Ho reminded himself every time he faced an insurmountable task. He eased his frustration with a cup of tea after eating the gamy fish his servant had cooked for him. He hated it but he always ate it. He was too hungry to be fussy.

"I'm so glad you liked my food. I should make more fish. It's good for you," Han said, filling up his half-empty teacup.

"Huh?" Chin looked at him vacantly. His mind was on other things.

"You know what they say—always give a man what he likes or he will eat somewhere else," Han mumbled, walking away.

"Wait!" Chin called. "Repeat what you said."

Han was surprised. "What did I say?"

"Give a man what he likes—"

"Oh! I said always give a man what he likes or he will eat somewhere else."

"Where did you hear that?"

"When I was a child, my mother would say it to my sister. Why?"

"Never mind!" He smiled impishly and enthusiastically leaped out of his chair. Chin remembered his own mother talking to his sisters in what he considered a cryptic language. Later he realized they were talking about the tricks most mothers taught to their pubescent daughters to get married and stay married. "You feed man's belly and under belly, he would not leave your door. None of you were born if I wasn't a good cook," his mother told his older sister, who'd begun to wear loose clothes to hide her developing body and argued against the need to learn cooking.

CHAPTER TWENTY-FIVE

Peter spent hours mulling over Kim Suk's revelations about his father. He tried to recall every single contact he'd had over the years with Shao Peng in case they'd ever discussed their families, but he couldn't remember one time. Shao was as private about his personal life as he was. Two people could answer his questions but one was dead, and he didn't know anything about his father's whereabouts except that he had moved out of Nanjing.

"Are you sure it was my father?" Peter asked her the next day when she came to the kitchen with Kim Man.

"That's what I heard."

"When is Li Kenong's wife coming back?"

"Her name is Su," she smiled. "I don't know. Why?"

"I want to ask her myself."

"Won't do any good. She already told me as much as she knew. I don't understand why you are so consumed by this. So what if your father and Shao Peng were friends?"

"There is no possible way they could have been friends. My father hated communism for as long as I can remember."

"Hey, Peter, I always wanted to ask you something."

"About what?"

"How did you join the CPC? Were you inspired by Karl Marx?"

"Who is he?"

She broke into laughter. "How could you be communist and not know him? You never read his book *The Communist Manifesto*?"

Peter shook his head. The name felt strange to his ears. He had never told her that, even though he could read just fine, he'd never read an entire book. It was a waste of time. Shao Peng once insisted he take a few books home and study them. After flipping through the pages, he had given up. Sitting in one place and concentrating didn't come natural to him. A month later, when returning the books, he told Shao that he preferred to learn from real life and not from some purple prose books. "I'm not a communist."

"Then why are you with the CPC?" she asked in surprise.

"I joined to fight Japs. I don't believe in this communist bullshit."

"*Bullshit?!*" Her eyes widened.

"Of course. I heard that Shao Peng went on and on about how good it is. But seriously, do you really want a few people in charge of your life, deciding how you live? Isn't that slavery? I want to live free. You believe in it?"

"Yes." She lowered her eyes. "It's the way for the poor and downtrodden to get justice."

"You want a man like your husband deciding for millions of people?"

She stood stock-still. Lines of worry appeared on her face. "You'd better watch yourself. Don't let anybody know your views."

"Well, you asked me." He began to prepare vegetable broth. "I hope you like my food."

"May I make a suggestion?"

He noticed that she'd lost most of her post-pregnancy weight by skipping rice and noodles. "What?"

"You should find yourself a nice girl. I think you feel lonely."

That came out of nowhere. How could she suggest it? She was either naive or a coldhearted bitch. Just because he wasn't sleeping with her didn't mean he'd stopped loving her. A night didn't go by when he didn't want her. He smothered a sigh. "Thanks for thinking about me."

"I need to check on Kim Jong." She dropped her eyes and left the kitchen.

Two days later, Peter was roused from his nap. He thought he heard someone at the front door, but when he checked, nobody was there. Had he imagined it? He headed back to his room and ran into Kim Suk coming out of the kitchen.

"I need to go out for a while. Could you watch Kim Jong? I'll take Kim Man with me."

Peter agreed with a smile, even though he would have preferred a snooze over a wayward Kim Jong. The boy's mood swings were out of control. Twice now, Kim Suk had asked Peter if some evil spirit possessed him. He dismissed the idea and begged her not to mention it to Kim Sung, who would commit her to a mental institution before she finished telling him. Kim Sung was still hardly ever home to witness his son in action.

When she'd gone Peter asked Kim Jong if he was hungry. The boy bobbled his head. *With this puny body I don't know where he puts all the food he eats,* he thought, and went to the kitchen to get a glass of milk. *Maybe it'll help him grow.*

"Peter! Open the gate!" Kim Suk shouted, banging on the door.

He opened it in alarm. She pushed past him into the house. Peter peeked outside to see if someone was there. Only the two guards, smoking and laughing in their truck.

Peter saw the fear in her eyes and asked delicately, "What's wrong? You're back so fast." She threw a swift glance at her older son, in his own world playing with his tin toys, and whispered, "Come to the kitchen. I need to talk to you."

He nodded and followed her.

She secured the baby in her left arm and reached into her coat pocket with her right hand, taking out a small piece of folded paper. "Read this!"

"What is it?"

"Read!"

Peter scanned the note. "*We checked into your request and concluded that the person of interest wasn't whom he portrayed. Advise you to keep your guard up!*"

"So?!" Kim Suk asked.

"What does it mean?" He handed back the note.

"I sent a request to see if Ko Hee had other living relatives besides Kim Sung," she whispered. "This is the answer. The man you met at Ko Hee's wasn't telling you the truth."

"Where did you get this? Is Li's wife back?"

"Never mind where I got it! Aren't you paying attention?"

"You're referring to Chin Ho? I don't understand why someone would pretend to be Ko Hee's relative?"

"I don't know, but I suspect he wasn't there to collect his inheritance!"

"Then what?" Peter asked, folding his arms across his chest. His mind still wasn't made up about the man. Chin was polite and friendly but he asked way too many questions.

"I don't know, but something isn't right. I can feel it."

"You're worried for nothing. The man seemed harmless. But if he tries anything stupid I'll break every bone in his body with these fists." He smiled and felt a rush he hadn't felt in years.

CHAPTER TWENTY-SIX

Dressed in his favorite white shirt and gray trousers, his hair combed, Chin Ho could have been a well-to-do businessman. On his way to Jin's, he ignored the prostitutes who promised him an unforgettable time.

"I have a younger girl available," a sallow and spindly man said, sidling up to him.

Chin was about to reply when, a few feet above his head, a window opened with a screech and Jin's head appeared.

"You son of a bitch! You steal my customers!"

The man showed off his tobacco-stained teeth. "You should retire those legs. You've already put too many miles on them."

"Tell your mother, you son of a bitch!" Jin hurled an empty tin box at him. He dodged the box and was ready to fling it back at her when Chin Ho told him to scram.

"Why? Is that your sister up there?" he snickered, puffing his puny chest.

"Don't listen to this pig! Let me open the door for you." Jin disappeared.

"Oh, she likes your dick."

"You need to leave," Chin said, spinning around.

The man stepped forward and prodded him in the chest. "You threatening me? I'll cut your cock! See how she likes you *then*."

"You asked for it!" He grabbed the man's arms and plunged his knee into his belly. The man groaned, curled up, and began cursing. Chin took a step back and kicked him between the legs. His victim dropped to his knees, holding his crotch, then rolled to his side.

"Come inside!" Jin grabbed his arm and pulled him in. "What's wrong with you? I have to live here with these reptiles. You fight and go home, but they come after me or don't let anybody come to me."

"Why don't you leave this place?"

"And do what?" she laughed. "Become a nun?"

"I can offer you a job," he said, scrutinizing her for a reaction.

She laughed again. "Doing what? I'm already working for you." She slipped out of her clothes.

Mesmerized by her curvy, petite body, his jaw locked as she sprawled on the bed. She had brown eyes, dark shiny hair, a thin long waist, and perky breasts with large dark nipples. He stared between her legs at her nest of hair and lowered his tongue to it, smelling her scent.

"You shouldn't," she squirmed.

He pinned her hands over her head and circled his tongue on the tip of her clitoris. She was getting wet. She was ready. He lifted his head and unbuttoned his pants. She pressed her thighs together. He grabbed her ankles and pulled them apart, then dragged her forward.

"Go in!" She licked her lips.

He raised her feet in the air and slipped deep inside. She tried to smile but the pain of pleasure was too intense. He gyrated against her pubic bone. Ten minutes later, he rolled off and lit a cigarette.

"You really missed me, huh," she said, wiping her breasts.

"Look at you, you're so young and pretty. Your face is like a doll," he said, blowing a white, puffy cloud into it. "You can make good money doing something else."

"Don't smoke in my face," she whined, moving away.

"Work for me!" He moved closer to her face.

"I already did," she smiled playfully.

"I can make you rich and powerful."

"How?" she asked, distrust written all over her face. She'd heard similar offers before. Men with loaded erections promise anything. She'd learned that early on.

"Will you travel with me to the Soviet Union? I'll pay you one year's wages in advance."

"What do I have to do there? Russians?"

"I can't tell you yet, but if you decide to come, I can promise that your life will never be the same."

"How can I trust that you're telling the truth?" She raised her eyebrows. "And why did you suddenly leave the other day without telling your story?"

"Oh that! I'm sorry. I couldn't handle your sob story. I came back but you weren't here."

"Liar! You men are all the same."

"I'm telling the truth! Another girl was here. She told me you'd gone somewhere."

"Did you fuck her?"

"No, but I thought about it," he grinned. "Where did you go?"

She answered sadly. "In a single day my whole family was butchered. I went to the funeral."

"What happened?"

"Nobody knows. One of my mother's neighbors went to our house and discovered my mother, stepfather, uncle, and aunt's dead bodies. Their throats were slit. I didn't even know my mother still stayed in contact with my aunt after what I told her."

"Aren't you happy they are dead? Let's celebrate!"

"I wonder if your heart is made of stone," she sighed.

"I don't know about my heart, but this is for sure made of volcanic rock!" he said, placing her hand on his erection.

"Again!"

"Can you blame me?" he whispered, aligning his body on top of her and dipping rhythmically.

He left Jin's after she promised to consider his offer. The street was packed with people. He walked until her house disappeared. A limping man approached.

"I hope I didn't hit you too hard." Chin handed him a few large-denomination bills.

The man smiled, counted his money, and said, "You've made up for it."

"Good. Just make sure nobody else goes up there."

"Don't worry about it."

"I'll see you in two weeks." Chin patted the man's shoulder and darted across the street, where his ride was waiting.

Am I getting too old? Jin examined her body in the mirror. She hadn't had a customer in days. Over the course of a week, she had used several techniques to lure them in—including coating her face with thicker makeup, exposing her breasts, standing in the window and licking her fingers—but nothing worked. She was getting desperate and worried. The rent was due in four days and the moneybag hidden under her mattress was empty. What if another prettier girl moved into this neighborhood and took all her clients? When she first came to the neighborhood, the older harlots had accused her of poaching their customers.

Worried about being cast out of the neighborhood, she sought the help of an old strumpet, who told her not to worry. "A new whore is like a new restaurant. Everybody wants to go there and try the new food, but a few days later people get tired of the same menu and want a new place to eat."

Aware that the woman was in her fifties but still had a steady stream of long-term clients, Jin asked, "How do you keep people from not getting tired of your food?"

The woman laughed. "I wish I had asked this question when I got into this business. I learned it the hard way, but you're smart." Jin smiled and repeated her question. "You change your menu! Add spices to your stale recipes."

She surveyed the street below and wished one of those prowling men would knock. Nothing was working. She slammed the window shut and burst into tears.

Jin didn't know if she was awake or asleep when she heard the knock at the door. At first, she dismissed the sound as a dream, but when the sound got louder and louder, she jumped out of bed and rushed downstairs.

"Hi, pretty." Chin Ho greeted her.

"I am so glad to see you, Ivan," she said, letting him in.

"Miss me?"

She replied with a broad smile and led him to the room where he ensconced himself on the bed. The room was cleaner than he remembered. The white bed sheet smelled of soap instead of body fluids. If it weren't for her unbridled beauty, he would have found a cleaner place to unwind long ago. "Did you think about my offer?"

"I'm still undecided," she said as she removed her blouse.

"Don't take off your shirt. I'll come back when you've made up your mind."

"Please don't go, I could use the money to buy groceries and pay my rent," she pleaded, tears in her eyes.

"Do you enjoy living like this?"

"No," she sobbed. The past few days had taught her a hard lesson. Without clients, she couldn't survive the sleazy district. She had spent hours weighing Ivan's offer, but it didn't make any sense. Why would someone want to help a whore? There were plenty of nice girls in the city. "I don't know what you see in me, Ivan. I hope you aren't fooling me. Can I trust you?"

"Do you have anyone better to trust? I know you've had terrible experiences with men. I don't blame you for having doubts. But you should give me a chance. I won't disappoint you. What do you say?"

She didn't answer and kept staring at him. She was out of options.

Chin observed her quietly. He was confident about his selection. Under the right circumstances she would blossom, he had briefed the general. "Be ready! I'll pick you up tomorrow afternoon."

Jin didn't believe that Ivan would return as promised until he knocked at her door the next day. "Are you all packed up?"

"No," she said, a little embarrassed.

"Why not? I told you I was coming to take you away."

"Let me do it now. It won't take long. I can get the rest of my stuff later."

"Later? You're not coming back here." He looked at her as if she were crazy.

"I can't leave my things… I haven't told my landlord yet."

"You want to take this junk with you?" he asked, circling the room. A noisy bed, which creaked relentlessly whenever he mounted her, a cumbersome closet with broken hinges, and a small table with uneven legs. Nothing was salvageable, not even to give away.

"It's not junk! I worked hard to buy this stuff," she protested.

"What if I pay you for all of it?"

"But you said it was junk," she frowned. "What will you do with it?"

"I really don't have time to explain everything, but here. Take this money. This should be enough for all this."

"Why are you giving me so much money?"

He consulted his watch. "Our train leaves in fifteen minutes. You can ask me all of your questions on the train."

"You promise not to hide anything from me?" she asked, throwing her clothes on the top of a wooden suitcase. "Start with your real name. Koreans don't name their boys Ivan."

He hid his admiration but he wasn't surprised. He'd known for some time that she was more than just a pretty face. She could probably do anything she set out to do, but she didn't know her capabilities. All that was about to change. She was destined to discover her true self. "My name is Chin Ho. Now will you hurry?"

"See? I was right," she smiled. "You men think street girls are stupid."

"I never thought that." He grinned. "Would I be taking you with me if you were stupid?"

"Maybe," she said, fixing her hair. "I'm ready."

After a few days of traveling by train, truck, and large boat, they arrived in Moscow, where two tall, uniformed men talked to Chin Ho in a language Jin didn't understand. They drove them in a jeep to a tall building.

"I'm freezing. What is this place?" she asked, climbing out.

"Academy. Follow me," Chin Ho smiled.

The next few days were full of surprises and revelations as Jin learned the real nature of her employment. At first, she was scared that she was there to learn how to seduce Kim Sung, but after Chin Ho's persistent and enthusiastic assurances, she began to see a better future.

"Can you imagine that one day you will become the wife of a country's leader?"

"No, I can't see that far," she answered honestly.

"That's why I brought you here. We'll educate you, teach you everything about Kim Sung, and at the end will arrange your meeting with him."

"You brought me here to become a spy like you?" she chaffed.

"You prefer red district?" he frowned.

She stared at him and shook her head. "What if he doesn't like me?"

"Don't sell yourself short. He'll bite his tongue the minute he lays eyes on you. You're beautiful," he said, suddenly standing up. "See you later. I need to get back to work."

CHAPTER TWENTY-SEVEN

"**S**ir, do you want me to wait here?" his driver asked.

Startled, Grigory Mekler realized he was home. Normally he was always on the qui vive, but today wasn't his day. He woke up with a big headache, attended a couple of meetings that were a total waste of time, and on the way home the car broke down near Crimea Street. Though the driver was a good mechanic, it still took him half an hour to fix the radiator hose. "No. You're dismissed. I'm done for the day. I just want to relax."

"Yes, sir!" The driver was about to jump out but Grigory instructed him to stay put. "Yes, sir. What time should I be back, sir?"

Grigory noticed the azure sky. He'd come home two hours earlier than usual. "Six will be fine," he said softly. He didn't want to tell the man that he was annoyed by his questions. His regular driver was on sick leave, but Grigory knew that was an excuse. Last week his wife had given birth and he wanted to stay home with his newborn son. He had confessed when the general called him to ask about his health.

He'd never fathered a child, but he knew it was an important event for the driver, so he granted him two weeks of absence.

At the door, a tall, curvaceous woman with ash brown hair and blue eyes, dressed in an elegant sable gown, kissed his cheek. "You're home early. Coming with me?"

"Where?" He knew his wife was referring to a dinner party she'd told him about the week before. Someone or other was getting engaged or married. He hadn't asked. Every time his gregarious wife mentioned the word party or function, he tuned out. She never blamed him. She'd known about his reclusive personality before accepting his marriage proposal.

"Nikolai Zlobin's daughter is getting engaged to—"

"I'm too tired," he said, indulging in a long, feigned yawn. Nikolai was an influential politician who took any opportunity to throw a party. Maria was his only daughter. He'd been trying for years to find her a suitor. She wasn't like any other normal girl. Before doctors could stunt her growth, she was well over six feet tall and weighed as much as her obese father. It wasn't her size, which annoyed Grigory. She used to visit his wife, and when she was busy, the girl would try to flirt with him. He never told his wife that one day he found her naked in their bed. He chased her out of the house and promised not tell anyone if she stopped visiting. He'd not seen her since and was happy about it.

"Is everything all right? You seem gloomy," his wife asked, rubbing his upper arm. "You're not feeling neglected, are you?"

"I'm just tired."

"Well, don't go to sleep early tonight. I'll take care of it," she whispered, rubbing her leg against his crotch.

One in the morning wasn't early, he thought about saying.

She'd made a similar promise last Thursday. He stayed up late but she didn't come home until three. "A man who rises up at five every morning of his adult life deserves to go to sleep early," he'd told her in the morning when she complained.

"I won't," he said, knowing he would probably fall asleep soon. He didn't want to spoil her mood. She would be too drunk later to remember his promise. She pulled his head down, kissed his mouth, and left.

He went to the library, tossed his hat on the table, and fell into his favorite armchair. His wife had given it to him on their twentieth anniversary. He thought about Andropov. He believed what his source, a close friend, had told him yesterday. "Yuri Andropov wants your job and he's working overtime for it." Slime! Grigory wondered if Yuri was motivated by their last interaction.

Chin Ho should be here any minute. This will secure my future. Stalin will never replace me when he learns what I've done to accomplish his goals. His eyes wandered over the shelves chockablock with books, new and rare. This was now his favorite room. Not long ago it was his bedroom, where his wife made love to him every night. Lately, her priorities had changed. Her social life and rituals were more important to her. On occasion he pondered asking her to curtail her late-night activities, but he couldn't. In all honesty he was the one who'd forced her to leave the house and meet other people—he was so busy working he didn't want her to be bored.

"Sir, a man is at the door."

He acknowledged his servant absently and sat upright. "Send him in."

Chin Ho strode in with a warm smile, head held high. "Good evening, General."

"Good evening. Close the door and have a seat."

"Thanks." Chin sat across from him on a wooden chair.

"Drink?"

"Please."

Grigory handed him a glass and sat down, legs crossed. "I'm impressed with your trainee. You picked a smart person."

"Thank you, sir. She is a very talented girl."

"That's what I heard from the academy instructors. You must be wondering why I asked you to come to my home instead of my office."

"I'm sure you've got a good reason."

"This could be our last meeting."

"Last meeting?"

"Yes." Grigory left his chair and strolled to the window behind his desk. Beyond it was the black night. "Someone thinks he can do my job better."

Chin stood up. "I beg to differ! You're the most qualified person I've ever met."

"Thanks. I called you here for your last assignment." He resumed his seat.

"Am I being discharged?"

The general smiled and gestured for him to sit. "I've been preparing you for a special task and now you've proven that I was right in choosing you. It'll be the toughest assignment you've ever had but rewarding beyond your wildest dreams."

"I'm ready, sir. I'll never disappoint you!" Chin's voice was husky with excitement.

"Get the brown envelope lying on my desk."

Chin Ho marched across the room, scooped it up, and returned, eyes gleaming.

"Open it and read it."

Chin Ho nodded, unsealing the envelope. His mouth agape, he emptied the contents on the table between them. He mopped his brow with the back of his hand and probed each item: a birth certificate, school records, numerous certificates of valor and bravery for fighting against the Japanese, medals, and a photo ID with his picture but a different name. "Bao Ju?"

"Yes. After today you'll forget you were ever Chin Ho or anyone else. You are now Bao Ju, a Korean who has been fighting the Japanese all his life."

"Why?" Chin asked, his eyes fixed on his photo.

"For the Soviet Union," Grigory replied, leaning back. "Let me explain…. "

CHAPTER TWENTY-EIGHT

News of Japan's surrender on September 2, 1945, after the U.S. dropped atomic bombs on Hiroshima and Nagasaki, initiated great festivities in *Vyatskoye*. The Soviet government threw a huge farewell party for Kim Sung and some of his Korean allies. Many influential politicians and dignitaries traveled from Moscow to attend. Kim Sung circled the room, rubbing elbows with his hosts and apologizing for his wife's absence.

"What a shame your wife couldn't attend this fabulous party." A woman with class and style gestured with a bare arm.

"I agree. Poor woman has come down with influenza." He bowed his head with equal grace and moved on to the next person. The room was as big and elegant as the people inside. With few exceptions (mainly military uniforms), the men sported dark suits and ties. The women wore sexy gowns and thick facial paint. An army of energetic waiters in white uniforms roamed the white-tiled floor with giant trays of hors d'oeuvres. The air was filled with lingering clouds of expensive cigar smoke and the smell of cologne and alcohol.

"How do you feel about the Americans dropping atomic bombs?" a bony young man asked.

Kim Sung smiled at his reporter's badge. "I wish the Americans hadn't stopped. Those *Jjokbari* should have been obliterated from the planet. The world has no place for such evil."

"May I quote you?" the reporter asked, scribbling in his notebook.

"Every word!" Kim Sung said. "Now excuse me."

"But what do you think about Hitler's atrocities on J—?"

"Today is a great day. Go enjoy yourself," he smiled, surveying the crowded room.

"Sorry, but I didn't get your answer," the reporter insisted.

"He answered your question. Now move along," a stern voice said over the loud noise.

"What a joy to see you again, General Mekler." Kim Sung extended his hand.

"The pleasure is mine. I hope you're enjoying the party." He shook his hand and glowered at the departing reporter. Two guards escorted him.

"I am very much. I was hoping to thank you for arranging it," he said earnestly. He'd met Mekler on occasion, when he'd gone to Moscow to convince him to increase funding for the Korean guerrillas who fought side by side with the Red Army. He didn't know the general's job description, but he knew he authorized money for his account.

"You deserve it. In a few short days you will rule a country."

"I'll never forget your generosity." Kim Sung shook his hand again, and after a further exchange about the war's end, went to mingle with some women, staring at him and laughing.

Before the clock struck midnight, General Mekler said goodnight to Kim Sung, who insisted he stay longer. But the general claimed he was too tired and left. By two in the morning most of the guests had departed, and at three Kim Sung announced he was leaving. A few inebriated women tried to cajole him to stay, but he refused politely. Normally he would stay and drink until he couldn't recognize the faces around him, but a few hours from now he had to be in Moscow for a private meeting with Stalin.

The sun would be up in a few hours. He walked toward his UAZ 469. "The weather is cool tonight," he mumbled, raising the collar of his overcoat and knocking at his driver's window. He woke with a start and opened the door.

"You're not paid to sleep!"

"Sorry!" The driver rubbed his eyes and started the engine.

"Home!" Kim Sung ordered from the back seat.

Kim Sung was dozing off when a loud noise startled him. "What was that?" he exclaimed, leaning forward. His eyes were red.

"I think it came from the engine," the driver replied, pulling over. The quiet street was narrow and lined with ghostly, deformed trees.

"Why are you stopping?"

"Smoke is coming from the engine. It's not safe." The driver jumped out.

A few days from now I'll never have to sit in this piece of shit again, he thought, watching the driver pop the hood. *I hope he can fix the damn thing. How can he check the engine without a flashlight?* He got out. "Hey! Don't you need a light?"

"No, he doesn't," a voice whispered behind his ear, and before he could swivel his head someone hugged him tightly, lifted him off his feet, and threw him to the ground.

"You mother—"

Four shadows appeared from the trees and began trussing him. He yelled, cursed, and threw punches, but his assailants overpowered him. After tying him up, they dragged him behind the trees and one of the assailants pointed a gun at his head. A fearful Kim Sung saw his driver, lying on the ground motionless, his hands and feet bound. "Who are you? What are you doing? You're making a big mistake. Do you know who I am?"

The black-clad assailants in facemasks pushed him against the tree. The person with the gun lowered his barrel.

"Thank you! Thank you!" Kim Sung exhaled, then began yelling in terror when two of the thugs poured something over him. He smelled kerosene. They were going to burn him! "I have lots of money! I will make you rich! Let me go! Don't hurt me," he cried in bewilderment. In a flash, a shadow leaped from the woods and, before they could retaliate, attacked the assailants, kicking and punching. Kim Sung had never seen a human jump or fight like that.

"He has a gun!" Kim Sung warned just as the goon took aim. The attacker dropped the man he was choking and disarmed the other man by breaking his arm.

"I'm taking you out of here," he said to Kim Sung when the assailants were writhing on the ground in pain. He threw him over his shoulder and carried him to a jeep hidden behind a tree. "Stay here," he whispered, and ran back behind the trees.

Kim Sung lay motionless on the back seat until the man appeared with his unconscious driver over his shoulder. He dumped the driver next to him and climbed into the driver's seat.

"Thank you. Can you cut me loose?" Kim Sung moaned.

"Oh, sorry." The man wielded a sharp knife.

"Where did you learn to fight like that?" Kim Sung panted. He'd never seen one man beat up five before. "You saved my life. Who are you?"

"I am Bao Ju."

CHAPTER TWENTY-NINE

Peter Chang awoke in a panic. Someone was pounding the gate relentlessly. He checked his watch. Five o'clock! Who's going crazy this early? He jogged to the door.

"What the hell took you so long?" Kim Sung barked.

"What happened, master?" He stared at his torn and dirty clothes.

"Never mind! Don't tell Kim Suk," he warned, dabbing his bruised forehead.

"Yes, master. Should I get you some hot water?"

"Bring it to my room."

Peter scurried to the kitchen, wondering what could have gone wrong at the farewell party. Did he try to flirt with someone's wife or daughter and got his ass handed to him? Before leaving, Kim Sung had had a huge fight with Kim Suk. He'd wanted her to wear a revealing dress, but she put on a traditional Korean dress. Peter thought she was lovely, but Kim Sung castigated her appearance and left alone. Peter saw rare tears in her eyes. She sent the woman home whom she'd hired to take care of Kim Man and went to her room without dinner.

"I brought you hot water, master," Peter whispered at Kim Sung's door.

"Come!"

He gently pushed open the door with his knee and carefully carried the steaming bowl. Kim Sung stood shirtless before a mirror, checking his forehead. His elbows were scraped mildly.

"Put the bowl on the table and leave."

"Should I make you breakfast, master?"

"You are still here?" he scowled.

Unsure if Kim Sung wanted breakfast, Peter went to the kitchen. It was still too early for Kim Suk or Kim Jong to come out of her room. He decided to clean the kitchen cabinets.

He didn't know the exact time when he heard the cough behind him. It was Kim Sung, dressed smartly, his face showing no signs of fatigue. "Go get my suitcase from my room. Tell Kim Suk I'm going to Moscow."

Peter wiped his hands on his buttocks. He found the medium-sized brown leather suitcase on Kim Sung's bed. He wasn't going for more than two or three days, he told himself, weighing the suitcase in his hands.

"You did a great job taking care of this house. I hope you're ready for a bigger one." Kim Sung praised him while nibbling on a rice patty upon his return to the kitchen. Peter had bought the treat to reward Kim Jong. The boy was showing a real interest in Kung Fu and behaving moderately better with his younger brother. Peter and Kim Suk hoped this change was permanent.

"Are we moving?" Peter asked, surprised. He'd heard the

news about the Japanese surrender but nothing else. That night his raw emotions kept him awake. He thought about his father, his relatives, and those fallen comrades who had suffered tremendously under the Japanese reign of terror. He dreamed about going back to China and meeting with his father. It still bothered him that his father hadn't stopped him from leaving the house. If Shao Peng weren't dead, he would go to his house and punch his teeth out for deceiving him. He wondered if Cui was already married and had children. If Kim Suk hadn't come into his life, he would have seriously considered settling down with her. Cui's eyes twinkled every time she saw him. He knew she loved him.

"Kim Suk didn't tell you we are going to Pyongyang? Give me the case, I'm already late."

How could she not tell him they're moving to Korea? I didn't want to go with them. He wanted to go back to China. He sat at the kitchen table, no longer curious about his master's injuries. Outside the sun shone in its full glory and the sky was clear blue. He stared at the door. When the waiting grew unbearable, he went to knock on Kim Suk's door. She opened it at once, wearing the clothes from last night. Her eyes were puffy and her mouth was lined. She looked older.

"What is it?" she asked, adjusting her rumpled dress.

"Can I make you breakfast?"

"You know I don't eat until—"

"I know. But since you didn't eat dinner I thought you might be hungry."

"Kim Jong is still asleep. You can bring some tea."

Kim Jong slept soundly several feet away in his bed. Kim Man was awake, playing with his toes.

He filled the kettle with cold water and put it on the stove. Then he took out a loose tea jar from the kitchen cabinet and placed it next to the empty porcelain cup. Kim Suk entered the kitchen carrying Kim Man.

"I thought I heard Kim Sung earlier. What time did he come back?"

"Very early in the morning. He told me to tell you he was going to Moscow for a few days. As soon as the tea is ready I'll bring it to your room."

She sat at the table. "I will have it here. I need to tell you something."

"And I wanted to ask you something."

"Ask."

"No. You go ahead."

She stared at him for a few seconds, and then dropped her eyes. "I'm pregnant."

CHAPTER THIRTY

Chin Ho wondered how to make his room darker so he could sleep. The giant window across from his bed was bare and the sun's late-morning rays were brilliant. His eyes were red and baggy, his face smooth but haggard. He pulled the cover over his face but the linen was thin. He kicked it away and thought about repositioning his bed. The room was crammed with furniture and closets he didn't need. It was one of many safe houses he could use without permission. The Soviet Union kept a large inventory of secret furnished houses for its spies around the world.

"Wait a minute! I know how to block this damn light," he said, jumping out of bed. He leaned against one of the steel closets and pushed it in front of the window. The room went dark. *Much better!* He lay down and closed his eyes. He hadn't been able to sleep in peace since General Mekler handed him this mission.

"We're changing your identity to Bao Ju to enable you to get closer to Kim Sung."

He set out to find ways to get acquainted with his target.

When he learned about the party, he cooked up a plan. The hired men weren't happy about getting beaten up, but he paid them well. He wasn't surprised when Kim Sung hugged him tightly and begged him to visit.

"There's no greater loyalty than putting your life in danger to save your leader," Kim Sung said after Chin Ho told him he knew who he was. "I can't believe I never heard of you. You are a great fighter."

"I was in Manchuria fighting the Japanese swine!" He dropped him outside his house.

"Yes, yes, I think I remember you now. You have a great reputation… I don't want anyone to know what happened tonight. You understand?" Kim Sung warned his driver, and then he shook Chin Ho's hand with a promise to meet him again. Chin Ho dropped the terrified driver back to his stranded vehicle, fixed some loose wires under the hood, and left him.

Hours later he opened his heavy eyelids. It took him a few seconds to get used to the dark. Bleary-eyed, he reached for his bedside table and switched on the lamp. "Shit!" he cried, shutting his eyes. The incandescent light was too strong for the small room. He reopened them slowly, arose from his bed, and padded to the closet hiding the window. He muscled it a few inches and stared outside to guess the time. It was dark. *How long have I slept? Where is my watch?* He checked his arm and saw a white imprint on his wrist. In sheer panic, he searched the pockets of his black trousers. He cupped his hand around his forehead to concentrate and then ran to his bed. His watch was under the pillow. He exhaled a long sigh of relief, scooped it up, and began shining it carefully with his white undershirt.

It wasn't the first time he had panicked about losing his watch. The last time it happened he was in Shanghai. He ransacked the whole house until he found it in his bedside drawer. His servant, Han, helped him, surprised to see his master so distraught. To everybody else it was an inexpensive watch; he could afford to buy a bunch of them. To Chin Ho it was his inestimable possession. No money could replace that watch—it had belonged to his father. His mother gave it to him a year before she died. His father wore this watch the day Chin had ridden on his shoulders coming back from school and the army truck hit him. The watch had survived the accident.

He strapped the watch back on his wrist. It was one a.m. *I slept so long. I hope there's some food around here.* He rubbed his stomach, wondering if he should visit the kitchen or write a couple of letters. He had been procrastinating the whole week. He would write first.

A week of resting and planning later, Chin Ho went to meet Kim Sung at his office in a nearby Soviet compound. Security was tight. Four tall, rigid soldiers stopped him at the entrance until they received clearance from Kim Sung to let him in.

"This way," one of the guards directed him to a nearby truck. He had parked his own vehicle a quarter of a mile away and walked.

Chin Ho smiled courteously and sat beside the driver. The UAZ 469, the official vehicle for Soviet military personnel, looped around the compound and, after passing a few canvas tents and cinderblock buildings, stopped at a small single-story building. Unlike the other buildings, this one had no guard at the door. He thanked the guard for the ride and entered.

"You are Bao Ju?" a female voice asked.

He spun around. An attractive Korean woman sat behind a desk by the door.

"Are you Bao Ju?" she repeated, leaning forward.

He walked over to her. She was in her early thirties and had a desirable face and stellar body. He placed his palms on her desk. The view was perfect. She was wearing a dress at least two sizes smaller than what she needed.

"You asked me something?"

She quickly sat up straight. "Your name?"

"Bao.... Ju." The name still felt alien to his tongue. He'd practiced so hard over the course of a desolate week to rename himself, but still his brain and mouth didn't coordinate.

"You can go right in," she pointed at the corridor ahead. "Second door on your left."

"What is your name?"

"Secretary," she said primly.

You don't get this arrogant sitting behind a hallway desk unless your boss is splitting your legs now and then. He smiled at his own bon mot and strolled down the tiled hallway. Before he could knock at the desired door, it opened.

"I think I have the wrong room," he said to the old man on the other side of the door.

"Come in, Bao Ju!" a familiar voice called out to him from behind the old man.

He went inside. Kim Sung came from behind his desk and grabbed his shoulders. "It is so good to see you again."

"Thanks. I hope I'm not interrupting anything." Ten other people were in the room and all eyes were on him. He was the youngest. Why were they lined up against the wall?

"We were just talking about you," Kim Sung smiled. "Have a seat."

He sat across from him. There were only two chairs in the room.

"These are my most loyal men, who will assume very important positions in my government. They have sacrificed everything to be with me.... You can leave now. I need to talk to Bao Ju." The men left the room soundlessly.

Kim Sung cleared his throat. "I wish I had known you earlier. I have heard great things about you but I didn't know you earned so many medals fighting those filthy *Jjokbari*. I'm sorry to snoop around to know more about you. I hope you understand that I need to be careful."

"I'm honored to be worthy of your consideration." He tilted his head in respect. Obviously, General Mekler had fed him his cultivated dossier.

"You worked hard for your country and now..." Kim Sung paused to clear his throat. "Now it's time to go back home."

"Go home?" He gulped.

"Yes!" Kim Sung was excited. "I need a man like you to teach the Korean people how to fight. You've already proven your loyalty to me. Now it's time to come with me to Korea and teach your people how to defend themselves against our enemies."

"I'm not sure—"

"I'll make you a general in my army. You have a long record of fighting experience. You'll have everything: power, money, and women. What do you think? The Korean people need a brave man like you."

Chin closed his eyes, pretending he was thinking. His heart beat vigorously. He couldn't be happier. The outcome was better than any he and General Mekler had anticipated. He slowly opened his eyes, glistening with tears he'd managed to fabricate, and raised his head. "If you think my presence will help the people of Korea, I will be honored to join you."

"You are a great man, Bao Ju. Let's have a drink." Kim Sung smiled broadly and pushed a button on the side of the desk.

~

In the Moscow training academy a man was admiring Jin.

"I know you got used to speaking only Chinese, but believe me your Korean is getting much better. Now repeat: *Jeo neum ga kkeum dok seo reur hap ni da....*"

CHAPTER THIRTY-ONE

Pregnant! Peter paced his room, feeling conflicted. *How could the baby be Kim Sung's? They hate each other. They don't even sleep in the same room. She must be having an affair. What a bitch! She used me and now she's using someone else.*

The door opened and Kim Suk walked in with Kim Man in her arms.

"What do you want?" he asked curtly, placing his hands on his waist.

She put the sleeping baby on his bed. "Why are you so upset that I'm pregnant? You are the one who ended our—"

"Who says I'm upset? I'm perfectly fine. You can sleep with whoever you want. I just want to know who you are doing *now.*"

"You know he is my husband and I can't refuse him if—"

"The baby belongs to Kim Sung?"

She closed her eyes as a stream of tears trickled down on her cheeks. "Yes."

"Congratulations," Peter said tartly. "I hope you and your husband have many more healthy children."

"He doesn't even touch me—"

"Wow! Getting pregnant without being touched… it could be a holy baby. Kim Suk, you're going to give birth to a prophet."

"Don't be stupid! It just happened. It was one—"

"I don't care. Don't tell me. I don't want to know." He held up his arm. "Now it makes sense why you were suggesting I get a girlfriend. You think of everything, don't you?"

"You are being unreasonable." She lifted Kim Man and stormed out of his room.

Yeah, get the hell out of my room. Who needs you? You conniving bitch! You made babies with me so I could never leave your pathetic life. I hate you.

Outside someone knocked on the door. Peter did a quick *Qigong* to calm himself and ran out.

"Why do you take this long to answer the door?" Kim Sung entered angrily. "Go pack up and help Kim Suk. We are leaving."

"Where—"

"Hurry! We don't have much time. Just pack a few clothes. The rest of the stuff isn't ours. We are going to Pyongyang."

CHAPTER THIRTY-TWO

General Grigory Mekler studied his wedding picture on the wall. He looked so young and energetic. *Anna's the same,* he thought. His wife got prettier with age.

She'd been pestering him all day to leave his room. This was the second day in a row he hadn't gone to work. He couldn't shake off the news he'd received two days before.

"Come on, darling! You haven't left the room since yesterday. What's wrong? You look terrible. You barely eat. You don't even shave."

"Nothing's wrong with me. I just want to relax."

"Relax? What did you do with my husband? He hated that word."

"Okay, okay," he smiled. "You made your point."

An hour later, he entered his living room, shaved and bathed. Anna greeted him with a smile. Slim and tall, she was ravishing in a body-hugging purple dress.

"Now you look like my husband." She approached him. She loved to smell his aftershave. He didn't like it; the smell was too strong for his Roman nose. He only wore it because she had bought it.

"Another party?"

"Yes. But I could stay home if you want me to."

"No, no. Let's not waste this pretty dress and makeup," he said, kissing her lips. "I need to catch up on some reading."

"Okay. But I don't know why I feel you're hiding something."

"Have I ever kept a secret from you? Go have fun." he said, pecking her cheek.

She grinned skeptically and walked away sinuously.

In his library, he picked up a book from his desk: *Animal Farm* by George Orwell.

His servant informed him about a visitor.

"Who is it?" He raised his brows. He wasn't expecting anybody. "Send them in."

He put the book back on the desk.

"Good evening, General. Sorry to come uninvited," Chin Ho said softly.

"What are you doing here?"

"I know I wasn't supposed to come, but is it true what I heard?"

"What did you hear?" Grigory asked stoically.

"You retired."

The general sighed. "News does travel fast." *I guess Anna will be home soon.* He hadn't told her and she'd probably hear about it at the party. They'd called it retirement, but really he'd been fired and replaced by none other than Yuri Andropov. Stalin himself had called him into his office and told him to leave with full government benefits. This house was his retirement gift. "You heard right. I am retired."

"But—"

"There is no but. It's true. Actually, I'm glad you came. I need to talk to you."

"I have news for you, too."

"Sit down. Drink?"

"Thanks."

Grigory went to his liquor cabinet behind the desk and fetched an unsealed bottle of vodka and two crystal glasses. Then he sat opposite Chin Ho. "Kim Sung was here in Moscow inquiring about Bao Ju's background. You must have inspired him."

Chin Ho smiled.

"The Soviet Spy Agency is being restructured into a new organization. I've heard rumors it will be called *Komitet gosudarstvennoy bezopasnosti.*"

"KGB?"

"Yes. Yuri Andropov will run it. I don't know how well you know him. He's a nationalistic son of bitch from *Tophet.* He plans to undo everything I did at the Agency. The girl you brought to replace Kim Suk may or may not be there tomorrow. You were a great asset during the war, but now that the guns are silent and I'm no longer your commander, I'm afraid I can't keep all the promises I made to convince you to change your identification. I feel terrible about it."

"Are you saying I'm not needed?"

"I'm afraid so. Word is Yuri Andropov will reclassify every agent and release the private contractors like you. I know he'll come to regret losing so many great spies who have ties to so many countries, but right now he's overzealous and irrational."

"That changes everything." Chin rose from his chair. "My

job just became a lot easier. Before coming here I was having second thoughts about my decision, but now…"

"Fill me in."

Chin cleared his throat. "Kim Sung has offered me command of his army."

"*Really?*" The general was surprised Chin had made so deep an impression on the Korean leader. "I'm glad that you are offered such a great opportunity. But I'm going say something, not as a your commander but your friend. I hope you don't take it wrong."

"Of course not. Please go ahead."

The general looked him in the eyes. "You're a good spy but you don't know a thing about commanding an army. You're better off in China."

Chin smiled. "For these same reasons I thought about declining his offer. Then I realized this gives me the opportunity to clean up my act and finally do something good for my own people. We know Kim Sung is a crazy man. Perhaps I could play some small role in keeping him sane."

The passion in Chin's voice convinced Grigory to drop the topic. Chin's mind was made up and he wasn't sharing all his reasons. It wasn't his fault. The general had trained him that way at the academy. Soon both men began talking about wonderful years they had spent together. At the end of their hearty conversation, a relaxed Chin asked, "What are you planning to do next? You are still young."

"My younger brother lives in the U.S. I'm thinking about leaving. There's nothing left for me here."

"Good luck to you, General. It was nice working under your watch. You taught me so much. I should go now."

Grigory left his chair. "It was my pleasure to get to know you, Colonel."

"I never understood why you call me Colonel."

"I call every non-military spy Colonel."

"That explains it." Chin Ho grinned, holding out his hand.

The general shook it warmly. "Where are you headed?" Intuitions told him it was their last meeting.

With great precision Chin planted his feet together, pushed out his chest, straightened his fingers, and saluted. "Pyongyang."

CHAPTER THIRTY-THREE

Jin admired her fancy dress in the mirror. Today was Sunday and in a few minutes, Dmitri would take her to the Academy dance studio to teach her a ballroom dance. Even though dancing was her bête noir, she liked the dress she wore.

"You look stunning," Dmitri exclaimed when she opened the door.

She smiled shyly. This was the first thing he'd ever said to her other than "good job." Before she'd arrived at this facility, she'd been a giggler, but Dmitri had changed that. It wasn't the only thing he'd changed. Now she sat differently, walked differently, talked differently, and most of all thought differently. Dmitri was her sole instructor. A man who knew it all. He could do things better than anybody else she'd ever known. He cooked better than her mother, whom she'd thought was the best. He knew more about women's clothes than she did. And he was an excellent makeup artist. Only one thing bothered her. Why didn't he ever notice her, even when two-thirds of her breasts were hanging out?

One day she deliberately pushed her ass against his crotch

to see what was down there and was surprised to feel a huge lump. Huge cock but no erection, she thought sadly. It had been three long months since she'd ridden one. She wished Chin Ho would come and take care of her needs, but he was gone and her instructor knew nothing about him.

Though the Academy was enormous—with its lofty ceilings, huge rooms, giant doors and windows, and extended corridors—there weren't many people around to talk to. Once or twice she tried to talk to the old man in military uniform who was always busy polishing the marble floors, but he didn't answer or lift his head. The second person whose acquaintance she tried so desperately to make was a behemoth woman who sat in the lobby behind a large, dark desk. Her first impression was that the woman was hired to complement the enormity of the building (she was taller than Jin even sitting down), but Dmitri dismissed that laughingly. When Jin greeted her on her way to the communication laboratory, the monstrous woman retorted she was too busy to carry on a conversation.

The last person who had refused to speak with her was a young, timid man in the kitchen. While Dmitri taught Korean culinary skills, the man cut the meats and vegetables, washed the dishes, and replenished the food supplies. Sometimes she saw a few men in uniform walk by her and smile, but nothing else. When she complained about this rudeness to Dmitri, he told her not to take it too personally and that everyone was doing their job.

"Don't you think this dress is a little too much?" she asked, trailing him. It wasn't as comfortable as her pink cheongsam, a single-piece gown with a split collar that she wore most days. Today Dmitri had insisted she wear this dress, which puffed out at the hips and had funnel-shaped lace cuffs with two flounces.

The decorative stomacher felt tighter around her flanks than when she first tried it on.

"Absolutely not!" he replied without slowing down or looking back. "You need to learn how to dress for every occasion."

The dance routine lasted over an hour. He was energetic and lissome; she was sluggish and sweaty. Her wet, sticky dress clung to her. She hated how it felt against her skin. "I need to get out of this," she said as he muted the music and came toward her with a white towel.

"You sure? You improved a lot from last week."

"I'm very sure. Thanks for the encouragement." She wiped her face with the towel. He was a bad liar, she thought. She knew today wasn't a good day. She'd tripped over her dress at least three times, and if it weren't for his quick reaction, she would have fallen on her face. She wondered if Kim Sung was an agile dancer like him.

"You go change. I'll see you soon." He smiled. His white collarless shirt had a sweat ring around it, but his starched khaki military pants still held their crease firmly. Was this his uniform? He never wore anything else.

She'd cleaned up and put on a relaxing Korean *Hanbok*. Her locks still damp, she dropped onto her bed. Dancing around Dmitri's chiseled body made her wet. He was well over six feet and had dreamy blue eyes, and his long face was always shaved to perfection. *He's so handsome. She* bit her lower lip while her right hand explored her pubic bone. *Oh, that feels good!* She suppressed a moan as her fingers touched the magic spot between her legs. If it hadn't been for one of her old clients in the red district, she would never have discovered how to pleasure herself. Her slow and gentle gyrating fingers became tense and restless as she reached climax. Her clitoris was distended.

Dmitri knocked at the door. "I hope you aren't sleeping."

Damn you! "What is it? "

"I need to discuss something. Let's go for a walk," his deep voice reverberated. She wished he were more talkative. She didn't know anything about him. A few times she had tried to dig deeper, to see if Dmitri was his real name. Or if he was married and had kids. But nothing fruitful came of it. He stared grimly and said his personal information was off-limits.

Jin hadn't been outside the building since she'd arrived. Several times she'd craved to go out and see the city, but he thought it a bad idea. She hadn't pressed him for an explanation. "You mean go out of the building and walk?"

"Yes," he nodded. He was tired and preoccupied.

"You want me to change or come out like this?"

"Whatever makes you comfortable."

They went to the front gate, where he talked to the guards and then led her outside. Although the weather was pleasantly warm and the sky clear, hardly anyone was on the street.

"Is it always this quiet?" she asked. It wasn't much fun to walk on an empty road.

"Only on Sundays."

For ten minutes she walked beside him, enjoying her temporary freedom and wondering why he was so nervous. He was constantly looking behind as if someone were following them. He was always composed and serene inside the Academy. No matter how many times she burnt the food or stepped on his toes while dancing, he never made a face. Something was wrong today. She could tell by the way he was behaving.

"What did you want to discuss?"

He slowed his pace and made sure no one was around. "I don't know how to tell you this…"

"Tell me what?" She stopped in the middle of road.

"I really like you, but—"

She smiled at him flirtatiously. *So that's why he brought me here.* "I thought you never noticed me. I like you, too."

"That's not what I mean," he said nervously.

Her face reddened.

"I'm told you are leaving today."

"Where?" She hadn't learnt so many things yet.

"We've been ordered to shut down our operation, and…" He studied her face. This wasn't easy. Of all the people he'd trained over the past five years, she was the quickest learner. Several of his students were now serving the Soviet Union around the world. Though the top brass were happy with him, Dmitri didn't like living a solitary life. Life had been full of zest when he taught linguistics at the Kremlin University. Men admired him and women adored him. He was a man of many talents. His hop was better than the dance choreographers and his cooking better than the women he met. He wished he had never attended the party where General Grigory Mekler's wife saw him dancing. A few weeks later, the general had summoned him into his office and assigned him to the Academy with strict instructions.

"… to send you back to China." His voice and his posture, wilted.

Her mouth agape and eyes filled with tears, she looked at him in sheer disbelief. He'd never told her she wasn't good enough. How could her dreams fall apart so suddenly? Chin Ho had promised her life would change forever. She wouldn't be living in this mirage if that bastard hadn't convinced her to leave Shanghai. Now what? Where would she go? The red district would never accept her back. She was considered a runaway whore. She hadn't told anyone she was leaving. Her life was over. "How could you do this to me?" she sobbed. "You told me I was a good student. All you men are liars! You think I'm not human. You throw me away like trash anytime it suits you. Take me to Chin Ho! I'll rip his heart out! He ruined my life!"

"I understand your anger, but believe me it isn't his fault that you are leaving this place," he said, trying to put his hand on her shoulder, but she slapped it off.

"Then whose fault is it? Tell me! Whose fault is it?"

Dmitri kept his head down and walked on. This wouldn't be the first time someone left the Academy without finishing training, but it was the first time he felt useless about it. General Mekler had given him full authority over the trainees. Once he'd kicked out four young men for not following his instructions. But Jin was part of an important mission. Dmitri had made some calls to verify his instructions, hoping this was a case of mistaken identity. How could they toss Jin out? But the person on the phone confirmed that the instructions were correct and he was to send her home immediately.

They stood outside the Academy building. "I hope you have a good trip. Your belongings are packed and in that truck." He pointed at the curb.

Jin cursed and wailed as she reluctantly climbed into the back seat. He tried to talk to her but she spat in his face.

When Dmitri returned to his room, a letter awaited him on the bureau. He opened it quickly. A short time later, with a lighter heart, he was packing. He had been relieved of his Academy duties and transferred back to the university. Not everything was so awful.

"Wake up. You've been asleep two days now," a sweet voice whispered in her ear.

"I hope you become a leper, Chin Ho…."

"Wake up. I'm the only one here. I'm Lee Sook-ja. Open your eyes," the woman said, jiggling her shoulder.

She woke with a start. "Who are you? Where am I? What's happened to me?" The last thing she remembered was being in the back of a military truck, crying her eyes out and cursing Dmitri and Chin Ho. The driver handed her a canteen. She had taken a few sips and … here she was.

"Why don't you wash first and then I'll answer your questions … the ones I know."

"Who are you? Where am I?" a fully awake Jin asked again, looking around warily. The room was nicely decorated with lots of mirrors. The bed was comfortable and oversized, covered with exotic linens and hand-embroidered pillows. There were no windows and no other ventilation except for the small entry door. She caught a glimpse of herself in the mirror. Her clothes were excessively wrinkled and her hair scattered in every possible direction.

The woman smiled, but it wasn't friendly. She appeared to be in her late fifties. Her wrinkled face was covered in makeup. Her thin hair showed her white scalp. She was short and her clothes were tight and revealing. "You should eat something. You must be hungry."

"I am not hungry! Tell me how I got here!" Jin was lying about her hunger. Her stomach grumbled ferociously.

"Your mouth might not be hungry but I can hear your

stomach crying," Lee said smiling. She left the room and came back moments later with a small tray.

"I told you I am not hungry," Jin said, staring at the steamy bowl of soup.

"You eat this while I talk, okay?"

Jin took the tray and put it aside. "Tell me first."

"My name is Lee Sook-ja, but people call me Cha. This is my house, and my business. I am respected among the elite politicians and military leaders. Two days ago, a man from the Soviet Union came here to ask me to hire you. He said you were tired and to let you sleep."

"Where am I?"

"That's a silly question. I told you it's my house."

"China?"

"No, you're in Pyongyang."

"I was supposed to go…" She left the sentence unfinished.

"The man who brought you here said you are experienced." The woman smiled slyly. "He also gave me this letter to give you."

Jin snatched the envelope from her hand and ripped it open. "*I know you're upset and probably want to kill me, but believe me I was as shocked about your leaving this place as you were. Sometimes we have no control over our fate and destiny. I know my government didn't comply with the promises it made you, but I also made you a promise to get you close to your target. Instead of China I sent you to Pyongyang's famous gentlemen's club. Every rich Korean man seeking companionship goes there. Kim Sung has become a new client of Cha. Please understand I didn't abandon you. You are now closer to your destination. I hope you succeed. You are a very intelligent and pretty woman. Take care of yourself, Kim Song-Ae. Dmitri.*"

A couple of tears escaped her eyes and landed on the letter as she folded it back to its original shape. After training her name was supposed to change to something respectful. Dmitri had suggested Kim Song-Ae. She liked it.

"Is this a brothel?" she asked Cha, expecting a harsh scolding.

"No! It's a place where very important people come to relax—a gentlemen's club." She sounded like someone had insulted her. "You're very lucky that I even considered hiring you. You know how many girls, including virgins from good families, want to work here? I only agreed because a very special person recommended you."

"Who?" *Chin Ho is the only person who would know these whorehouses.*

"We never name names, we just provide relaxation. Just try one client, and if you don't like it go wherever you want. I'm not asking you to do something new. I was told you are very good with men."

"I need to think."

"Fine, but remember you can make lots of money when you are this young. Imagine all those powerful people licking between your..." She smiled. "I'll come back this afternoon. Think as much as you want, but don't forget that an opportunity like this comes once in a lifetime."

Jin knew too well that her choices were limited. She had no money, and no family, and she still wasn't sure about her personal belongings. *Maybe I should stay to make some money and then go back to China,* she thought, staring at the large mirror over her bed.

Cha was ecstatic about her decision, and convinced that once she tasted the money and power she'd stay permanently. "It's temporary until I save some money," she told the overzealous Cha, who went on and on about her rich clientele and seemed indifferent to her personal life.

"Of course. Whatever you say."

"Something is bothering me that I'd like to ask you."

"Go ahead. I'm here to take care of you."

"I thought your hiring was selective. Why would you hire me without knowing anything about me... and after a Soviet man brought me here unconscious?"

"I'm not interested. I only care that you're healthy down there," she said, pointing between her legs. "As I told you, you come highly recommended, so I'm sure you're healthy."

Jin said nothing. She had always been careful with her clients. Men with rashes and boils weren't even permitted to sit on her bed or touch her. She washed herself with cold tea leaves and rose water every time she had sex.

"I should think of a name for you."

"Does it matter?" Most prostitutes didn't use their real names. Jin had. She wasn't one of those who played bad girls in the red district and then returned home to play good girls.

The woman laughed. "Of course, sweetheart! This is high society. Your name has to match the people you serve."

She thought for a while. Jin Sun hadn't brought her any luck. It was time to drop the jinxed name. "Kim Song-Ae."

"Good choice! It's very pretty and suits you well."

The next morning Cha entered her room unannounced and offered a tour. She accepted immediately. She was tired of lying in bed and cursing Chin Ho.

"My parents built this house," she said, searching Jin's face to see if she was impressed with her twenty-room, over-decorated mansion.

"It's a very nice house. I haven't seen any girls, but last night I did hear some noises."

"The girls don't live here. They only stay a month or two and then they must stand on their own feet." She stopped suddenly before a big wooden door. "You heard noise from your room?"

"Yes, I could hear faded moans and laughs. What's behind here?"

"This is the passageway." Cha swiped her hand across the image of a nude woman, meticulously carved into the door.

"Passageway?"

"Yes. This is the door that leads to the world of wealth and power."

Jin nodded silently. She understood the passage would lead to the bawdy house.

"You are wise. You don't ask stupid questions like other new girls," she applauded.

Later that evening Jin spent hours transforming herself into Kim Ae for a nighttime guest.

"Ravishing!" Cha said, styling the thick shiny black hair that nearly covered her back.

"Thanks. Sometimes I think I should cut my hair. It's too long."

"Don't ever do that! I've never seen prettier hair than yours."

Jin sadly thought about her mother. She used to say the same thing when she fixed her hair.

"By the way, can you beat a man?" She braided the hair into a thick rope.

"What do you mean?" she asked. Coming back from her

mother's funeral, she did slap an old man on the train when he put his hand on her breast. She didn't know where she got the courage. Men had groped her without her consent before. Perhaps her mother's death made her realize that she was all alone in the world and had to defend herself from vultures before they tore into her.

"Don't get scared, but some men enjoy being beaten by a pretty girl."

"Are they crazy? I don't want to meet sick men," she said, her voice trembling.

"No, no! They're not crazy! It's a sexual fetish, enjoying a woman beating them."

"I never heard of that before. What if they beat me, too?"

"Nobody touches my girls! Not even the most powerful clients. So don't worry. I'm here to protect you." She rested her hand on her shoulder. "You look so pretty. Wait here for half an hour, then walk down the passageway, straight through a small hallway. You'll see a tawny door on your left. You will meet your client in that room."

She nodded obediently. Her heart told her Cha was a caring woman, but she wasn't going to listen to it. It had made her trust Ivan. That bastard!

Thirty minutes later she entered the slightly dark passageway, her heart pounding. She walked briskly down the hall, slowing as she neared the door. She counted six color-coordinated rooms. She gave herself a final appraisal, took a deep breath, and entered the room.

"Wow! Cha has found a jewel!"

"You son of a bitch!" She jumped on him.

CHAPTER THIRTY-FOUR

When Peter disembarked the Soviet ship in Pyongyang, he couldn't believe he was still alive. The sea journey had wrecked his health. He'd spent most of his days throwing up and visiting latrines. Peter hated those roguish Soviet sailors on the bottom deck who constantly made fun of his seasickness. He wished Kim Sung had arranged better accommodation for him. On the other hand, the Kim family survived the treacherous Sea of Japan in their upper-deck luxury room without any serious illness.

After spending a few days recovering, the first thing Peter noticed about the new house was its size. It was three times bigger than the previous house. *No way can I take care of this mansion by myself*, he thought while unpacking. Kim Suk wasn't around to give him a hand or advice. She was too busy resting. Knowing the trip had made him so sick; she should have asked him about his health. He decorated the house the way he thought appropriate and she didn't even comment.

Everyone else, including little Kim Jong, was excited about the six-bedroom house, which included a swimming pool and three servants quarters. According to Kim Sung the house had belonged to a Japanese general who'd escaped back to his country. The couple decided to continue living in separate rooms. Kim Jong had his own room, too.

"You're a big boy now," Peter told him.

"What happened to all our stuff?" Kim Sung asked after Peter had unpacked everything they'd brought from *Vyatskoye*. "The place feels empty!"

"Master, this is all we have," Peter replied.

"We have to buy more furniture. You make a list of things we need and I will have my secretary order them," he said. Instead of making the list, Peter gave the message to Kim Suk.

He needed to get out of this place as soon as possible. But how? Kim Sung liked him too much to fire him. Maybe there was a way to get kicked out! A deviant smile spread across his face before it went pale. He couldn't leave the boys alone. Kim Man wasn't safe around Kim Jong. *I should wait until he's older and can defend himself.*

A week later Kim Sung came home early. He'd been extremely busy organizing his party and hiring people to start a Korean Army. Since the Japanese departure, the Korean Peninsula was divided into two regions. North Korea was controlled by the Soviet Union and South Korea by U.S. forces. Communists from both China and the Soviet Union saw Kim Sung as an ally to propagate their ideology and promised to help him unify the Peninsula. But the U.S. and its Western allies considered North Korea the brainchild of Stalin and the enemy of capitalism and vowed to defend the South against any incursions.

Peter was watering some dying plants in the courtyard when Kim Sung entered with a thin woman in her early sixties and asked about his wife. Peter looked across the brick court-yard where he had seen her earlier, sitting on the chair. She was gone now. Lately she'd been constantly whining about her morning sickness and afternoon fatigue. He thought she was faking to get his attention. "I'll go check, master."

"Stay!" he ordered. "This is Peter Chang, a very loyal servant."

Peter bowed respectfully.

"And this is Jung Soon. She is a midwife and house helper. She will help you and Kim Suk." Kim Sung smiled. "Wait here!" Peter and Jung Soon exchanged stares as Kim Sung went to fetch his wife. She broke the ice.

"How old are you?"

"Old enough," he replied tartly. Her question felt stupid and odd. He knew he needed someone to help him care for this vast house, but she didn't seem up to the task. She was way too old to scrub and clean.

"It's a big house."

You noticed! He grinned. *She's already scared. I give her a week before she gets her tail out of here.* "Six rooms!" He lifted his brows and bobbed his head.

"Only *six?*" She swiveled her beady brown eyes in all directions. "I thought it had more."

"This is the woman I told you about," Kim Sung said from a distance. Kim Suk and Kim Jong followed him. "She's an excellent cook and has delivered many babies."

Jung Soon hurried toward Kim Jong. "Master, you've a beautiful—ehhh!"

"Kim Jong!" Kim Suk screamed. The old woman was bent over her shin, almost crying. Kim Jong had kicked her hard. "What's wrong with you? Are you crazy?"

"Nothing's wrong with him! He's excited!" Kim Sung defended his son. "Are you okay?"

"I'm fine, master," Jung Soon said, recovering.

"I was asking Kim Jong!" Kim Sung scowled.

Peter kept a straight face. If Kim Sung hadn't been around, he would've slapped Kim Jong across the face. He understood that parents loved their children unconditionally but Kim Sung's behavior was appalling. He was encouraging his son to act like a savage. The boy was getting used to the idea that he could do anything and not get punished. Peter got chills picturing him as a grown-up.

Jung Soon was a great help and an excellent cook. Within a few days she had taken over the kitchen and become the sole caretaker of Kim Suk. Peter was happy with the arrangement. He hated cooking and washing dishes. Kim Sung approved of her work but not her refusal to live in. She insisted on staying in her own house. She came to work before dawn and stayed until she served dinner. Watching her in the kitchen, Peter envied her. She was quicker and more productive than he had ever been.

"I don't understand how you cook, wash dishes, and clean all at once?" he finally asked.

"What do you mean?" she laughed, filling soup bowls. "I hope Kim Suk likes this soup."

"I was taught to do one chore at a time."

"You can do one thing at a time if you plan to spend all day in the kitchen. Could you take this to soup to her? My foot is bothering me."

"Of course! Sit here." He gently pushed her into a chair at the kitchen table.

The woman pushed away his hands. "What are you doing?"

"Taking off your shoes so I can see better."

She quickly withdrew her feet. "I don't like to remove my shoes."

"Just trying to help." Puzzled, Peter picked up the soup tray and fled. She was probably embarrassed by the hole in her socks. It would be stupid of her if she thought he was.... He shivered in disgust.

Jung Soon made sure Peter had disappeared, then lifted her foot onto the chair. She swiftly pulled down her sock and removed a folded paper stuck to her ankle, then deposited it into her bra and grinned triumphantly.

CHAPTER THIRTY-FIVE

"Get off me! What are you trying to do?" Chin Ho tried to grab Jin's hands. She was wrapped around his waist, punching him.

"You swine! You son of a bitch! You lied to me!" she sobbed. Her small fists had no real force but long fingernails were brutal. He felt a burning sensation on the back of his neck. *I'd better stop her before she skins me.* He slipped his hands under her armpits and, with a sudden jerk, tore her hands apart and threw her on the bed, pinning her to the mattress.

Jin wrestled ferociously. She'd dreamt of this moment. Had she known he was the client behind the door, she would've packed a dagger to carve his face. Everybody she ever cared for had betrayed her. This time she was going to act upon her feelings. She was done being a pincushion. "I'll kill you, bastard!"

He sat on her thighs and held her arms to her sides.

"Let me go! Son of a bitch!" She couldn't push him off.

"I will if you promise to be civilized and let me explain." He stared into her bloodthirsty eyes. She looked a lot different now than when she'd entered the room. Her neatly styled hair spilled all over her face, her makeup had smudged, and her mascara blackened her eyes.

"Get off me!" She was growing exhausted.

"I'm getting off. Now be nice!" He rose to his knees. His hands still held hers.

She didn't move but kept her gaze fixed on him.

"I'm letting you go." He released her hands and jumped off the bed.

She stayed there, put her hands over her face, and began to sob.

Touched by her wailing, he sat next to her and looked around the semi-dark room, sparsely furnished with a large bed and a small table holding bottles of oils and lotions. "Don't cry. It wasn't my fault they made you leave the Academy."

"It was my fault. I trusted you!"

"I know you trusted me." Her skimpy dress had moved up to her thighs. He placed a hand on her bare knee. "That's why I brought you here."

She pushed his hand aside and sat up. "You brought me here? Why?"

"Because I promised you," he whispered. Then he explained.

She watched his mouth intently, but her eyes couldn't hide her bewilderment. "How do I know you're telling the truth?"

His head, slumped over his lap, lifted. "Did you get Dmitri's letter?"

She nodded, brushing her hair from her face. "You told him to write it? Why didn't *you*?"

"I was out of town."

"Why did you send me to a brothel instead of— Never mind. I know why! You think I'm a whore and I belong here."

"Don't say that. I didn't know any other place in Pyongyang. Dmitri suggested this place as temporary housing."

She shook her head, her violent anger replaced by remorse. Ivan had come back to restore her trust in men. Overwhelmed by her fluid emotions, she began weeping again. "I'm so sorry to scratch your face. I thought you had abandoned me."

"Don't worry. I guess I deserved it for not coming after you earlier." He grabbed her elbow hastily. "Get up. You are leaving this place."

"Where? What about Cha?"

"She already knows."

~

Two weeks passed in the small but cozy house where Chin Ho had brought her. A few times she wanted to thank him but stopped herself. He was the reason she was there. He had told her to call him General Bao Ju, but she wasn't sure about it.

"In Shanghai you were Ivan, in Moscow you were Chin Ho, and now in Pyongyang you are Bao Ju?"

"It's complicated," he'd said, smiling. "Can't you tell by my uniform I'm General Bao Ju?"

Late one afternoon Jin fought boredom with a fresh bottle of vodka. She'd been a teetotaler before living in Moscow. Dmitri introduced her to drink. At first she complained it was too strong and burnt her throat, but later she developed a taste for it. It helped her not to think.

The door rattled and opened inward. "You're already drinking." Chin Ho came in holding a large box and the house key. She secretly admitted to herself that he had never looked better. The military uniform accentuated his manliness.

"What else is there for me to do? I'm bored to death." She looked gorgeous in her blue chiffon dress. "You want to drink with me?"

"No, thanks." He placed the box on the table.

"What's in it?"

"Your dress for tomorrow's party."

"What party? Let me see."

"I thought you were bored at home so I decided to take you to a party."

"Thanks. This is very pretty." She held the red dress next to her body.

"You'll look nice in it."

"Thanks." She put the dress back in the box and sat next to him. Her eyes were wet.

"What's wrong? You don't like it? I can bring you something else."

"No. I like it. I've never worn such a pretty dress before." She forced a smile.

"Why tears?" He touched her shoulders.

"You are so nice to me. But I don't know anything about you. Can't you be honest once in your life and tell me about yourself? You change your name and profession everywhere you go—businessman, spy, and now army general. Who are you?"

He gazed at her silently and rose. "It's for your own good

not to know me too well. I'll pick you up tomorrow night. Be ready."

Chin Ho couldn't sleep, thinking about what Jin had said. *She doesn't realize it but she knows everything there is to know about me. Well, maybe not everything...* He grinned and fell asleep.

Jin went to bed excited. It was about time she got out of the house. The next morning she woke up early and started getting ready for the party. Dmitri had told her a lot about social gatherings and night parties, and even had her attend a mock party at the Academy. Tonight was the real deal and she was ready to dazzle.

Chin whistled when she opened the door. He was on time and dressed as General Bao Ju. "I have never seen you this pretty." His expression made her laugh.

"You like my it?" She spun around, showing off her low-cut sleeveless dress and stiletto heels. Chin hadn't said much about the party details. However, the dress he picked out told her that Kim Sung was either the host or the main guest. Dmitri had coached her that Kim Sung was attracted to Western clothes, especially women's clothes.

"Splendid!" He smiled. "I'm not sure if I should take you to the party or the bedroom."

"How about both?" She pecked his cheek. He hadn't touched her since she left China.

His eyes lit up. "I don't want to tire you out before the party. How about afterward?"

She agreed with a seductive stare and followed him to his motorcar.

Jin earned plenty of admiring glances and whispers. Since a general accompanied her, nobody dared to flirt with her. During dinner Chin introduced her to Kim Sung as Kim Ae and walked away smiling. Kim Sung put away his plate and was all over her.

The journey has begun, Chin Ho mumbled from a distance. This wasn't the first time he had given up his whore for a better cause. But he had to admit that watching Kim Sung rub his greedy hand against her leg made him a little jealous. He wondered if he should've told Jin what he'd done to her family. He didn't just kill them. He took the time to castrate her uncle and stepfather before he stabbed them in the heart. With her mom and aunt, he was quicker and didn't make them suffer. After both women confessed they knew their husbands were raping the girl, he snapped their necks. Dismembering was painless to dead victims. Most people wouldn't understand what he'd done. To them he'd be a monster. A psychopath. But Chin had a good reason. He understood how rape felt to a child. His uncle Kwan was caught in the act. Chin Ho still carried a pain that shredded his soul. He had been too young and weak to defend himself. As he grew older, he promised himself that if he ever came across a child rapist, he would remove him or her from the face of the earth. And nobody could ever accuse him of failing to keep his promises. Jin would vouch for him. She would have picked a different profession if she hadn't been robbed of her childhood innocence. She had deserved better. It was her time.

"General Bao Ju, would you have a drink with us?" Kim Sung called to him. He was practically glued to her shoulder.

He nodded, walking toward them. He would drink to that.

Lying in bed, lonely and somewhat tipsy, Chin thought back on the night. Kim Sung had offered to drive Kim Ae back to her house. Chin had known what that meant, and a few minutes later had driven home. Now he wished he hadn't. He almost crashed his motorcar into a roadside wall.

He hadn't seen Kim Sung's wife at the party. While her husband was hunting other women, she was busy with Peter Chang. He smiled. He was sure Kim Suk and Peter Chang's days were numbered. It was just a matter of time before the Soviets told the Korean leader of his wife's infidelities and past. That would be a bad day for those two. Peter Chang would be cut up into pieces and fed to the boars. Kim Suk's death would be equally painful. Her husband was a merciless man. Chin Ho had seen an evil in Kim Sung's dark eyes. Would he feel guilty if his suppositions became reality? Nothing was his fault. Chin shook his head in denial and closed his eyes.

CHAPTER THIRTY-SIX

Peter Chang had mixed feelings about Jung Soon. The woman had completely taken over the kitchen and housecleaning. He was fine with that. He had more free time to spend with the kids. His efforts to bridge the distance between the two young boys were a great success. Apart from occasional tantrums and misbehavior, six-year-old Kim Jong got along well with his younger brother, who was only three but already the same height. Kim Jong wasn't happy about that until Peter told him he was a lot stronger than his younger brother. What irritated Peter was that the woman had taken complete charge of Kim Suk. She delivered all her meals, cleaned her room, and carried out the dirty dishes. Had it not been for Kim Suk's sporadic moaning and grunting in her room, which he heard when teaching Kung Fu to Kim Jong in the courtyard, he would've thought she didn't live in the house. In previous pregnancies, on the advice of her doctor, she walked around the house. This time she'd confined herself to bed. The midwife told Peter that Kim Suk was having a difficult pregnancy because the baby was probably a girl. He thought Jung Soon was stupid to make such an assertion. He never heard such a thing.

One day in the spring of 1946, just before lunch, Peter headed for his room to fetch a set of nunchakus that he'd made by tying two plantains on each end of a string. Kim Jong was too young and unreliable to handle the real wooden weapon. Peter still feared his violent temper. Jung Soon came after him and asked him to feed the kids. Kim Suk wasn't feeling well.

He was engrossed in watching the boy eat when he heard his name. Jung Soon was screaming. Peter warned Kim Jong to stay in his chair and dashed toward the room. The midwife directed him to get hot water and clean towels. Kim Sung was in labor and there was no time to take her to the hospital.

Peter was terrified. Kim Suk dug her nails deep into his arms and cried out in pain. He wished he weren't there. Jung Soon seemed unaffected by her screams and kept shouting, "Push! Push!" Twenty minutes later she placed the baby, covered in traces of blood and vernix, on the mother's chest. Peter picked up the water bowl, soiled towels, and ran from the room. It was good to be a man. He could never survive the pain of childbirth.

Kim Sung didn't know about the birth until he came home at night. Jung Soon transferred the baby to his arms. "You have a beautiful daughter."

"Daughter!" he said unhappily. "You hold her. I'm tired." He gave the baby back to Jung Soon.

Disheartened, Kim Suk asked him, "What should we name her?"

"Does it matter? Name her whatever you like." He grimaced and left.

"What do you think about Kim Kyong-Hui?" she asked Jung Soon.

"That's a beautiful name."

Kim Suk looked at her daughter silently and wished her a better life than her own.

Kim Sung's cold demeanor troubled Peter. He showered his boys with all kinds of gifts and clothes. However, he never brought a single gift for his newborn daughter. Even Kim Jong, who hated his baby brother when he was born, liked to be around his sister. Kim Man remained quiet. He was different from his older brother. He never asked for or cried about anything. When his older brother broke toys, the younger Kim enjoyed putting the toys back together. Peter wished he could help his older brother learn to behave. He often found himself comparing the boys: Kim Man was a gentle breeze, calm and serene, and Kim Jong, an ominous cyclone, slowly churning over the Yellow Sea, swelling to wreak havoc.

The summer of 1947 was hot and humid. Peter was feeling lackadaisical and went to his room to escape the sweltering heat.

Kim Sung wasn't pleased when he tried to beat the heat in the swimming pool. "Pool isn't for servants!" Peter was a good swimmer and wanted to teach the youngsters. Teaching from the outside of the pool wasn't practical or safe. What if something went wrong? Kim Suk didn't know how to swim, and he'd never seen Kim Sung in the pool. Peter had to caution the kids to stay away from it. It had no safety barriers.

He asked Kim Sung to cover it with a tarpaulin. He declined without any explanation.

Peter was haunted by painful memories. His neighbors' oldest son drowned in the Yangtze River right in front his eyes. He had warned him not to go too deep. The boy was always trying to prove that he was a superior swimmer. By the time Peter reached the spot where he last saw his head appear and then disappear under the water, it was too late. The body was never recovered. This horrific experience taught him two things: never bet against the water and never overestimate your skills. If he were as good a swimmer as he used to boast he was, the tragedy could've been averted. He blamed himself.

Lying on his bed in the heat, Peter daydreamed about going back to China to talk to Shao Peng's servant Hu Yaobang or his friend Kang Sheng. According to Kim Suk, both men were present when his father went to see Shao Peng. Peter knew Shao was close to both Hu and to Kang. Chances were good that he told them something about his father.

A sudden scream interrupted. Peter bolted from his room and chased the noise to the east side of the house. He felt his heart in his throat when he saw Jung Soon by the swimming pool, holding Kim Man's wet head in her lap. He wasn't moving. Kim Jong stood a few feet away, white as a ghost.

"*What happened?*" Peter screamed, snatching the boy from her and shaking him. "Breathe! Breathe! Kim Man, *breathe!*"

Jung Soon was weeping in short grunts. "He was floating on the water when I came to call him. Oh, gods, make him live."

Peter lifted the boy's yielding body. "I need to take him to the doctor!"

"What's going on? Jung Soon, you left the baby alone in her room." Kim Suk walked toward the pool. "Why are you all here?" She asked, then screamed. "Why are you holding him like this? What happened to my son? What happened? Why isn't he moving?"

Without answering, Peter sprinted for the main door of the house. He heard a loud thud behind him as Kim Suk collapsed. He continued running, the boy in his arms.

Peter fell to his knees when the doctor told him Kim Man was dead. His worst fears had materialized. He'd wanted to protect him from his older brother but he had failed. Kim Man was gone.

Kim Man's death sent Kim Suk into a chronic depression. She secluded herself and blamed Kim Jong for pushing his younger brother into the pool. Kim Man couldn't swim. She spent hours sitting by the pool, crying. Kim Sung and Kim Jong were the only two people who accepted the tragedy and moved on.

"You were right, he is evil," she told Peter when he went to her room to deliver her lunch. She had lost a significant amount of weight. Her cheeks and eyes were sunken, as if she were terminally ill.

"I never said he is evil and you shouldn't either. He is your son." He helped her sit up, fighting his own sorrow. Kim Man's death had devastated him. A night didn't go by when he didn't cry, remembering boy's face.

"He drowned my Kim Man." She sobbed.

"Maybe it was an accident." He exhaled deeply. There was no point in tormenting a grieving mother. He already knew the prickly truth. An indifferent Kim Jong told him that Kim's favorite toy, a small metal car Peter had given him on his third birthday, fell in the pool and he went into the water to get it. He asked him why he hadn't yelled for help. Jung Soon discovered the boys by accident on her way to the kitchen. The boy grinned but said nothing. Peter searched every corner of the pool and found nothing. The day before he had found the toy hidden under Kim Jong's bed. Peter felt ashamed when he thought of drowning the evil child in the same pool.

"It wasn't an accident! Nobody believes me," Kim Suk wailed.

He couldn't leave her in this condition, Peter decided in great anguish. His dream to go back home and find his father was put on hold indefinitely.

CHAPTER THIRTY-SEVEN

"I missed you so much," she said, gently rubbing her hand on his genitals.

Having sex with married men never bothered Jin. Most of her clients were married, and the ones who said they weren't were liars. From her second-story window she saw them remove their wedding rings and shove them into their pockets. If those idiots only knew she was aware of their gambit. Their rings might be gone but the evidence of them remained—white, untanned bands on their fingers. But as long as they were paying her, she didn't care about their personal lives. One wise working girl told her, "Their wives should thank us for sending them home happy. We do all the work and they get to have kids, spend their husband's money, and get to be called wives. Shame on them if they complain."

Though Jin agreed, this situation was different. Her goal wasn't to sleep with a man. She didn't need anyone but Chin Ho to satisfy her womanly needs. He hung twice as large as Kim Sung. She'd spent months preparing to woo Kim Sung into marrying her. At first, Jin felt bad for his wife. When Chin made her dream about the luxurious lifestyle and the power that came along with it, she succumbed. She was only human.

"I missed you too, Kim Ae," Kim Sung replied, fondling her breasts. He lay naked on her bed and she sat next to him. It was the first time in the two weeks after his son's death that he had come to visit his mistress. Not long after General Bao Ju introduced them, he fell head over heels in love with her and gave her a house close to his residence.

"You poor thing! I know your son's death is hurting you. Let me help you," she whispered, lowering her head over him.

He wiped his hand on her bareback and watched her closely. He knew he was in for a treat.

She put the tip of his shaft in her mouth and began rolling her tongue on it. His flaccid penis began to harden. She tightened her lips and began stroking and sucking it simultaneously.

"Oh, you are good!" he moaned.

She took him out of her mouth, smiled naughtily, and spit his viscid fluid back onto it.

"Ahhh! You are so good."

The sight of her licking his own fluids was too exciting for him and he couldn't hold back. He held her head down and kept it there until he filled her mouth. "Stay there! Don't move," he begged. The sensation was overwhelming.

She waited a few seconds for his body to normalize, then removed him from her mouth. Her lips were pressed tightly.

"Swallow it!"

She opened her lips. "I already did!"

"Get me a towel. You made a mess down there," he smiled, touching himself.

"I'll be right back." She went to the closet. *I can't wait until you marry me. I will be the wife of a leader. What a life I'll have! Clothes, jewelry, servants, mansions... I should thank Chin Ho.*

"Hurry up! I have to go."

"This early?" She returned with a white towel.

"Yes, I have an important meeting. Don't be upset! I'll come back in few hours.

"Promise?" She reached for his lips.

"Of course!" He kissed her cheek instead and left.

After a long bath, Jin returned to her bed naked. She felt slightly upset that Kim Sung didn't kiss her on the mouth. Chin Ho was different. He kissed her everywhere. She thought about him. He hadn't visited her in months. The last time she saw him he had helped her move to this place. She remembered their last conversation. He had looked tired. Working with the army had added years to his face. When he said it was the last time he could visit her, she cried on his shoulder. But she knew it was necessary.

"I'm sure you have slept with lots of women. But why are you so nice to me?" she asked him, standing next to his motorcar. He dropped his eyes and then, after a brief silence, took an envelope from his pocket. "Listen, if this doesn't work out I want you to move back to China. In this envelope, you will find my Shanghai home address and a key. I've instructed my servant to help you. That house belongs to you now."

"Why are you so generous to me?" She grabbed his arm, tears rolling down her cheeks.

He looked in her eyes. "I made you homeless once but it won't happen again. I keep my promises. Good luck."

Feeling cold, she put on a silk robe Kim Sung had brought her. Chin Ho's envelope was still in the bottom drawer of her bedside table. She didn't blame him for doubting her relationship with the Korean leader. He was a man of flaws and cruelties. When Dmitri warned her about his bad temper and the way he treated his wife, she told him she wasn't anything like Kim Suk. Finding a caring and loving husband wasn't her dream or goal. Financial security was more important than anything else. If she had to fake love to get what she wanted, she would do it in a heartbeat.

Having no interest in Kim Sung's affairs, she knew she had already crossed the first major hurdle. Emotional detachment was key to her success. What other profession besides being a prostitute would have taught her that trait? Surprisingly Kim Sung had been nice to her. If it was temporary because he lost his son or he genuinely liked her, she couldn't tell. All she knew was to sexually deplete him so he couldn't do anyone else. For her plan to work properly, he needed to visit her every day. And the way she had pleasured him this afternoon, he was bound to come back soon for more. She was sure of it. The girl who had taught her this technique, oral fantasy, told her that no client would ever leave her once she had used it. Until today, Chin Ho had been the exclusive recipient of the oral fantasy.

CHAPTER THIRTY-EIGHT

It took him exactly fifty minutes to transform from Chin Ho to General Bao Ju. He looked at himself in the mirror and wondered if those lines around his eyes were new. Being a commander wasn't easy, but he was successful at it. He was thankful to his mentor, Grigory Mekler, who had been kind enough to send him books on military training before he left for Pyongyang. Chin knew they were only for the Soviet commanders and that Grigory had taken a huge risk in sending them to him, and he never thanked him properly. The books were written in Russian, not a problem for him, and in great detail. He read each cover to cover and enjoyed the looks on the faces of the other Korean generals when he demonstrated his impressive, advanced military knowledge. Chin also attributed his success to his spy training, but his years of association with Grigory were immeasurably beneficial.

When he returned to the bedroom to wake up the girl, he was surprised. The bed was already made and the girl had moved to the kitchen.

"What are you doing?" His voice startled the shapely girl.

"Mmm. Making breakfast for you."

"I don't eat breakfast. Get your purse! I'll take you back," he said, walking out of the kitchen. He had picked up the girl from Cha's brothel the night before. Usually brothels didn't let their girls go out. But he insisted that Cha make an exception. Knowing his military status and his personal ties to Kim Sung, she reluctantly agreed to send a girl with him. Normally it was contrary to his personality to harass a brothel operator. They were the ones who kept the best girls for their best clients. He never wanted to lose his spot on that list. Since his return from China after a few days' visit, he wasn't feeling too great. Events happened in Shanghai that he couldn't tell anyone. He had tried hard not to worry too much. It wasn't the first time he faced a difficult choice. His mind kept taking him back to Shanghai. Even the girl who was new in the business noticed his disinterest. Perhaps that was the reason she was trying to cook him breakfast. He had told her it wasn't her fault that he suddenly lost his mood. He was under a lot of pressure, he assured her unsuccessfully.

After dropping off the girl, he was driving back to Kim Sung Military Camp One (the Korean leader named all the training institutes after himself) when he saw the rickshaw stalled in the center of the narrow street. "Idiots!" he mumbled and got out of the vehicle.

The street was empty. "Hey, move this rickshaw out of my way!" he shouted, moving closer to see who was blocking the street. To his surprise, nobody was around. Leaving the two-wheeled conveyance unsupervised was odd. Anybody could have stolen it. He pushed it to the side of the road and wedged a small rock under each wooden wheel.

When he returned to his vehicle, the door was open. He

didn't remember leaving it that way. "What is this?" he said to himself, picking up an envelope from the driver's seat. He looked around carefully and then dug out the handwritten letter. His face went white.

A young man peeked from behind a large bushy tree. The man in uniform had driven away in a hurry. Nevertheless, he looked around carefully and then retrieved his rickshaw. He wished he could earn this kind of easy money every day.

CHAPTER THIRTY-NINE

By 1949, Kim Sung had consolidated his power in North Korea and become prime minister. His successful political career had minimal impact on Kim Suk. She remained sorrowful, and no one ever saw her smile. Kim Sung forced her to attend some political functions but she barely spoke—merely sat in silence.

After Kim Sung proclaimed himself Supreme Leader, they moved to a new mansion with countless servants, one assigned to every nook and cranny of the house. Peter Chang and Jung Soon weren't excited, having nothing to do. Kim Jong and his sister had separate nannies. Jung Soon spent her days circling Kim Suk. Peter's only task was teaching Kung Fu.

Kim Sung was in his office one morning when his secretary reminded him about his nine o'clock meeting. He preferred having them in the morning. A handful of his staff knew where he spent most of his afternoons. No one dared gossip about him. People were scared and cautious. Two lower-level staff members, responsible for collecting and delivering his mail, were discovered headless in a nearby sewer after they were heard making fun of their leader's increasing girth.

Twenty minutes after nine he walked into the conference room with a procession of staffers.

"Hello, Mr. Prime Minister," Yuri Andropov said, standing up. He was the only person in the room and looked displeased with Kim Sung's late arrival.

"I hope you haven't been waiting too long." Kim Sung sat in one of the leather chairs at the huge oval table, freshly picked flowers in a vase sitting in the middle. On the west wall was a giant, framed picture of him looking at the sky as a colorful rainbow hovered over his head.

"It's fine." Yuri forced a smile. "I need to talk to you in private."

Kim Sung looked at one of his staffers and they all fled without a sound. "Please feel free to talk. Nothing leaves these walls without my permission," he said, trying to impress his guest. Andropov wasn't only running a Soviet intelligence network but was also a close friend of Stalin. Rumors said he wasn't a nice person to be around and that he'd climbed the success ladder by stepping on his friends and allies. Some Soviet generals weren't too happy with how he had treated his predecessor, Grigory Mekler.

"Thanks." Yuri nodded and opened the green folder he'd brought with him. "Are you satisfied with the arms supply?"

"I am. But we could use more tanks and some of those American jeeps," he said slyly. During the war, the United States had given the Soviets plenty of cargo vehicles. The most famous was the jeep. It ran much smoother than the Soviet UAZ-469. Most of them ended up in the hands of greedy politicians and generals.

"I'll make a note of it." Yuri wrote something inside the file. "We're somewhat concerned that the money we sent for infrastructure is being spent on jails and camps."

"You know jails and camps are important for controlling the traitors and anarchists. Didn't your government populate Siberia with similar camps?"

Yuri gave him a blank look and moved on. "What do you think about the South? The Premier wants to know if your army is capable of taking them over."

"Of course we are capable. All we need is a source of money and arms. We can overrun the South tomorrow if you get us what we need."

"I will let our cabinet know and get back with a decision," he said, closing his folder. "That was the official business."

"Anything about the Americans?" Kim Sung asked.

"What do you mean?"

"Do you think they will get involved if we attack the South?"

"Only if you are winning." Yuri leaned back. "Don't worry about them. You have our full support and arms."

"Mao Zedong has also promised me his support."

Yuri removed his glasses and leaned forward. "You trust the Chinese?"

"Why wouldn't I? Don't you? We fought hard together against those *Jjokbari*."

"I'm going to tell you something that's been on my mind since I discovered it." Yuri crossed his arms. "We didn't tell you this before because we didn't want you to do something irrational and ruin your political career."

Kim Sung's face turned stern. "I'm listening. Continue, please."

"Did you know General Grigory Mekler?"

"Of course. He's retired."

"Correct," Yuri said bitterly. "He was in charge of your protection and your interests."

"I didn't know." Kim Sung looked surprised.

"If he had been watching over you the way he should have, we wouldn't be having this conversation." Yuri's face was tense.

"Will you be more clear? I don't follow." Kim Sung was irritated.

"Your wife and your servant Peter Chang are both working for Mao."

Furious and stunned, Kim Sung jumped to his feet and slammed the table. "Yuri Andropov! You had better have ironclad proof to accuse my wife or I'll—"

"I know you are upset. That's why we waited this long to tell you. Let me show you General Mekler's report."

⁓

The man standing outside Kim Sung's conference room door suddenly looked ill and fell to his knees. Two men carried him to another room and gave him a glass of water. The man breathed slowly. One of the men suggested that he go home and relax. The sick man hesitated but then agreed and walked away holding his stomach.

Outside temperatures were unbearably hot. Most streets were empty as people stayed in the shade, avoiding the heat. But a few human rickshaws, some hardworking day laborers piggybacking large brown bags and wearing no shoes, and men with bicycles hauling sacks of merchandise behind their carrier stands were forced to be out on unpaved dusty roads to meet their financial burden. Some shopkeepers, who were lucky enough to afford a permanent brick-and-mortar store, were still open, their front doors covered with make-shift awnings. But street peddlers and people with temporary shopping stalls were the real victims of the weather, since nobody wanted to stand in the sun haggling.

The man flagged a rickshaw and hopped in. Ten minutes later, he paid the young man and waited until he disappeared from sight. He crossed the street to a tumbledown house. In five minutes, a young woman in her early twenties came out, frightened and panicky. She hired a human rickshaw and jumped on. Fifteen minutes later, the exhausted rickshaw man dropped her off in front of a mansion. She rushed to the front gate, where four army guards stopped her. She explained hastily. One guard gestured for her to stay put and went inside. He came back with Jung Soon in tow. She hugged the girl and took her inside.

A few minutes later, the mansion emitted thick clouds of smoke. The guards at the door ran inside. The young woman stuck her head out of the gate and looked around cautiously. She waved her hand, and then led two shadows out of the mansion.

Moments later three guards carried out two children, and the frantic Jung Soon followed. She was crying, "Kim Suk! Kim Suk! Find her!" The scene was chaotic. People were running everywhere. Some were yelling, "Water! water! People are inside! Help them! Help them!" The mansion was engulfed in a raging fire and the sound of horrifying screams grew louder and louder.

CHAPTER FORTY

Kim Sung paced the room like a hungry lion. His fists were clenched tightly and his eyes were red. He couldn't believe what he had just heard. If the man before him was a Korean, he would have cut out his tongue and fed him to the boars piece by piece. Even if his information was correct. "You're telling me that my wife was meeting with Li Kenong's wife in secret and passing information?"

"Unfortunately it's true. Li Kenong's wife often came to visit her daughter in *Vyatskoye* and met with your wife."

"How can you be certain?" Kim Sung leaned on the table. The evidence was overwhelming. He knew Grigory Mekler was reliable. He wouldn't fabricate all this. They were friends. He even invited Kim Sung to his home and introduced him to his lovely wife. He still remembered her smell.

Yuri Andropov smirked. "Li Kenong's daughter is married to our—"

Chaotic sounds were heard outside the conference room and someone knocked.

"What the hell is going on? Come!" Kim Sung barked.

A frightened, distraught man in his early thirties declared, "Sir, your residence is on fire."

"What?!" Kim Sung stormed out of the room.

"Mr. Prime Minister!" Yuri Andropov ran after him until an armed soldier stopped him at the end of a long hallway.

"Sir, you have to wait here," the soldier said, blocking the door.

Yuri gave him an angry look. He was in no mood to take orders. His plan to slowly reveal to the Korean leader his wife's infidelity with his servant had been foiled by some damn fire. "Do you know who I am?"

The soldier didn't respond or budge. He stood tall and alert.

"Mr. Yuri Andropov!" a throaty voice called.

He swiftly turned and saw a short, skinny man in civilian clothes approaching.

"I'm the Supreme Leader's communications advisor."

"Why is this guard not allowing me leave?" Yuri asked acidly, alternating his glare between the soldier and the man.

"Sorry for any miscommunication, sir. This exit is only for our Supreme Leader. If you like I can escort you to the main exit."

Yuri thought for a few seconds. He should just leave now and return tomorrow to let him know the best part of the story. He was looking forward to seeing his reaction. Humiliating people with big egos was satisfying. "Thank you. I hope the Prime Minister's family is safe."

The man didn't agree or disagree. "This way, sir."

"One moment. I left my files in the conference room." Yuri knew their value.

"You stay here, sir. I'll get them for you."

"No, I'll get them myself," Yuri insisted. He dashed the fifteen feet to the conference room. "Where are my files?!" he screamed at the communications advisor in the doorway.

"I don't know which files you are referring to, sir."

"Don't play dumb! All my files are gone! Who took them?" Yuri was sweating. He was furious. He hadn't even had the chance to tell Kim Sung about the blood report.

"Maybe you left your files somewhere else, sir. Nobody entered this room except you and our Supreme Leader."

"Go! Ask someone. I need my damn files." Yuri gritted his teeth. Only one other person knew the contents of his files, and he was now retired and living in the U.S. Mekler's face flashed across his mind as he dragged himself from the room.

At midnight, Yuri Andropov was still awake in the Soviet state house, three miles north of Kim Sung's office. His body and brain were tired but a comfortable sleep was nowhere near. Losing his files in the prime minister's office could ruin his reputation and his fast-paced career. Stalin looked up to him as a man without flaws. He had no doubt in his mind that Kim Sung ordered someone to steal them. He didn't want the Soviets to know too much about his personal life; particularly things that would destabilize his future or make him look weak. Yuri shouldn't have let the files out of his sight, but his biggest mistake was not making copies. He wasn't sure if Grigory had made any. At the time, he thought copies could fall into the wrong hands and create problems. Since he never discussed the files with anyone but Grigory, it was important to forget the whole episode. Kim Sung would read everything himself and get rid of his wife and servant. Wasn't that the reason he had traveled to Pyongyang?

A soft knock at the door made him turn his head. "Yes, who is it?"

"Sorry for the inconvenience, sir, but the informant came back," his military attaché said.

Yuri sat up straight and asked the man to enter. "What did he say?"

"Kim Sung's house burned to the ground. No official statement was issued, but I'm told that he has lost his family in the fire. Again, we have to confirm the last part."

He dismissed the man and went back to bed, thinking he would leave tomorrow unless he had to attend the funeral. He saw no reason to inform Kim Sung about his lost files. It would be like telling a robber he was robbed.

CHAPTER FORTY-ONE

The girl ahead was walking fast. Peter could easily have matched her strides if it weren't for Kim Suk. She was slow and calm.

"Will you tell me what's going on or are we going to keep walking until we reach China?" Peter asked again, looking back at the dark, smoky sky. He'd been shining his shoes when Jung Soon burst into his room and told him to flee the house. At first he thought she was joking, but then Kim Suk and a young girl he'd never seen before marched into his room and said the same thing. He was still in doubt until Kim Suk dragged him from his room. Smoke poured out of the kitchen and an adjacent room. Servants ran around the house yelling, "Fire! Fire!" He wanted to push Kim Suk away and run to get the kids when Jung Soon told him they were safe and then cursed him to leave. Confused by all the mayhem, he followed Kim Suk and the girl out of the house. That had been half an hour ago.

"Just follow her!" Kim Suk persisted. She was breathing hard and her clothes were wet. Her cloth shoes weren't made for the street. If it weren't an emergency, she would have worn better shoes and clothes. The gray tunic felt too baggy. At least Peter was wearing strong leather shoes and his black pants and white shirt looked comfortable. Her husband insisted all the male servants wear the same uniform. Female servants were allowed to wear whatever they liked, except for loose garments. She hated the way Kim Sung ogled the housemaids. If it were up to him, he would ban their clothing and make them walk around nude.

In twenty minutes, the girl led them to a posh section of the city and stopped in front of a big house with a metal gate. Instead of knocking on the door, she gave it a feline scratch. It opened at once, as if they were expected. The girl bowed her head to an old woman and motioned them to follow her to a room across the large courtyard. They entered a heavily furnished room.

"Thank goodness you are safe!"

"What the hell is he doing here?" Peter asked Kim Suk. She was still calm but he was seething. "You know him?"

"She does." Chin Ho smiled slyly. "Please sit down. You must be tired in this heat."

The young girl left the room. Kim Suk sat across from Chin Ho. Peter stayed on his feet, his face red and sweaty. He was getting sick of other people making decisions and not sharing with him. "I need to know what the hell is going on! Who are you? Why are we here?"

"You are here because you are both dead."

"Dead?!" Kim Suk croaked, exchanging a look with Peter.

Chin Ho stood to meet the young girl, who had returned with a black leather briefcase. "Let me see." He looked inside and smiled. "That's it!"

"What do you mean?" Peter frowned.

Chin Ho returned to his seat. "Does he know I'm a general?" he asked Kim Suk.

She shook her head.

"General of what?" Peter asked incredulously.

"North Korea."

Peter felt his heart jump out of his chest. He wiped his face. "Is he telling the truth?"

Kim Suk nodded.

"No need to be alarmed. I am here to help you." Chin Ho set the briefcase on the table.

"Why are we here, Kim Suk? Why did you drag me here? I'm leaving!"

"Wait, Peter! It's not her fault. She told you as much as she could. If you sit down, I will explain why you're here."

"Talk!" Peter pulled a chair close to him. "But be aware I can sniff bullshit from a mile away. Now go on!"

"Good for you!" Chin Ho replied, sarcastically. "First of all, I'm not your friend. The truth is I hate both of you, and if I could shoot you and take you back to Kim Sung for all your infidelities I would. But—" He sighed, shot daggers at Peter, and continued. "I've no choice but to help you out of this country."

"Why is that?" Peter placed his elbows on his thighs and rested his chin on his fists.

"Apparently," Kim Suk said, "when he was snooping around to get to know more about us in China, the CPC was following him to get to know him. Do you remember the message I received about him from China?"

Peter stared at her but said nothing.

"Commander Li Kenong told him if anything happens

to you or me they would kill his sisters back in China. His sisters are hostages."

Chin Ho shifted in his chair, a painful grimace on his face. He didn't know his trip back to Shanghai to meet his sisters would turn out to be such a disaster. He was walking along the street to their house when a small group of armed young men ambushed him. With guns to his forehead, he didn't put up a fight. They blindfolded him and whisked him away to a house. There they tied him to a chair and removed his blindfold. The man in front wasn't familiar, until he told him his name was Commander Li Kenong. Chin Ho had heard this name several times from Grigory over the years. "He's a ruthless Chinese guerrilla," the general had said, and read him a news headline: Four Chinese traitors beheaded in broad daylight. Li asked Chin Ho why he was collecting information about Peter Chang. He tried to dodge the question, but Li told him he would bring in his sisters and have his men rape them in front of him if he lied. Chin Ho relented right away and told him the truth. Li Kenong reacted with shock and rage and told him if Peter Chang or Kim Suk ever suffered harm because of him, his sisters would pay the price. Two days later they kicked him out of China and warned him never to come back.

"Is that true?" Peter's question startled Chin.

"It's not important. My job is to protect you—" Chin mumbled. The letter he discovered in his car told him about Yuri's visit. He was instructed to get ready for any situation. His sisters' lives were tied to these two. If it weren't for them, he could have ended up on the streets selling sweet potatoes or shining shoes. After the day his mother came home holding her chest, and collapsed and died, his sisters became mothers. They continued to support his education. War and poverty didn't bring them any suitors but they didn't care. All they seemed to care about was Chin's school. The girls had put their own lives on hold to make him succeed. They didn't want him to turn out like his other brothers who left home and never returned. Chin had the resources to find his brothers now but decided not to. They'd abandoned him when he needed them the most. After finding success, Chin had given away most of his wealth to his sisters. Last he heard, respectable men wanted to marry them. One of the reasons he went back to China was to meet his younger sister's suitor. His sisters never knew his real profession. They thought he was exporting spices and teas to faraway countries.

"I still don't know why we're here. Aren't you worried about the kids, Kim Suk?"

She sidestepped his question. "Jung Soon works for him. She brought the girl to me and said we had to leave the house immediately. A Soviet man told Kim Sung about our connection to the CPC."

"How do you know she works for him?" Peter's brain was stuck on her first sentence. How could a nice little old woman be a part of this operation? He wouldn't have guessed in a million years that she was involved.

Kim Suk glanced at Chin Ho. "Jung Soon told me. She occasionally brought me his messages."

"So you've been communicating with this man and you never bothered to tell me?" Peter felt betrayed again. Obviously, she enjoyed keeping him in the dark. "You hired Jung Soon? Why?" He turned to Chin.

Chin answered yes but refused to elaborate further. He wasn't going to tell him or her why he sent the old woman to their house. It would surely cause problems. They would become furious to learn that Jung Soon's initial job was to spy on them. To help Jin he needed to know the depth of their affair— whether they were lovers or sex partners. Jung Soon had told him they were neither. She never saw them doing anything inappropriate. But that was hard to swallow because he knew they had made two kids together. Chin wondered if Peter had gotten bored with her and stopped seeing her. It was a plausible explanation and he could relate to it. He could barely stand the same woman more than a few days. Of course, Jin was an exception. She had found ways to keep him hooked. Her menu changed often. "Read this." Chin Ho held out the briefcase that the girl had brought in earlier.

"What is it?" Peter pulled out some files. "What is this? I can't read Russian!" He recognized the alphabets. Kim Sung had brought books and magazines home with similar writing. He overheard him telling his wife to read Russian books. The communist philosophies in them were more coherent and inspiring.

"Let me see." Kim Suk snatched the files from him. Her face turned ashen and her lips started trembling after she finished reading. "Where did you get this?"

"One of my men stole it from Kim Sung's conference room. These files belong to Yuri Andropov. He came to see your husband to share the contents with him." Had his vehicle not broken down three miles from the meeting venue, he would've stolen the files before the meeting. He had never planned to take this route to rescue them. But after what Yuri said he had to take emergency steps to contain the damage. He was hoping Kim Sung would never find out why his house burned down. Andropov had to be prevented from revealing what he knew.

Chin Ho opened his mouth to say something when Kim Suk interrupted. She was sweating heavily. "How much has he told Kim Sung?"

"Don't worry. Yuri never got to tell him about the blood." Chin Ho took the files back.

"Are you sure?" She was crying. "I don't want anything to happen to my son."

"What blood?" Peter asked.

"I'm very sure! And Andropov will never tell anyone that he lost his most important files in North Korea," Chin Ho chuckled. "He cares more about his career than his country."

"What blood?!" Peter shouted, standing up. He'd had enough. He felt like an outsider.

"It's a file—" Chin Ho paused to look at Kim Suk, who'd dropped her head. "The file shows that you are Kim Jong's father, Peter."

"Oh!" Peter's face turned red. He fell back in his chair. Deep down he hadn't wanted to believe he'd fathered Kim Jong. The boy was nothing like him. He was an evil child. *How about Kim Man? Was he my son, too?* The thought pricked his heart. The boy reminded him of his own childhood. His mother used to say that Peter was a quiet and trouble-free baby until he turned twelve. Then she began calling him a trouble-seeker.

Kim Suk felt Peter's anguish and felt guilty. Instead of telling him directly, she'd dropped hints that both boys were his. How could he not know?" "I should've told you this earlier. I thought you already knew."

Peter buried his head in his arms. He felt like crying. But then strong men never cried, he reminded himself.

Studying the situation, Chin Ho cleared his throat and said, "I ordered Jung Soon to take the children out and set the mansion on fire, so no one would find your bodies. And Kim Sung won't hunt you down to your graves. You two know him better than anyone else."

Grinding his teeth, Peter mumbled something under his breath.

The young girl returned and whispered in Chin Ho's ear.

"Thanks!" he said. "I have to leave. I'll see you in two days. Don't leave this house!"

Peter watched him leave and then walked over to Kim Suk. He touched her shoulder. "Why didn't we bring the children with us? I should go back and get them."

"No! No!" She grabbed his wrist. Her eyes were red and swollen. "He will kill you."

"I don't care. What kind of mother leaves her kids behind?" Peter knelt beside her.

"A woman like me!" she sobbed. "They'll have a better life with him. Kim Sung will provide them all the comforts of life. I can't rob my children of their fortune." She continued weeping.

Peter Chang held her shoulders firmly and jolted her. "You have me! I care about you! I love you, Kim Suk!"

CHAPTER FORTY-TWO

Kim Sung stood behind a phalanx of armed guards, watching his soldiers with pails and hoses fight the fire. His glorious mansion was veiled by thick smoke. The army had cordoned off the entire neighborhood. The Supreme Leader's house burning to the ground was a bad omen.

"I wish I were dead in that fire instead of the mother of this nation," Jung Soon wailed, beating her chest. The two children had already been taken to the Prime Minister's office.

"Are you sure she was in her room?" Kim Sung asked. After seeing the children, he seemed in good spirits. Everybody else around him was in disarray.

"Yes, Supreme Leader. She was taking a nap in her room," she sniffed. "Poor Peter! I saw him burning and crying for help."

"Don't cry. You are a brave woman. You saved my children." He patted her shoulder and addressed a soldier. "Take her to my children. They need her."

"Yes, sir!" The soldier saluted him and took the weeping Jung Soon away.

"This house was new. How could it burn so fast? Where is General Bao Ju?" he grunted.

"He is directing the soldiers to seal the neighborhood, Supreme Leader," a two-star general answered.

"Tell him to meet me in my office."

A heavily decorated soldier guarding the door saluted briskly. Kim Sung examined him head to toe, assessing his alertness, nodded, and entered his office.

The large room had a high ceiling and only one window, positioned high enough to prevent anyone from seeing in. A number of colorful portraits hung on the walls, most with the same theme: the savior. In one picture, Kim Sung wore a sad smile as a gaggle of hungry children wrapped themselves around his arms and legs, staring at his face for help. Another showed him feeding an old Korean man with his hands. But the one he cherished most showed him sitting on a wide, golden platform, the sun peeking out from behind his left ear, creating the illusion that his face was emitting the shiny rays upon the sea of people, assembled to shower him with their love and respect. It was titled "The Angel of Prosperity." Among the portraits were numerous framed posters with quotes from the Supreme Leader written in golden ink.

The room boasted fewer than a dozen chairs, each resting a few inches from the wall and more than fifteen feet away from Kim Sung's low-profile pine desk. This was decorated with one small metal picture frame encasing little Kim, an empty frame that he'd hoped to fill with his newborn child, and two brown folders.

He admired his artwork, then slowly took his chair,

flipping open the folder marked with a red cross that occupied most of its hard cover. He read silently, his facial expression changing from a smile, to anger, and finally to a caustic grin, before he closed it.

"May I come in, sir?" The strong but humble voice echoed in the room.

"Yes! Come in, General Bao Ju," he beckoned. "What did you find out?" He leaned back. He was dressed in his favorite gray *Zhongsheng* suit.

"Sorry, Supreme Leader, but nothing survived the fire. Only bones and ashes are left. This nation will mourn your great loss."

His face turned stern. "I don't want my nation to know their mother died helplessly in a fire. My own house burnt to the ground. You know my enemies will laugh at me."

"I will never allow it, Supreme Leader. With your permission I would like to take this matter into my own hands."

"What do you have in mind?" Kim Sung asked cautiously.

"We will use this horrific news to bolster your image, Supreme Leader."

Kim Sung's dull eyes sparked. "I'm listening! Sit down and tell me."

"We will wait one week and then announce that the Supreme Lady of the nation passed away during childbirth."

"But she wasn't pregnant," he frowned.

"I will have all of our newspapers run a story tomorrow that the Supreme Leader has a surprise gift for his nation. The mother of the nation is pregnant and ready to deliver the baby soon."

"I like the way your brain works. I should promote you again." Kim Sung smiled.

"Supreme Leader, do I have your full permission to carry out this mission?" General Bao Ju stood up.

"Of course! If anybody makes trouble, shoot him in the head." Kim Sung laughed. "Do you know how many senior officers I passed over to choose you?"

"I am honored to serve you and your family, Supreme Leader."

"Thirty-five!" he said, wanting to search his face, but Bao Ju kept his face down. "I bypassed many of my senior officers to give you this honor. Do you know why?"

"You trusted me, sir?"

"No! I picked you because I trusted my judgment. I always know who is the right person for the job. It is a divine gift. Kim Jong has it too. His mother never understood it."

"The nation is fortunate to have you as its leader. I wish you a thousand years of health."

"Carry on, and tell the guard to send in General Cahng. I'm very unhappy with his work."

The thought of losing his wife and Peter Chang at the same time had made Kim Sung happy. He hated Kim Suk and had wanted to expel her from his life on numerous occasions but was afraid of the repercussions. She knew too much about him and could ruin his reputation in front of his enemies. He hadn't disliked Peter Chang until Yuri Andropov told him about his CPC affiliations. He was glad they didn't survive the fire. He didn't know how many servants he'd lost. He remembered Kim Suk complaining once that they had more than fifteen. "This place is like a zoo!" she'd said.

You bitch! You got what you deserved. And I already know

who I'm going to marry, he thought, opening the folder bearing the red cross to read it again.

"I'll kill them like pigs. I'll crush them to nothing!" He slammed the folder so hard on his desk that he could hear the uniform of the guard outside rustle in panic. "Sons of bitches!" He ground his teeth in anger and at the same time growled "Yes!" to the knock at the door.

A man in his late fifties stood in the doorway, his head down in respect and fear. "I'm so sorry I'm late." He was the senior General of the North Korean Army, who received daily briefings about the opposition.

"Weren't you in charge of building my mansion, which has now burned to the ground, General Cahng?" Kim Sung did not offer him a seat.

"Yes, Supreme Leader." The general's voice shook.

"Good! Now, you prepared this folder, right?" Kim Sung touched the red cross.

"Yes, sir, I made it cautiously," he said, but his voice lacked conviction. He was terrified. Barely five feet tall, he had a bony face and thinner arms than most men his age.

"I don't understand why there are more names in this folder than before. I thought you were doing your job properly." He tossed the folder at him, papers flying everywhere. The folder contained the names of high-profile Koreans who didn't see Kim Sung as a good leader and considered him an opportunistic politician who rode to the top on Stalin's shoulders.

"I will round them up and shoot them myself, one by one, your greatness!" The general was on his knees, collecting from the floor the handwritten memos he'd compiled after reviewing intelligence reports and talking to his lower-ranking officers. The hard, white marble floor hurt his old knees. Kim Sung sneaked up behind him and kicked him hard between his buttocks. The general groaned in agony and fell on his face. Kim Sung wasn't finished with him yet. He repeatedly and violently kicked him until General Cahng's blood-soaked body stopped moving. He lay on the floor, his face deeply gashed and a streak of blood oozing from the back of his head. His army uniform was printed with Kim Sung's black shoe marks.

"Bastard!" Kim Sung tried to spit on him but his mouth was as dry as sand. He trudged back to his seat, his gray suit covered in blood and his heart beating from the physical exertion, "I am their leader! How could someone dislike me?" He gazed across his desk in disgust. "Traitors!"

He slapped his hand on the table and padded carefully toward to the exit, avoiding contact with any more of Cahng's coagulated blood, which had already stained his shoes.

I need Kim Ae today. She knows how to make me feel better.

⁓

When Kim Sung left in a state of bliss, Jin collapsed on the bed, exhausted. For some reason he'd arrived in a good mood. After spending an hour to satisfy him, all she wanted was a long nap, uninterrupted and dream free. Three nights in a row she'd dreamed of snakes crawling all over her body. Each time she woke up sweating and trembling. Though her life was nothing short of a nightmare, with vultures tearing at her body as long as she could remember, the nights were when she felt safe; the quilt on top of her body was a temporary fortress.

A knock at the door made her jump out of bed as if she

had actually seen the snakes slithering there. She knew the knock well but never expected it. She ran toward the door, her breasts spilling out of her orange gown. "Chin Ho!" she said, pulling him in and wrapping her arms around him. "I thought I would never see you again."

"How are you, Jin?" He peeled her away gently. "You look beautiful."

She blushed, covered her breasts, and stared at his face. He looked so different. His playful, shiny eyes were dull and sad. "What happened to you? Are you sick?"

He smiled. "I'm fine. Just a little tired. Kim Sung was here?"

She nodded. However, for some reason she felt bad that he knew about it. Kim Sung had left his hat on the table.

"Listen, I won't take too much of your time. I need to tell you something."

She wished he hadn't said that. He could take as much time as he wanted. He was the only true friend she had. "Tell me!"

Chin sat beside her on the chair and told her about Kim Suk's death and then his meeting with Kim Sung. "Soon you will be his wife."

Jin was stunned. Kim Sung never mentioned it. It worried her that he was probably happy because his wife had burned alive. She was going to make sure her life wouldn't end in the same manner. As long as Chin Ho was on her side, she had no fear. He would protect her as he had in the past.

"I need to ask you a favor." He stood up.

She looked up at his face and slowly rose. "Of course."

Their eyes locked. "Can I come to you if I need your help?"

"What?!" She burst into laughter. "Why would you ask such a silly question? Of course! I would do anything for you."

He moved forward and kissed her on the lips and then left without saying good bye.

She stood there perplexed, wanting him to come back and kiss her again. In the next life, she would not sell her body. She would become a good girl, find Chin Ho, marry him, bear his children, and grow old with him. Tears were rolling down her cheeks. She would take a life or give a life. All he had to do was ask.

CHAPTER FORTY-THREE

A week passed for Peter Chang and Kim Suk in the house. The young girl, Lin, was an exceptionally good host. She cooked, cleaned, and refused to accept any help in the kitchen when Peter offered. Chin Ho visited twice. The second time he told them it would take a few more days to get them out of the country. Peter was worried about Kim Suk's mental health. She was on an emotional roller coaster. Sometimes she sat quietly for hours, staring at nothing, and then began crying and, after that, laughing hysterically. The uncertainties of the present and the future kept Peter awake most of the night. In his mind, he had gone to China several times, but not like this. There was no Kim Suk in his plans. She was supposed to take care of her children and attend those high-society parties with her husband. Now she was stuck with a man who could not offer her the luxuries of life she'd gotten so used to. All he had was love and empty pockets. Not enough to live a meaningful life.

Close to midnight, while Kim Suk and Lin slept, Peter was glued to the radio. The newscaster was overcome with emotion. "*The whole country mourns the loss of our great mother and a great daughter of our nation. Our first lady, who will be remembered for eternity, passed away in childbirth. The baby girl was stillborn. In this difficult time we praise our nation's Supreme Leader, the father of our country, Kim Il-Sung, who protects us from the evils of South Korea and its allies. We pledge our lives and the lives of our future generations to stand by our father, his children, and the children of his children."*

At one o'clock he went to bed. He was drifting off when he heard a whisper.

"Are you sleeping, Peter?"

"No." He got out of bed. Chin Ho was by the door. "What's happened?"

"Everyone else sleeping?" They went into the courtyard. "Cigarette?"

"Yes. Kim Suk isn't doing well." Peter lit one. He hadn't smoked in a long time.

"I can imagine what she's going through." Chin Ho looked at the full moon. "Will you promise me something?"

"What?" Peter asked, puffing smoke.

"Help my sisters. They've been through some hard times."

"What can I do? I have no influence. You're the man with power and wealth."

"Don't underestimate yourself. You're a legend in China. I know! I heard people talking about you. So what do you say? Will you help them?"

"I can't make any promises. But I'll try. May I ask you something?"

"Go ahead."

"Have you ever done anything you feel proud of?"

Chin Ho laughed silently. "I don't know where

you're going with this question, but yes, once I avenged a wronged girl."

"What did you do?"

"I sent away her abusers permanently. How about you?"

Peter thought for a moment. "I did something like that, but mine was personal."

"I guess we're alike," Chin Ho admitted, reluctantly. "Do you want to talk about how we ended up here together?"

"Not really. Why?"

"This might be our last night together."

"Do you mean it?"

Chin Ho smiled. "Tomorrow, when the whole nation is mourning the loss of their beloved first lady, you and Kim Suk will leave forever."

"Okay. In that case, take a seat. You first."

The next morning the young girl woke him up and told him it was time. Kim Suk was standing by the door, her eyes red and face puffy. A few days had added a few years to her age. Peter held both her hands and asked her if she was ready to leave. She replied with tears. He looked around the house—Chin Ho wasn't around—and took Kim Sung to the military truck parked outside. The driver helped them climb in the back and hide behind the large shipping crates. Some hours later, they were out of North Korea.

EPILOGUE

What!? I flipped through the book. I'd reached the end. I read the last page repeatedly. *This story isn't finished! Too many questions need to be answered.*

It was three in the morning. I'd spent my entire Sunday, plus a few hours of Monday, reading it. *I need to ask Ron to finish the story,* I told myself on the way to bed.

If it hadn't been for my smart phone, I would have slept through the next night.

The number was unknown. "What is it?" I barked.

"Would you like to participate in our poll?" a female voice asked politely.

"No!" I yelled, switching it off. I looked at the display. It was four o'clock in the afternoon. I jumped out of bed, took a quick shower, stuffed the book in my backpack, and jogged to the park. Ron was sitting in his usual place.

"I finished your book," I announced.

He smiled, revealing his few teeth. "You liked it?"

I smiled. "Very much. Do you know that this book could cause an uproar around the world? You wrote some crazy things. But why didn't you finish the story?"

"What crazy things?" he asked, clearly disturbed by my comment. "It's a true story!"

"Okay, what happened to Peter Chang and Kim Suk?"

"Nobody knows. No one ever saw them again."

"How about Chin Ho? Whatever happened to him or his sisters?"

Ron laughed. "Chin Ho's sisters lived happily in China until they died. Nobody harmed them. After the Korean War, Chin Ho escaped from North Korea. Rumors were that Kim Sung's wife, Kim Ae, helped him."

"Did Peter ever meet his father and find out that Shao Peng was his biological father?"

"Peter's father died the same year as Shao Peng. I don't know if he ever found out about his real father."

"How about Kim Suk's kids? You should write an epilogue to answer these questions."

"Why don't you visit a library and see what happened to Kim Jong and his sister?" Ron raised a hairless brow bone. "Your generation is so blind to history and world affairs."

"Huh!" I scratched my head. He was right and I was the living example. Before reading his book, I didn't know anything about North Korea, and the only thing I knew about South Korea was that my smart phone was made there. Ashamed, to the library I went! I wrote down all the information I needed to discuss North Korea with Ron. After several hours, I reviewed my notes.

"After the death of his beloved wife, Kim Jong-Suk, Kim Sung married Kim Song-Ae. Kim Sung had three more children with her. After Kim Sung's death in 1994, his son, Kim Jong, became the leader of North Korea. Kim Suk's daughter, Kim Kyong-Hui, is alive but in poor health. In 2012, Kim

Jong died of a heart attack. His son Kim Jong-un now rules the country."

Although I didn't read about the Korean War, I was still proud of my research. *We read if it interests us,* I thought. I went back to the park to prove the old man wrong. But he wasn't there.

Two months later, I returned. The bench was empty. I shrugged and went home. Months later I saw an old woman sitting on it. I'd seen her talk to Ron on occasion, so I approached.

"Hi there. Could I ask you whatever happened to Ron?"

"Who, dear? Ron?" She looked puzzled.

"Yes, the man who used to sit here. Sometimes you two talked."

"Oh, he died a few weeks ago, dear. Such a nice man! A while back, before you met him, he told me he saw your picture on the jacket of his favorite book. He loved your work…"

I missed much of what she was saying. My head spun until I could no longer stand.

"… but his name wasn't Ron," she said. "It was Chin Ho."

The End